R. Tourtellotte

The Elusive Booths of Burrillville

An Investigation of John Wilkes Booth's Alleged Wife and Daughter

by

Joyce G. Knibb & Patricia A. Mehrtens

Original Cover Art By

Nick J. Ackermann

Published 1991 By

HERITAGE BOOKS, INC.
1540-E Pointer Ridge Place, Bowie, Maryland 20716
(301) 390-7709

ISBN 1-55613-479-7

Dedicated to A.A.S.M

Without whose help
this book would
never have been
written.

We would like to take this opportunity to thank all those who aided us in our pursuit of the Burrillville Booths. The majority of the people who helped in our search are acknowledged in the text as they appear. In particular, our indebtedness extends to the Burrillville Historical and Preservation Society as well as to the Pascoag Free Public Library for allowing us to utilize their files and research materials. Special acknowledgements are also made to Marjorie Colony and Rosamond Putnam, descendants of our Burrillville Booths, for all the information they allowed us to see and use regarding their relatives. Thanks also go to our editor, Laird C. Towle, who has not only shown patience but has aided our progress while we unraveled this New England mystery.

CONTENTS

ILLUSTRATIONS

All Illustrations are placed after the page number listed.

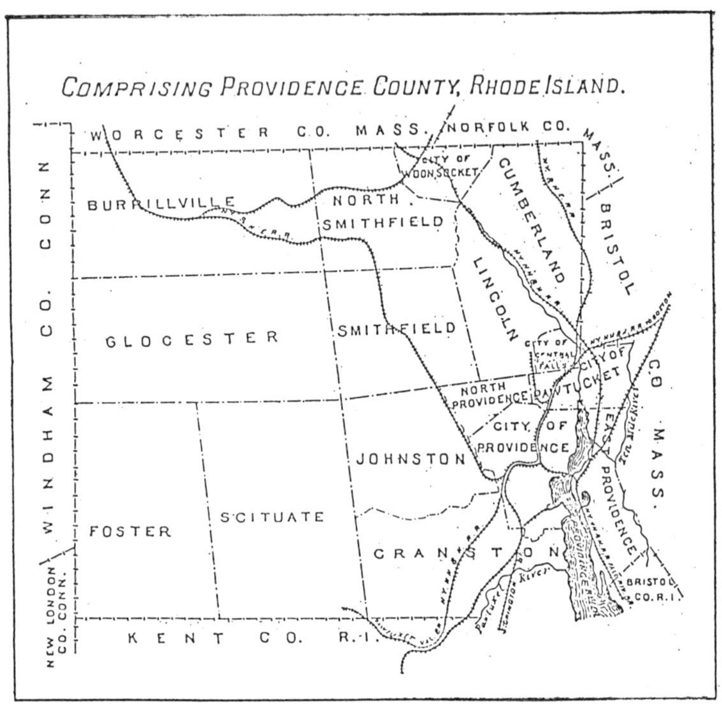

Burrillville and the surrounding area.
Notice its proximity to Massachusetts and Connecticut.
Map of Providence County, Rhode Island
1895 Everts & Richard
Philadelphia, Pennsylvania

INTRODUCTION

For over a decade, we two, admittedly, amateur historians have been searching out local fact and fiction in an attempt to bring some attention to the history and the traditions found in Rhode Island's most northwesterly territory, the town of Burrillville. The early history of this area has as much to do with the borderlands of Massachusetts to its north and Connecticut to its west as it has with the remainder of Rhode Island. Even today, residents of Burrillville feel that other Rhode Islanders view our corner as the outlands and, somehow, not as much a part of the Ocean State as the remaining cities and towns.

We do share in common the renown characteristics of contrariness, independence and tolerance that the founders of the Colony of Rhode Island initiated, and which following generations propagated up to and including our present time. If the early settlers in Providence and Newport possessed these qualities in abundance, then those who penetrated into the hinterlands were even more so. The unusual tolerance in that time period, which only the truly independent can have, might explain in part the easy acceptance of two captivating strangers who, during the latter half of the eighteen hundreds, came to dwell amongst the native swamp Yankees who inhabited the farmlands in this northwestern corner of Rhode Island.

In compiling and recording the history of Burrillville's approximately fifty-six square miles, we have ventured into some unlikely spots, have scanned materials not seen by human eyes for decades, and have undertaken sizable and long-range projects in order to bring our town into focus. One of these, a funded three year humanities project, involved recording the recollections of selected lifelong residents to obtain a comprehensive study of life in the villages of Burrillville between 1900 and 1950. It was the casual remark from one of those whom we interviewed which prompted this compilation and cast the two of us into the role of historical detective tracking down the whereabouts of John Wilkes Booth between 1859 and 1865 in order to capture the elusive Booths of Burrillville. So as not to mislead, we hasten to acknowledge that J. W. Booth is a peripheral figure in the history of our local Booths. We let the historians, writers, and other aficionados of Booth—and there are scores of them—provide their primary sources to us in order to pinpoint his whereabouts in specific places at specific times. Our essential interests are in the two strangers who came to Burrillville and how they affected those who lived here. In documenting the drama of their personal lives, we inadvertently reveal how little human nature has varied from their time to ours. The social, moral and economic climes are startlingly different. Human nature remains much the same.

Our material is presented in the chronological order of our findings and in a straightforward fashion. Rather than weave a particular theme or theory, we present the documentation as found, leaving the interpretation to the reader. The insertion of compilers' notes gives us an opportunity to express our personal commentaries and/or opinions. Our trail can be followed as we gather and record the necessary facts and figures to unravel this little-known knot of regional history.

Anyone who has attempted historical or genealogical research will be familiar with our exaltation over a crucial "find," the frustrations over the almost obligatory brick walls, and the unexpected surfacing of letters, diaries and the like which kept us on the trail littered with dusty documents and computer printouts. Also recognizable is the uncomfortable feeling, which grew as we steadily progressed, that truths and facts (hardly ever the same thing) are not easy objects to package.

Before we begin our search, a few last words on the geography of our town is in order. Burrillville was incorporated in 1806 after separation from the town of Glocester, which was originally separated from Providence in 1731. Within each township, areas were designated by those who lived there as a certain village or hamlet. Sub-divisions within these were numerous to the point of confusion. Our study is chiefly concerned with the villages of Pascoag, Bridgeton and Wallum Lake. However, we do not confine ourselves to just these locations or to the surrounding territories. Our search broadens with each new discovery, and the strange twists and turns are documented as they occur.

Chapter/File 1

BEGINNINGS

In this northwest corner of Rhode Island in the town of Burrillville, there is a tradition amongst certain families that the wife and daughter of John Wilkes Booth fled from the South to our village of Pascoag after Booth assassinated President Abraham Lincoln in 1865. It was said that Booth visited his wife, Izola (born Martha Mills), and his daughter, Ogarita Rosalie, at least once after the tragic event. Izola Martha's half-brother, Alonzo Abram Standish Mills, and his mother, Caroline Mills Brown, lived on a sizable farm in the outermost section of the village.

The local angle to the Booth myth was reinforced by the discovery of some "missing" journals written by Alonzo Abram Standish Mills. These gave us names, dates, and facts which verified the existence of Izola Martha, Ogarita Rosalie and others associated with them in our community. Because some of these facts were contrary to what we had already read and heard, we decided to take the information one step further and double verify the story as presented.

Our search led not only to all the standard places used to research historical facts but also to interviewing local figures with ties to this family. We gleaned information from local newspapers of that time frame and took interesting side trips to other parts of the northeast, all for verification of the facts on hand. Our journey begins with the following interviews.

***Source**: Miss Hazel Rosalie Hopkins (1912 -) resides in Ross Village (Bridgeton, Rhode Island) at her girlhood home. A retired social worker, formerly supervisor of Homes for the Aged and Convalescent Homes for the Rhode Island Department of Social Welfare. Miss Hopkins has a remarkable memory for family* *genealogies and historical events both local and national. She related the following:*

The wife of John Wilkes Booth and his daughter lived for some time at the "Wilson Place" in the village of Bridgeton. Booth visited his wife (Izola) and his daughter (Ogarita Rosalie) at least once. Izola declared openly to be the wife of JWB, and stated that she and her daughter fled the South after the assassination of Lincoln (April 14, 1865). They claimed the name of Wallingford, temporarily, on their way for refuge to the "end of the world" by stagecoach from Wallingford, Connecticut, their last stop before heading for Burrillville.

The mother was said to be a stage actress, and her daughter was budding into one with appearances on stage in Providence. Ogarita gave birth to a child, and a year later married William Ross Wilson, a man much older than she. This was said to have been a marriage of convenience and offered protection from public controversy to the daughter and granddaughter of John Wilkes Booth. (*Family members of John Wilkes Booth were harassed for several decades after the assassination.)

Exactly when and where they lived is hazy. At one time they were living with Alonzo Mills and his mother on the Brown farm, a short distance up the road from the Wilson's complex of homes, barns and mills. (*Ogarita lived on Wilson Hill after her marriage to Mr. Wilson.) Into this Yankee hinterlands, Izola and Ogarita were well received amongst the ladies, and their names are sprinkled through families down to the present generations. (Compilers' note: The continuation of the names "Izola" and "Ogarita Rosalie" is to be wondered at as several of these local ladies sent and lost brothers and sons to the Civil War defending the Northern cause. We do recognize the fact that not everyone in the North at that time was pro Lincoln or pro war. Hereafter, an asterisk in parenthesis (*) denotes compilers' note.)

Source: *Name withheld upon request. A Burrillville native whose grandparents and father lived in one of the Wilson houses "on the hill" related the following.*

My grandfather said that his father and uncle played poker with Booth at the "Wilson Place". (*The implication was that the poker player named Booth was actually John Wilkes Booth, the assassin of President Abraham Lincoln. There were other Booths living in this community: A prominent landowner in this village was

Seth Ross, who married his second wife, Rebecca Booth, in 1790. Jacob Booth [age 25, occupation, painter] appears on the official Burrillville Militia Enrollment Records in 1862. The "Wilson Place" was located on the outskirts of Pascoag, later designated as the Bridgeton area.)

Source: *Shirley [Patterson] Greene (1926 -) grew up on Wilson Avenue in Bridgeton. Well known local historian and certified genealogist. Former editor of the Rhode Island Genealogical Society's quarterly, Rhode Island Roots. Mrs. Greene related the following in a telephone conversation.*

The Booth story was staple lore in her family and throughout the villages in this section of town. It was said that Booth visited his wife and daughter after the assassination of President Lincoln in 1865. She could not verify the account in any way except to point out that it was generally accepted by the older generations to have some truth in it.

Source: *Martha Ogarita Sayles (1904 -) Native of Burrillville. Lt. Colonel in the Army Nurse Corps during World War II. Dean of the School of Nursing at the University of Rhode Island, retired. Miss Sayles writes to Hazel Rosalie Hopkins the following in a letter dated September 17, 1986.*

"First before I forget. The story told me about Ogarita is a bit different (*apparently from Miss Hopkins' version). Mother's sister's name was Eva Ogarita and that is how it got to me. As I heard it Gram (*Marthae [Hawkes] Ross born in 1857) gave it to her because a friend of hers was an Ogarita Wilson who lived up on Wilson's Hill. There were rumors that she was connected with Wilkes Booth some way and that he came in the dark of night at least once to visit. I cannot vouch for the authenticity of this, but it is the explanation I got for my unusual middle name . . ." (*At first, Miss Hazel Hopkins did not realize the significance of her own middle name, "Rosalie." However, she was aware that her mother's middle name, Izola, had always attracted attention from outsiders. We question why no one has written about these Burrillville Booths previously . . . if the story is true. Yet, we cannot ignore the reliability of the above sources.)

Source: *Ruth Shinsel in a letter dated October 31, 1966 written to Hazel Rosalie Hopkins.*

"We are most grateful to you and to your two kindly aunts for your encouragement and aid in our very difficult research. (*One of the aunts was Florence Adeline [Angell] Taft born in 1879, and the other "aunt" was actually Hazel Rosalie Hopkins' mother, Nora Izola [Angell] Hopkins born in 1889.) Having learned since our visit with you, some considerable facts and corrections, we are now ready to proceed to further investigation. In comparing names you mentioned with statistics in our possession, we quite fully understand why those names were used . . . we found out one of the reasons the life has been so difficult to trace, and will have to repeat some of the searches because of incorrectness of some of the data on hand. We appreciated your resolution and your assurance that we would hear from you. We can only assume that you have so far not heard or seen anything that might help us further. We expect that my husband and I will have to go up to Stamford and Providence again within the next couple of weeks . . . ."

(*The above researcher is careful not to mention any proper names and hardly any proper places with the exception of Stamford and Providence. How are these cities associated with our local lore? This letter is included only to indicate that others have also been hunting in Burrillville for answers. Miss Hopkins related that periodically the Ross Village area is visited by outsiders looking for information on Alonzo Mills and Izola Martha Mills. The resolution of which Mrs. Shinsel writes is the information which Miss Hopkins has given to us. Apparently, Mrs. Shinsel is chasing down the Booth story. Her visit was previous to the centennial of Lincoln's assassination, and she implied in conversation that the research was being done for a television program on that subject. It is encouraging for us to hear that "outsiders" appear to have some inkling of the stories that we have heard locally concerning J. W. Booth, his wife and daughter. We wrote to Mrs. Shinsel, who lives in Washington, D. C., but have not received a reply to date. Documentation and verification of specific facts are needed. We begin our quest at the Burrillville Town Hall and its records department.)

Source: *Burrillville Town Records filed in 1879. Births - Volume 1A (1852-1897) p.77.*

Name of child: Izola Louise Wallingford. Born November 15, 1878 in Burrillville. White/ first child. Parents: George H. Wallingford born in Providence and Ogarita Wallingford, no place of birth given. Residence of both: Burrillville. No occupation given for father or mother. (*According to this record, Ogarita was married to

George H. Wallingford at this time, though we have been unable to find any record of a Wallingford living in Burrillville. Would this discredit the Wallingford, Connecticut, part of Miss Hopkins' account? We were given to understand that both mother and daughter were temporarily using this particular last name. At least this entry places Ogarita in the Burrillville area.)

Source: *Burrillville Town Hall Records. Marriages - Vol. 1A (1864-1900) p. 53.*

William Ross Wilson and Ogarita Elizabeth Wallingford, both of Burrillville and both white, married October 12, 1879 by Rev. William Fitz. Groom born in Burrillville, age 64 at time of marriage and occupation listed as a farmer. His parents listed as James and Deborah Wilson. Bride born in Providence, age 20 and no occupation. Her parents listed as Charles Still (Bellows) and Martha Louise Bellows. First marriage for William and Ogarita's second. Marriage registered by Alvah Mowry, Town Clerk. (*Note that Ogarita's middle name is not listed as Rosalie but as Elizabeth. We assume that Martha Louise is Izola Martha [Mills] Booth and has married a man by the name of Bellows. Curious . . . are they hiding the fact of their previous names or do they no longer claim to be the Ogarita Rosalie and Izola Martha previously noted? Please note that Ogarita is listed as being born in Providence, something we did not expect to find. Background: Reverend William Fitz was a leading figure in this community, and Alvah Mowry was Town Clerk for thirty-six years. This is mentioned because we have learned from experience that entries in records—town, state or otherwise—are not always what they seem. The clerks register what has been given to them. Sometimes the facts are not presented correctly by the persons filing the information, or misspellings take place in the transition from paper to permanent records. Therefore, more than one source will be searched for verification of these facts.)

Source: *Representative Men and Old Families of Rhode Island, Volume III. H. H. Beers & Co. (Chicago, 1908) pp. 1838-1839.*

William Ross Wilson was born on the family farm in Pascoag (Bridgeton) January 24, 1815. (*The name Pascoag prior to 1894 included all the villages that later became known as Bridgeton.) He was one of seven children born to James Wilson of Thompson, Connecticut and Deborah [Ross] Wilson of Pascoag. (*William Ross Wilson was related to Marthae Ross, grandmother of Martha

Ogarita Sayles.) William was educated in the local schools and at an academy in Oxford, Massachusetts. He went to Morenci, Michigan, in the late 1850s where he engaged in business with his brother, George W. Wilson. Returning to Burrillville, he assumed with another brother, James M. Wilson, the management of the home farm along with a grist, saw and shingle mill. He was a man of superior business qualifications and of high integrity and honor. . . was overseer of the poor in 1856 . . . a member of the town council from 1861 through 1862. He lived on the homestead (Ross) farm with his two unmarried sisters, Almira E. and Sarah. He married but had no children. (*Please note that his wife's name, Ogarita, is conspicuously absent, which is unusual for this source.) He died July 23, 1902 esteemed and respected by all who knew him. (*We cannot but wonder why he chose to marry a twenty year old when he was sixty-four . . . especially with her touted association with John Wilkes Booth . . . and with William listed as an enrollment officer for the Burrillville Militia in 1862 and 1863.)

Source: *Burrillville Historical and Preservation Society's Cemetery Files. In 1976 the BH&PS surveyed and recorded individual graves in more than 130 cemeteries.*

Historical Cemetery #50. Wilson (*Family) Lot: East Wallum Lake Road, in front of NET pole #17. 250' in off road, close to reservoir (Wilson's). 60x60. 25 burials. No veterans. Poor condition. Granite post and iron pipe fence. Owner, unknown. (*We have learned from experience to check cemetery files with cemeteries in order to verify the actual burials as listed. We visited this site in 1987. A good many of the Wilsons are resting here. The only non Wilson is a Mary Dean, wife of Joseph Dean, who died in 1801 at the age of twenty-six. Unfortunately, two of the larger monuments have been toppled face down and cannot be read. We assume one of these to be William's grave.)

Source: *Pascoag Herald dated July 25, 1902. Bound and unbound copies of this newspaper were stored in the Pascoag Free Public Library. (*Both of us are trustees of the Ladies' Pascoag Library Association . . . One of our fathers-in-law, Cyril W. Knibb, purchased the office where the Herald was published in Pascoag and donated the copies to the library. One of our fathers, Joseph G. Zifchock, bought the equipment and operated a printing business there.)*

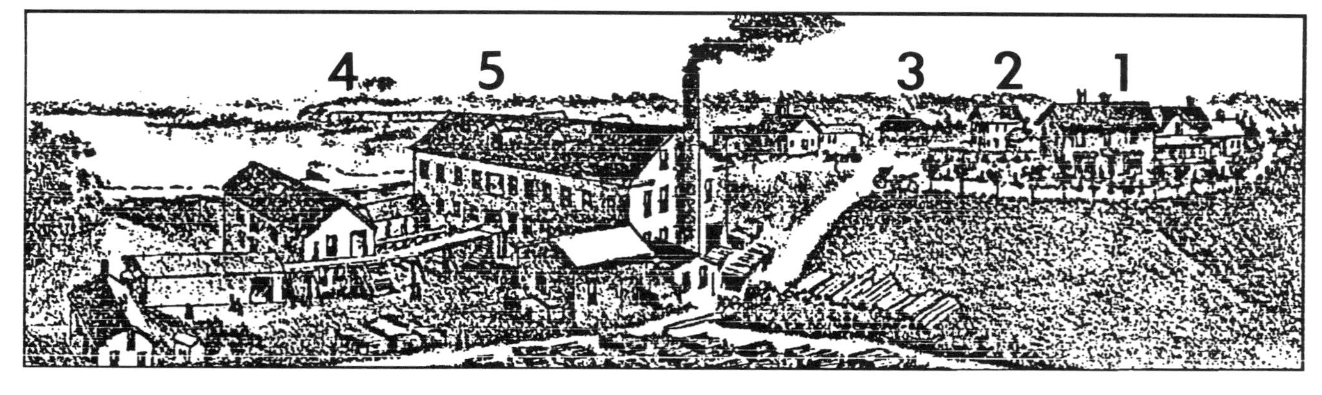

Map of Pascoag and Vicinity - 1895 - O. H. Bailey & Co., Boston
1. Residence of Herbert M. Wilson
2. Residence of William R. Wilson
3. Ross Homestead
4. Providence & Springfield Railroad
5. Wilson's Yarn, Lumber, and Grist Mills

William Wilson dead . . . an old and much respected citizen of Burrillville died at his home above Bridgeton after an illness lasting only a few hours. The cause of death was an abscess on the liver which broke into the abdominal cavity. The deceased leaves one brother of Webster, Massachusetts, Marvin Wilson, and one sister, Myra (*Almira?) of this place. . . (He) has always been regarded by his fellow townspeople as an upright, honest and energetic man. He hasn't been in ill health for any period of time. Tuesday night he did his chores and retired early but was taken with internal pains during the night and died Wednesday at one o'clock. (*Strange, no mention made of Ogarita, or whether or not he was a widower.)

Source: *Pascoag Herald dated August 1, 1902. (*Herald was started in April, 1892 by Arthur Fitz, son of the Rev. William Fitz, the minister who married William and Ogarita in 1879.)*

The funeral of William Wilson was held from his old home on Friday afternoon. There was a large gathering of relatives and friends which was a true tribute to the universal esteem and respect borne the deceased. Rev. Walter Ela of the Laurel Hill M. E. Church officiated. The service was simple, yet impressive, and was a fitting finale of a life so well lived as the one just ended. Interment was in the little family plot on the old farm. The bearers were Herbert Wilson, Marvin D. Wilson, Howell G. Wilcox and Charles F. Wilcox. (*According to this newspaper account, William Wilson was indeed buried in what is now Historical Cemetery #50 and lies beneath one of the toppled stones. Up to this point, we have been unable to locate Ogarita's final resting place.)

Source: *Town of Burrillville Records Deaths - Volume 2 (1901-1928).*

William R. Wilson, single, white, male, died July 23, 1902 in Pascoag at the age of 87 years, 5 months, 30 days. (*The designation of single means that he was either divorced from Ogarita or that his relatives have chosen to ignore the marriage of 1879.)

Born in Burrillville, Rhode Island of American parents, James and Deborah [Ross] Wilson. According to the attending physician John J. Lace, he died of old age and was buried in Burrillville by undertaker W. R. Waterman.

(*This last entry ends our easy findings . . . we have reached our first brick wall. As we cannot discover any more local documentation regarding the Burrillville Booths, we are awaiting verification or negation of the newspaper dates and names in our possession taken from Alonzo Mills' journals. We decide to turn to the history of the Booth family to see whether or not Izola and Ogarita fit into the pattern of their lives.)

Chapter/File 2

JOHN WILKES BOOTH

From our early history lessons, we knew that John Wilkes Booth assassinated Lincoln in 1865. Whether or not he had a wife and daughter was of little concern to us. We vaguely recalled that the Booths were an acting family, and that Edwin Thomas Booth was the ultimate "Hamlet." The Burrillville lore initiated our search for the verification of the relationship between our local family and the better known Booths of Maryland.

Source: *Encyclopedia Britannica, Volume 3. The University of Chicago, Encyclopedia Britannic, Inc. (United States, 1946) p. 890. (*We give this summary for its brevity and its general acceptance to refresh the reader's memory.)*

Booth, John Wilkes (1839-65) American actor, assassin of President Lincoln, was born in Harford Co., Maryland, in 1839. He was the son of Junius Brutus. His brother, Edwin Thomas Booth, was an actor of prominence. He sympathized with the South in the American Civil War, and in 1865 organized a conspiracy to assassinate the President, the Vice President and members of the Cabinet. On the night of April 14, 1865, while Lincoln was watching a play from a box at Ford's Theatre in Washington, Booth stealthily entered the box and discharged a pistol at the head of the President from behind, the ball penetrating the brain. Brandishing a huge knife, the assassin rushed through the stage-box, leaped down upon the stage, and escaped from the building. He was pursued, and twelve days later was shot in a barn where he had concealed himself.

Sources: *(*A reference list is found at the end of this chapter/file from which we composed the following. An attempt was made to relay only the material that is generally accepted as being more or less factual, though we are beginning to think there is "no such thing as a fact." After having read a considerable amount of material on Booth, the assassination, and the aftermath, as written by those from both the 19th and 20th centuries, we are convinced that those who write of past events should refrain from weaving themes and schemes with only a few sticks with which to build their castles. We label our opinions and commentaries as such.)*

John Wilkes Booth (1838-1865) was one of ten children (six of whom survived to adulthood) born to Junius Brutus Booth and Mary Ann Holmes, whom Junius married on May 11, 1851, a month after his first wife, Adelaide, divorced him. Junius and Mary Ann sailed from England to America in 1821. (In 1846, Adelaide and her son Richard sailed to America to find Junius Brutus.) Eventually, Junius found a suitable secluded spot in Harford County north of Baltimore, Maryland, where the family lived in a rough log house until a more imposing home known as Tudor Hall was built. (*Note that John Wilkes birth is listed at times as 1839. . .see first source above. Modern researchers support the 1838 date.)

Junius Brutus was recognized in England as an actor of some renown. In America his fame grew rapidly, and he was soon considered one of the major tragedians of his day. Physically, he was on the short side and "thickset;" nonetheless, he mesmerized his audiences with his commanding voice, dramatic poses and the famous "glittering" Booth eye. As stage performances became more and more demanding, this rather brilliant though erratic and eccentric man became more and more addicted to "drink." His visits home for rest and recuperation were few and sporadic. In 1852, while returning from a tour in California, he died aboard the steamer J. S. Chenoweth, heading up the Mississippi for Cincinnati. (*The Gold Rush State was reached via waterways and over the Isthmus of Panama.) He was buried in Baltimore Cemetery. Edwin erected a monument of polished marble in the shape of an obelisk in memory of his father. This monument and the bodies buried there were later removed to a plot in Greenmount Cemetery in Baltimore. (*We mention this as it is disputed later who was and who was not buried in that location.)

The son, Edward, (1833-1893) at the age of fourteen was assigned the task of being his father's guardian and dresser, i.e., keeping Brutus from "drink" and low company. (*Previously,

Junius had the audacity to employ his legitimate son Richard. As Junius Brutus Booth did not marry Mary Ann Holmes until 1851, all of their children would have been considered illegitimate.) Edwin, whose style was less bombastic and more learned than his father's, was to become the truly great American tragedian, having received his education—on stage—from his father and other leading actors and actresses on those long and varied engagements.

John Wilkes Booth was left at home with his younger brother, Joseph, his mother, and sisters, the lovely Asia and the withdrawn Rosalie (*for whom Ogarita Rosalie was named?) to manage the farm as best they could. John's early associations with boyhood chums in the country and schoolmates in the city (Baltimore) imbued him with Southern manners and beliefs. The elder brothers were less provincial in their thinking as they had left home early and traveled across America and to Australia as well. By all accounts, John was given free reign and considered the darling of the family. As a young man he was associated with the Know-Nothings, became an impromptu member of the Richmond Grays, who guarded John Brown before he was hanged, and was an outspoken—even to the point of being arrested—supporter of state rights and slavery. Most of the family members moved north. Edwin settled in New York and Boston, Asia in Philadelphia, Junius Jr. in California then New York, and mother Mary Ann and sister Rosalie wherever Edwin placed a home at their disposal. John, alone, counted the South as his home, living in Baltimore, Richmond, and Washington, DC.

The years 1858-1859 found John working with a stock company in Richmond, Virginia. (*By addition and subtraction of the documented dates on Ogarita Rosalie, Izola would have had to marry John Wilkes during this time period.) Shortly afterward, he toured and captivated audiences throughout the South. It was said that Junius Jr. ruled the stage in the West, Edwin in the East and John in the South. But, John is soon encroaching on his brother's territory with appearances in Boston, New York, Chicago and Philadelphia. His good looks, southern charm and athletic and passionate stage performances quickly had a bevy of ladies pursuing him. His many liaisons with actresses led to dangerous near misses when one of them slashed at him with a knife and another reportedly shot at him. He was also known to have associated with ladies of the evening, Ella Turner (Starr) of Washington for one. We read that he was supposedly and secretly engaged to the daughter of Senator Hale of New Hampshire. All who knew John Wilkes Booth, before and after the assassination, declared that he was a man of considerable charm, gentle of manner, generous to friends, and a man of many accomplishments. But, mention was also made that he was "excitable" and eccentric in his fervor for the Southern cause. History does not record that he was ever married or ever recognized any children as his own.

In the latter half of the year 1864, his appearances on stage lessened. We are told that he earned $20,000 a year as an actor. (*This certainly takes him out of the minor league as far as actors are concerned.) He invested money in the oil fields of Pennsylvania (*the Texas of its day) and land speculation in lower Maryland. His business agent, Joseph H. Simonds, succinctly, informed John that he could earn more money on the stage. Booth's whereabouts are a bewildering array of crisscrossing between Baltimore, Philadelphia, New York, Boston, Montreal, and the near west. His home base was the National Hotel in Washington, DC, whose register provides knowledge of his erratic comings and goings.

During this same time period it is believed that he, as well as others before him, were plotting to kidnap the President, escort him to Richmond, and demand as ransom the release of the much-needed Confederate prisoners-of-war scattered throughout camps in the North. Whether or not Booth received money and/or condonation from either Jefferson Davis at Richmond or Jacob Thompson in Canada—where a Confederate contingent was wreaking havoc and mischief on the northern Union borders—has never been clearly established. Strange as it may seem, John Wilkes Booth, wearing his Southern heart and loyalty on his sleeve, crossed the lines in order to perform in the theaters of the North and the South. We do know that he assembled a motley band to implement the planned abduction. Among these were two friends from Maryland, Michael O'Loughlin and Sam Arnold as well as George A. Atzerodt, David Herold, and Lewis Thornton Powell (Paine/Payne), who roamed about Washington. Included in this group were known rebel sympathizers, Mrs. Mary E. Surratt and her son John, a courier for the Confederates. The kidnapping attempts were foiled as Lincoln was never where Booth expected him to be. (*For those who would like to further pursue this type of information, we suggest a combination of Clara E. Laughlin's *The Death of Lincoln - The Story of Booth's Plot, His Deed and the Penalty*, Theodore Roscoe's *The Web of Conspiracy; The Complete Story of the Men who Murdered Lincoln* and William A. Tidwell's *Come Retribution* for starters . . . see reference listing at end of this file.)

It was said that Booth became distraught over the failure of his well-laid and costly plans, together with the information of the

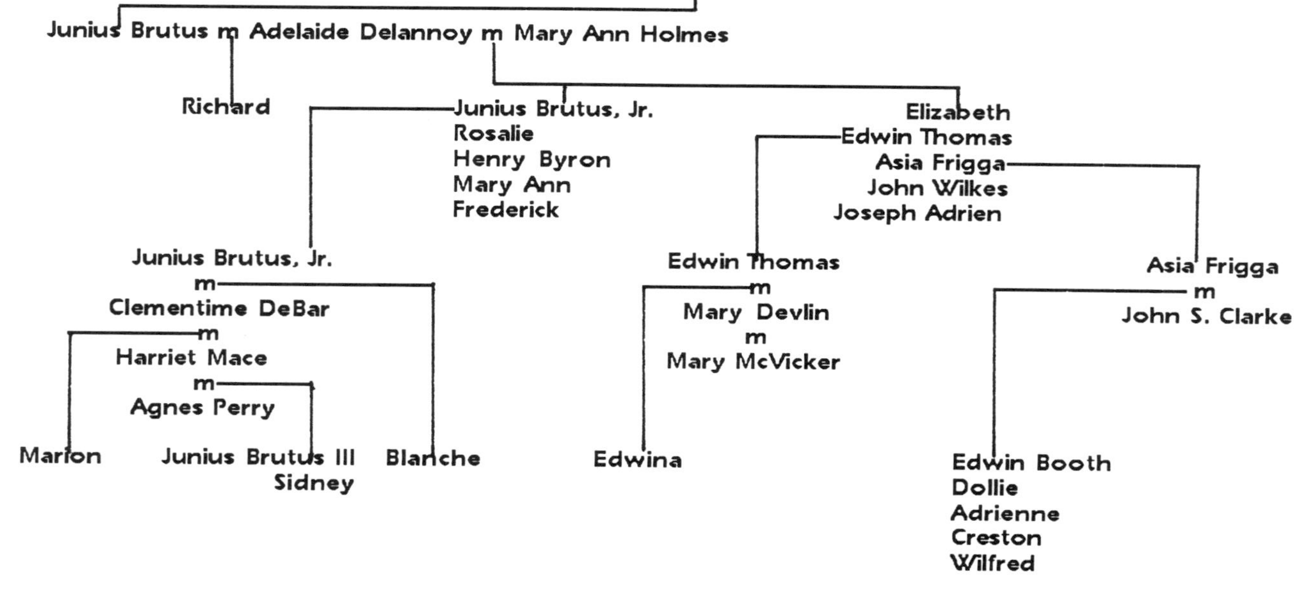
Booth Family Tree
Richard Booth m Elizabeth Wilkes
Junius Brutus m Adelaide Delannoy m Mary Ann Holmes
Richard
Junius Brutus, Jr.
Rosalie
Henry Byron
Mary Ann
Frederick
Elizabeth
Edwin Thomas
Asia Frigga
John Wilkes
Joseph Adrien
Junius Brutus, Jr.
m
Clementime DeBar
m
Harriet Mace
m
Agnes Perry
Edwin Thomas
m
Mary Devlin
m
Mary McVicker
Asia Frigga
m
John S. Clarke
Marion
Junius Brutus III
Sidney
Blanche
Edwina
Edwin Booth
Dollie
Adrienne
Creston
Wilfred

defeat of Richmond on the third of April 1865, and Lee's formal surrender at Appomattox on the ninth. On the morning of April fourteenth or on the previous day, he heard that President Lincoln and General Grant were to attend a performance at Ford's Theatre on the evening of the fourteenth. Booth was well acquainted with this theater and had free access to it. He hastily made plans that might have seemed preposterous to the faint of heart—or the sane—but they partially succeeded. He would assassinate the President and General Grant in their theater box; Lewis Powell would do likewise to Secretary of State Seward at his home with Herold acting as Powell's backup. George A. Atzerodt would dispose of Vice President Johnson in his hotel room.

General Grant changed his mind about attending the theater and was thus spared; Booth accomplished his deed and fled; Powell wounded Secretary Seward, but not fatally, along with four others; while Herold pursued Booth along the so-called escape route to Virginia. Atzerodt either lost courage or never intended to follow through with his part in the assassinations. Booth with a broken leg spent twelve days with Herold eluding those who pursued them before Herold surrendered and Booth either shot himself or was shot by a soldier (Boston Corbett) in a tobacco shed on the Garrett farm near Port Royal, Virginia. John Wilkes Booth's dying words were for his mother, not for a wife or any daughter. He said that he died for his country, i.e., the South. Atzerodt, Herold, Powell, and Mrs. Surratt were all hanged for their trouble. Samuel Arnold and Michael O'Loughlin, along with Dr. Samuel Mudd and Ned Spangler, were sentenced to Dry Tortugas off the coast of Florida. O'Loughlin died there. Dr. Mudd, who had set Booth's leg during his escape, was pardoned in 1869 by President Andrew Johnson. Ned Spangler, a stagehand at Ford's Theatre and Samuel Arnold were also pardoned shortly thereafter. Mrs. Surratt's son skipped the country. John Surratt was captured in Egypt and brought to Washington, DC, for trial in 1867. After a confused three months' trial, charges were dropped against him. (*With all the notoriety of the Booth family and in particular John's lifestyle and deed, we question why Izola in 1865 would lay claim to being his secret wife as suggested in local lore.)

It is not difficult to imagine the near panic by the government and the public, during these events and their immediate aftermath. Historians and others have harshly criticized the actions of the government during this period. (*We reflect upon those who write of such things who have lived through the assassination of President Kennedy and the attempted assassination of President Reagan. The smugness of hindsight by those who write of past events can be irritating and hints at a severe case of myopia.) Investigations and alleged conspiracies mushroomed around the death of Lincoln and the attempted assassinations of government officials. We include a brief listing of these so-called conspiracies as we have by now stumbled upon a book—via footnotes and references—by the alleged granddaughter of John Wilkes Booth, who proposes that he was the pawn of one of the following: (1) Secretary of War Stanton arranged it all as he wanted the power and the glory for himself . . . he knew of Booth's role. (2) Vice-President Johnson wanted to be president and to rid the government of certain members of the cabinet . . . as did Stanton. (3) Jefferson Davis and Jacob Thompson were responsible for the kidnapping plot and the assassination for obvious reasons. (4) The Knights of the Golden Circle, for reasons known only to them, used Booth, a member, to implement the crimes. (5) The Catholic Church was responsible as they were opposed to everything President Lincoln stood for and believed. (6) John Wilkes Booth was the sole mastermind of both the kidnapping plots and the assassination.

Along similar lines of popular thinking and writing, John Wilkes Booth was alive and well (*and we are not privy to whether he was or was not) having escaped the Garrett barn and left behind a willing stand-in for the final act. Booth was later spotted all across America, Mexico, England, Italy, Bombay, Ceylon and the South Pacific . . . to mention only a few places, despite the account that his body aboard the monitor Montauk was identified by friends, theater associates, his doctor and others, shortly after his death. Four years later (*after Edwin finally received permission to receive the body of his brother, which had been buried in a building in Washington, DC, known as the Arsenal and formerly used as a penitentiary) Booth was again identified by family members (*probably the younger brother, Joseph) and friends who were theater associated. This was done by standard forensic methods. In 1869 the family put John Wilkes Booth's body to rest with his brother and sisters and his father in the shadow of the obelisk now standing at the Greenmount Cemetery in Baltimore.

(*This has been a rather long file, but one we felt was necessary in order to give identification to the temper and fervor of the second half of the 19th century with its dramatic and romantic events and the participants who played them out. It might seem as though we have strayed far afield from our northwest corner in Rhode Island with its less exaggerated figures of the Wilsons, Alonzo Mills and his mother Caroline working their farms on

John Wilkes Booth - Noted for his flashy style.
Photo by Silsbee, Case & Co.
From the Richard & Kellie Gutman Collection

Wallum Pond Road, but they too were a part of this era and even more so when Izola and Ogarita came into their lives bringing the tragic name of Booth with them. In truth, the above file is a good preparation for the one to come entitled "Izola." We turn to Miss Forrester's *This One Mad Act* and allow her to tell us where her grandmother, Booth's alleged wife, fits into the picture. (*Miss Forrester is actually Izola Louise Wallingford, born in Burrillville on November 15, 1878.) As previously noted, we include the following references for your information.)

References Used and Suggested Reading

Bryan, George S. *The Great American Myth.* New York: Carrick & Evans, Inc., 1940. (*Myth-buster Bryan destroys a few of the conspiracy theories engendered by Booth's assassination of President Lincoln.)

Bishop, Jim. *The Day Lincoln Was Shot.* New York: Harper & Bros., 1955. (*Gripping account of that infamous day, April 14, 1865, though the author himself admits it is more fiction than fact. Much of what he wrote was actually based on historical accounts.)

Clarke, Asia Booth. *The Unlocked Book - A Memoir of John Wilkes Booth by His Sister.* New York: G. P. Putnam's Sons, 1938. (*Written by Booth's sister then given to a family friend whose daughter had it published several years after Asia's death. It is a poignant account of Asia's view of her brother.)

Forrester, Izola. *This One Mad Act . . . The Unknown Story of John Wilkes Booth and His Family.* Boston: Hale, Cushman & Flint, 1937. (*Supports the concept of a conspiracy and Booth's surviving the Garrett Farm episode. Gives a romanticized history of the author's family and their relationships with the Booth family.)

Furnas, J. C. *The Americans. A Social History of the United States 1587-1914.* New York: G. P. Putnam's Sons, 1969. (*Read the selection on the Civil War era for a broader perspective of life in America during this time period.)

Gutman, Richard J. S. and Kellie O. *John Wilkes Booth Himself.* Dover, Massachusetts: Hired Hand Press, 1979. (*This team produced a fine collection of photographs starring John Wilkes

Booth. They also tracked down the photographer, the location of the studio and the dates when the photography was done.)

Hanchett, William. *The Lincoln Murder Conspiracies.* Urbana and Chicago: University of Illinois Press, 1983. (*This author picks up where author Bryan left off to discredit the conspiracy theories as written by others.)

Kimmel, Stanley. *The Mad Booths of Maryland,* 2nd revised and enlarged edition. New York: Dover Publications, 1969. (*Kimmell's book is still considered the best overall biography of John Wilkes Booth and his family especially during their Harford County stay.)

Laughlin, Clara E. *The Death of Lincoln - The Story of Booth's Plot, His Deed and the Penalty.* New York: Doubleday, Page & Company, 1909. (*A straightforward and interesting account of events surrounding Booth's act written by one who had known family members and associates.)

Roscoe, Theodore. *The Web of Conspiracy - The Complete Story of the Men Who Murdered Lincoln.* Englewood Cliffs: Prentice-Hall, 1959. (*The author relates his conspiracy account and of the men who "murdered" Lincoln.)

Ruggles, Eleanor. *Prince of Players. Edwin Booth.* New York: W. W. Norton & Company, Inc. 1953. (*Mainly about Edwin Booth and his tragic life on and off stage with an account of Edwin's relations with his brother John Wilkes.)

Samples, Gordon. *Lust for Fame: The Stage Career of John Wilkes Booth.* Jefferson, No. Carolina, and London: McFarland & Company, Inc. Publishers, 1982. (*The author concentrates on John Wilkes Booth's stage career. There is a complete listing of Booth's stage appearances in chronological order.)

Sandburg, Carl. *Abraham Lincoln - The Prairie Years and the War Years.* New York: Harcourt, Brace and Company, 1954. (*Author Sandburg has his own view of the assassinator Booth. The book should be read in its entirety whether you have interest in the Booths or not.)

Stern, Philip Van Doren. *The Man Who Killed Lincoln.* New York:

Random House Inc., 1939. (*This book has had a meteoric rise and fall of followers from the author's accounting of the man who killed Lincoln. Fascinating reading just the same. Though Stern's account of the assassination is fictionalized, his lengthy "Afterword" contains the documentation of his sources and the controversial information which surrounds Booth and his demise.)

Tidwell, William A., Hall, James O. and Gaddy, David Winifred. *Come Retribution - The Confederate Secret Service and the Assassination of Lincoln.* Jackson and London: University Press of Mississippi, 1988. (*Just when one thinks that the grand conspiracies have been put to rest along comes a trio who support a Confederacy conspiracy with Jefferson Davis, Jacob Thompson and John Wilkes Booth having interesting rolls. A hefty book, with many pages of documentation, which examines the covert actions of both the South and the North.. All accompanied by the forceful logic of circumstantial evidence.)

Townsend, George. *Life, Crime and Capture of John Wilkes Booth.* New York: Dick & Fitzgerald, 1865. (*Townsend was a correspondent for the *New York World* and a peer to the Booths and all the leading characters of this tragedy.)

Wilson, Francis. *John Wilkes Booth - Fact and Fiction of Lincoln's Assassination.* Boston and New York: Houghton Mifflin Company, 1929. (*Francis Wilson was an actor himself and knew Edwin Booth personally. His attempt to bring a balance to the distorted image, as portrayed by others, of John Wilkes Booth as a man and as an actor, succeeded.)

Note: There are scores of books on the above subject matter. Almost any book on Booth and/or the Civil War will contain a lengthy reference list or bibliography. We warn that books published before the 1930s, or even the 1940s, will probably not be found in local libraries due to present library policies of discarding books which do not have a "popular" turnover leaving little except modern fiction, recent biographies and the latest "show and tell" books. It will be necessary to obtain many of the above books from private collections, college and university libraries, or Civil War archives.

Chapter/ File 3

IZOLA

Imagine our delight when we read Miss Forrester's book—acquired through the Northern Rhode Island Interrelated Library System—and saw in print the local names and places that we have been documenting. The relationships amongst Alonzo, Caroline Mills Brown, Izola and Ogarita were revealed by this book, and it opened a new area of knowledge to us. The following account of Izola's association with the Booths of Maryland and with her family members in New England owes a heavy debt to Miss Forrester.

Source: *This One Mad Act. . .The Unknown Story of John Wilkes Booth and His Family by his granddaughter Izola Forrester. Hale, Cushman, & Flint (Boston, 1937).*

According to Miss Forrester's account, Izola Martha Mills was the daughter of Abram Standish Mills of Southport, Connecticut, owner and captain of a trading schooner in the China trade. Her mother, Izola Maria Mendoza of Cordova, Spain, died in childbirth off the coast of Martha's Vineyard. The child was given shortly after birth to Abram's sister, Fanny, and her husband, Henry D'Arcy of Baltimore, and raised in the South. Abram Standish Mills married Caroline Jenkins eight years after the death of his first wife and fathered Alonzo A. S. Mills. Caroline in turn married Mr. Edward Brown of Providence, Rhode Island, after the death of her first husband, Abram. Izola's half-brother, Alonzo, lived with his mother and step-father on the Mills farm in Pascoag. Alonzo was Izola's closest relative in the North except for her grandmother, Sarah Standish Mills, who lived in the vicinity of Fairfield, Connecticut.

John Wilkes Booth met Izola Martha [Mills] D'Arcy at a ball in Richmond, where, it is said, they became infatuated with one

Family Tree as viewed by Miss Forrester

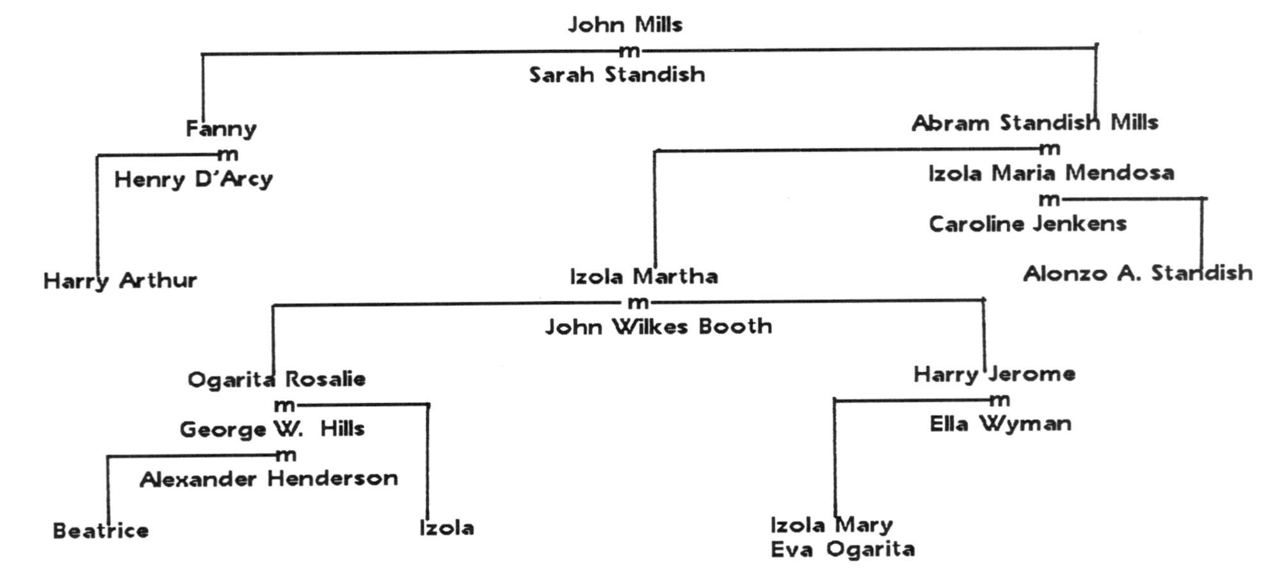

another. Despite the protestations of the D'Arcys, she eloped and wed the "actor" in Cos Cob, Connecticut, where the groom's brother Edwin, who was at that time on stage in Australia, had built a home in 1858. Miss Forrester relates that her adopted father, George Forrester, was shown the old record of this marriage by the widow of a Methodist minister in Cos Cob. It read, "the uniting in holy matrimony on January 9th, 1859, of J. Wilkes Booth and Izola Martha Mills, by the Rev. Peleg Weaver, at North Cos Cob." Harry Arthur D'Arcy, her cousin, accompanied them and acted as a witness. The couple later secured a home in the Shenandoah Valley, Virginia, between Martinsburg and Winchester (*This location is twice the distance to Richmond as it is to either Baltimore or Washington, DC) where Ogarita Rosalie was born on October 23, 1859. (*Ogarita's records at the Burrillville Town Hall list her name as Ogarita Elizabeth with her place of birth as Providence, Rhode Island.) Booth returned to Richmond, Virginia, where he was acting with a stock company. According to Miss Forrester, it was not unusual for actors and actresses to pose as being single to their public.

Izola lived in the Valley from 1859 until the spring of 1865. Booth returned, infrequently, often accompanied by Harry D'Arcy, both of whom were now involved with "special missions" for the Confederacy. (*Booth was also on stage from New Orleans to Boston and visited Canada as well during this six year period.) She acquired some nursing skills when she volunteered to aid doctors who occupied her Southern home and used it as a hospital for Union troops. Her cousin, Harry D'Arcy, was captured somewhere in West Virginia and shot as a spy. After the war, Aunt Fanny moved to Boston upon the death of her husband, Henry D'Arcy. After Lincoln's assassination, Izola fled the South with Ogarita and her black nurse "Aunt Sarah" to the home of a family named Stevenson, who lived near Baltimore, Maryland. Aunt Sarah had a son named Henry who was valet to Booth and accompanied him on these "special missions" for the South. (*In skeletal form this reads like a romantic novel or a Civil War soap, but Miss Forrester is most convincing and offers some documentation for her account.)

The author concludes that Booth (*her grandfather) was only a cog in the wheel of a complex conspiracy instigated by the Knights of the Golden Circle, a branch of Freemasonry that flourished in the North as well as the South, to rid the government of President Lincoln and certain members of his cabinet. Her contention is that Booth's devotion to the Southern cause and revenge for its defeat led him to this "one mad act." As do several others, she believes that John Wilkes Booth escaped the Garrett Farm in Virginia and went into exile where he was aided by the Knights of the Golden Circle until his death in 1879. (*For those interested in learning more about the foregoing, we suggest reading Miss Forrester's book and William Hanchett's *The Lincoln Murder Conspiracies* . . . see references from Chapter/file two.)

Between 1865 and 1868, Izola Wilkes or Martha D'Arcy (*known to us as Izola Martha Louise Mills) is living near Pleasant Valley, Maryland, not too many miles from Tudor Hall. (*The Booths were no longer in residence there.) A secret trip to California unites Izola for a year or so with her husband though details on this are hazy. John H. Stevenson, a member of the secret brotherhood, Knights of the Golden Circle, accompanies her on her journeys. Her daughter, Ogarita Rosalie, is at the Sacred Heart convent in Baltimore. Auntie Rosalie (Booth's elder sister) visited the nine-year-old girl and writes to Izola that she is doing fine and grows to look more and more like her father every day. (*Throughout the book, Miss Forrester speaks of the letters, money and gifts that flow from Rosalie and her mother, Mary Ann [Holmes] Booth, to Izola and Ogarita. She also suggests that there has been some sort of a disagreement between Edwin Thomas Booth and Izola Martha.)

A letter to Alonzo in Pascoag places Izola Martha in Baltimore in the fall of 1869. There is an unidentified epidemic in the city, and once again she is nursing the sick and laying out the dead. (*Izola is often found thus, and we wonder about her association with the medical world.) In January of 1870 or 1871, she gives birth to a son, Harry Jerome Dresbach Stevenson, who in fact is John Wilkes Booth's son. Miss Forrester repeatedly states that Harry was the best proof in the world that Booth was not killed, and that he was often identified as the son of John Wilkes Booth by agents, actors and friends of the Booth family. Stevenson generously allows the child to use his name. (*There is some doubt whether or not Izola later married John H. Stevenson. The author states so and then has her Uncle Harry saying that Stevenson merely was aiding the family as a member of the secret brotherhood.) In 1870 Izola gathers her family and moves to Boston, "leaving the South forever." (*We do find it curious that Izola, Ogarita and young Izola are frequently going to Boston in the 1880s to visit Mr. Stevenson at his residence at the Tremont House. Young Izola thinks he is her grandfather, but that grandmother is no longer married to him. Everyone eventually appears to end up in Burrillville or Boston, and we know that we too will be "going up" to Boston.)

From Boston, letters are sent and visits are made to Pascoag during the early 1870s. It is difficult to pin point when Izola, Ogarita, and young Izola stayed on the Brown farm with Alonzo and Mrs. Brown . . . and whether or not they were all there together at one time. Miss Forrester acknowledges that she was born on the "Mills" farm in Pascoag (1878). (*We know that they all were familiar names and faces to the people living in Burrillville during that decade.) In the early half of the 1880s, Izola moves to Canterbury, Connecticut about 25 miles across the Rhode Island border where she lives with her most recent husband, Edwin S. Bates, a much younger man. She is living in the mansion of a former mill owner located near Little River. Here, Ogarita, now married to Alexander Henderson, returns from theatrical engagements to restore her energy. (*We assume that she has divorced William Ross Wilson whom she married in 1879.) At times, young Izola and her half-sister Beatrice, the daughter of Alexander and Ogarita Henderson, go on tour with them. Apparently, Harry, young Izola and Beatrice attend the local schools in Canterbury. Miss Forrester obviously considered this home and recalls her favorite haunts and activities while there.

In the fall of 1887, Izola Martha [Mills] D'Arcy Booth (Stevenson) Bates dies of a heart attack at the age of fifty-one. She is buried beside the little Methodist Church—where she was known to have occasionally preached—in the center of Canterbury Plains as Mrs. Edwin S. Bates. Without their strong anchor, the family dispersed. Ogarita took the girls and went to Chicago, and Harry was boarded at a local minister's home (*by whom?). Terrace Hall, as Izola called her home, and its contents were sold at auction upon her death. The house was destroyed by fire a few years later.

(*Throughout the account of her grandmother, Izola Forrester refers to her as an actress of some renown. She tells of the trunks filled with theater costumes, props and playbills and of her association with actors, actresses and agents. Yet, she never identifies one specific place or time where her grandmother—under any of her many stage names—strutted the boards as Medea or Lady Macbeth. Through the eyes of a child, Izola Martha Mills D'Arcy Booth etc. was a mysterious blending of warm heartedness and uneven temperament.)

Prayer meetings as well as staged theater productions were held in Izola Martha's home. She was willful and wayward as both sides of her family declared. This handsome—also ample as shown by her pictures—and dramatic woman displayed a great deal of courage towards the many adversities that faced her during her lifetime. She emerges as the one figure who provided safety, security and seclusion for her family from the harshness of the times and the profession they had chosen. (*Small wonder that the memory of her still haunts those who live in this northwest corner of Rhode Island.)

(*We confess that it has been a struggle to suspend all of our disbelief with all that the author has related; though, we do not take her many years of research lightly. She—just as we are—gathered her material from the recollections, writings and documentation of others. There are several discrepancies in her book which we will deal with when necessary. She writes movingly and skillfully pulling the reader into the drama and romance that swirled around her mother, Ogarita, and her grandmother, Izola. Having recorded and transcribed the recollections of many elderly people, we know that sometimes youthful memories can be molded into myth . . especially when events and names have been repeated, again and again, by past generations. We have been given a sizable amount of data to ponder and to document. One of us cannot resist the temptation to leave the ledgers behind and cross over the border into Connecticut to see the places that Miss Forrester wrote of so winsomely. Our first plan of action is to telephone a person who formerly lived in our area, but now resides in Canterbury, to see whether she has any information regarding the elusive Izola Martha.)

"Izola" Martha Louise Mills
Booth's alleged wife

Chapter/File 4

CANTERBURY

Beginning our pursuit of the elusive Booths of Burrillville, we historical detectives had the following distinct advantages over those who have been trying to verify or disclaim a connection between our Booths and the more nationally recognized Booths of Maryland: (1) Researching local and regional history has been our avocation for more than a decade. (2) Names associated with this local lore and legend were known to us as were several of the descendants of their families. (3) We recognized the name of Alonzo Mills as we had read transcribed portions of his journals . . . but viewed them only as a curious documentation of local history at that time. (4) The fact that we are both natives of Burrillville acquaints us with a great many of the people who lived here or had moved from this area. One of the latter provided the introduction and information needed to pursue our search in Canterbury, Connecticut, where "Izola" Martha lived out her remaining years.

Source: *Susan [Bailey] Burroughs (1941-) is a native of Burrillville (Bridgeton) and "brought up" on Wallum Pond Road known as Wilson Avenue during the first half of the twentieth century and as East Wallum Lake Road from 1950 to the present. Susan married a Canterbury native and subsequently moved to Connecticut.*

When called and asked about the gravesite of Mrs. Edwin S. Bates, Mrs. Burroughs said, "Oh, you want to know about John Wilkes Booth and the burial beside our church (*Calvary Baptist). Everyone knows about that around here. Call Mr. Linwood Tracy; he can tell you all about it." (*Everyone seems to have known about Izola excluding the two who are attempting to document her life story.)

Source: *Linwood Tracy (1911 -) Custodian of the Canterbury Plains Cemetery.*

An appointment was made to meet Mr. Tracy at the cemetery, which is in tiptop condition. One can look down the rows of individual mounds of old gravesites with a few family headstones scattered amongst them. At one time the townspeople had placed a sizable urn on Izola's grave, but it disappeared several years ago. . . much to Mr. Tracy's chagrin. He added that during the spring family members of Izola often come to visit her grave, and that they are associated with a theater in New York City . . . one being a director of stage productions. (*Interesting indeed!) He promised to call if they ever return.

Not too distant from the Calvary Baptist Church, Mr. Tracy points out a modest white cottage where Izola ran a "maternity hospital." (*This is yet another account of her medical abilities.) When Izola Martha lived in Canterbury (1882-1887), she was well thought of, in spite of the fact that her dubious past was well known. (*This is counter to Miss Forrester's belief that Izola led a secluded life, did not mingle with the local society, and was considered a mysterious person.) Mr. Tracy gave directions to the site of Terrace Hall near Hanover where Izola lived with her children and grandchildren. Its location is several miles from the cemetery and church.

(*This distance throws some doubt on a poignant scene from *This One Mad Act* when young Izola [Miss Forrester at age nine] walks cross country in the snows of November to find her mother, Ogarita, kneeling at her mother's grave, a final goodbye before they depart for Chicago . . . possible but not probable. It is a good hike from Terrace Hall to the cemetery on Canterbury Plains.)

Even with directions, the site of Izola's last home is not easy to find, and it is certainly secluded as Miss Forrester related. Terrace Hall, which burned before the 1900s, has been replaced by a new home owned by a family named Olsen. The long road winding its way up the high embankment and cutting through a secondary growth of trees is still there. Across the road are the ruins of a mill with several stone foundations and a sizable stepped dam used for the overflow from Little River. In all honesty, it is not difficult to imagine the Victorian mansion and the indomitable Izola Martha standing on its porch either welcoming or waving goodbye to her brood.

(*One of the satisfactions of doing historical research is the opportunity to visit the sites that are read about and researched to the

Canterbury Plains Cemetery
Mr. Linwood Tracy near Mrs. Izola Bates' Grave

Canterbury near Hanover
Site of Hilbert's Mill near Fort Ned.
Photos by the authors.

nth degree. Mr. Tracy's final advice was to go to the *Norwich Bulletin's* office and check their files . . . as several articles were written about Izola during the centennial of Lincoln's assassination.)

***Source:** Jim Scott, "After Lincoln's Assassination. The wife of John Wilkes Booth lived and died in Canterbury." Norwich Bulletin-Courier, April 11, 1965. Sec. 3. pp. 2-5.*

(*This article recaps much of what we have covered in the file entitled "Izola" though the following bits and pieces are new.) There is no trace of Izola's activities between 1869 to 1871 until letters begin to come from Boston to Alonzo in Pascoag when she writes of the great Boston fire (*date not given).

Izola lived in the mansion once owned by a man named Hillbert, who operated the woolen mill and was said to have committed suicide in his home after the mill and other buildings were destroyed by fire. Mrs. Edwin Bates died the night of November 9, 1887 in Canterbury. Bates was her third husband; her second was John H. Stevenson and her first John Wilkes Booth. Bates spent his time at his home on Chestnut Hill (*Connecticut). Stevenson was a resident in a Boston hotel; he died of a heart attack on a train heading west in 1889.

Miss Forrester (Izola's granddaughter) describes the ring on her grandmother's hand with the two hearts of gold and the inscribed initials, "J.W.B. to I.M.M." Izola was buried with this ring on her finger.

Miss Forrester admits to the gaps in her published story, *This One Mad Act,* but attributes this to the fact that many people had died before she could interview them and that all written evidence in the case (*of the Booths) was deliberately destroyed or withheld. Miss Forrester was a feature writer and journalist for some of the "biggest" and "most powerful" newspapers and magazines of her time (1878-1944) and spent over forty years unearthing information linking her to Booth, according to Mr. Scott. Izola Forrester returned to Canterbury and boarded with a family near Barstow Road. She later rented a dwelling there. By the early 1900s, she was a successful writer. (*Reporter Scott's information, for the most part, is from Miss Forrester's book.)

***Source:** Susan Slosberg, "Local Lore Perpetuates Century Old Mystery." Norwich Bulletin-Courier, Sunday, April 11, 1965. (*Section and page not listed on copy, same edition as previous.) This article continues the story with the following additions.*

Linwood Tracy relates to reporter Slosberg much of what he told us. His picture and one of the church and cemetery are included. This is not the original Methodist Church where Izola was said to have preached. Mr. Tracy was born in the house once owned by Izola. Terrace Hall has since been destroyed by fire. (*Via telephone Mr. Tracy said that he was born near the first home that Izola owned in Canterbury and not Terrace Hall, which he had never seen.)

The researchers at the University of Virginia told Susan Slosberg that Lincoln's assassin was never married and that various women connected with him were prostitutes. (*This last statement is a bit heavy. We already know about Ella Turner, and we read of others in this profession with whom Booth associated. But, he was also in and out of love with actresses and was reportedly engaged to a senator's daughter. The old double standard reigned. Also, historians agree that in the South, especially Richmond, Booth was accepted by the "better society.") The reporter also relates Miss Forrester's account of the Knights of The Golden Circle, Booth's escape, and doubts about the identification of the body as Booth's.

(*The librarian of the *Norwich Bulletin* was kind enough to send the above articles to us. We were willing to go to Norwich and turn all the pages of the *Bulletin* between 1880 and 1887; unfortunately, these years are included in the editions that were damaged by floodwater. These papers are being reclaimed according to the librarian. The state library in Hartford has only a few of the *Norwich Bulletins* that we need, but we will check them out.)

Sources: *Linwood Tracy and Records at the Canterbury Town Hall.*

We two historical detectives continued our search by traveling to Canterbury to meet with Mr. Linwood Tracy and to take pictures of Martha's gravesite. Mr. Tracy mentioned the fact that a colored assistant of Martha's was buried in this same plot. He had no further information on this assistant. Mr. Tracy also brought a snapshot of the urn that had been placed on Mrs. Edwin S. Bates' final resting place. The urn was manufactured at the Barstow Foundry once located on Barstow Road not far from where Martha ran her "lying-in hospital" situated on a sizable farm. The house is still standing though "not recognizable due to changes and a fire over the years." (*If Martha had been living here when she died, the snowy November graveside scene in Miss Forrester's book would have been possible as the "hospital" is not far from Canterbury Plains Cemetery.) Obviously this was an early farmhouse as are several others scattered throughout the pleasantly rural area. Perhaps it should be mentioned that the Prudence Crandall House is also in the same locale. Her house was famous (during the eighteen hundreds infamous) for being "the first school for Negro girls" in New England.

Canterbury Plains is aptly named as the terrain is in mock contrast to the gently rolling hills of Connecticut state. At the Town Hall, housed in the basement of a school, we are greeted by a helpful and pleasant Town Clerk, who checks out our identity and status as genealogists. We turn to the early index of Births, Deaths and Marriages to find that Canterbury was sparsely settled in the eighteen hundreds. We do find "Izola" Bates' death record as listed in Volume 4, which is currently out being preserved for posterity. Marilyn E. Burris, Town Clerk, agrees to forward a copy to us for a slight fee, which we are more than happy to pay. This is the first official verification of Martha Louise Mills' use of the name Izola. Again, we wonder who gave this information to the incumbent Town Clerk in 1887. There are only a few other names which ring a bell. Benjamin Pierce married a Sarah Mills in August of 1758. This time frame is unfortunately not right for our Sarah Standish Mills, the elusive grandmother of Martha and Alonzo. There are three Bates, Joseph P., Alford (?) and a Mary along with some Wilsons. None of these appears related to our case. We need to recall that the same basic Anglo-Saxon names appear and reappear throughout our regional and national history.

Turning to the Probate Court records, we are amazed to find that Izola Bates is not listed. Why? Miss Forrester and Mr. Tracy have her owning property with a sizable amount of land at Terrace Hall near Hanover and also at the hospital on the plains. Of course, it is up to the family or their legal representative to decide whether or not to go through probate. But this absence poses many questions. It should also be mentioned that there are no tax records available for that time period according to the Canterbury Town Clerk.

Even more puzzling are the land records, where there is no mention under any of her varied names of any transactions from 1880 through 1887. Did she have just a lease or maybe only a handshake agreement on the purchase of these properties, which in those times was not at all unusual. Possibly. All of this cannot be fantasy. The lack of information obtained was somewhat disappointing. Sometimes the lack of evidence can tell you as much as the discovery would have done. The day was not a total failure as it was filled with sunshine as we drove the twenty-five miles over the hills and dales of eastern Connecticut. No one can blame "Izola" Martha for "removing" herself and family to this delightful and still sparsely settled countryside. Driving back to Burrillville, we fall to talking about Alonzo and his more fruitful records, which require a careful and closer study to provide us with the clues necessary to discover who our elusive Burrillville Booths actually are. But first, a little background on the gentleman who has perked our interest in this subject by his fascinating journals, not to mention the impact they have had on our investigations.)

Chapter/File 5

ALONZO

As previously suggested, the daily recordings of Alonzo Abram Standish Mills have given us an advantage over those who have been and still are covering the same ground in order to resolve this mystery. By now it should be clear that Alonzo is half-brother to "Izola" Martha Louise Mills, uncle to Ogarita "Rosalie," and great-uncle to Izola Louise Wallingford (*Miss Forrester, the author). We know that they all lived on the Brown Farm at one time or another. There are still a few local people who are able to recall Alonzo, and from all accounts he was a well-known and interesting figure in this town.

This chapter/file begins with some background material on Alonzo which we hope will "fill in the lines" to make our journalist into a very real individual. We continue with samples from his journal along with some revealing notations made by Alonzo himself on the situation at hand.

Source: *Hazel Rosalie Hopkins continues to be an inexhaustible well of information and contributor of valuable materials and photographs.*

Alonzo Mills was considered to be rather eccentric. (*This would take "some doing" as the Bridgeton-Wallum Lake section of Burrillville was known for its abundance of local characters . . . possibly due to the distance from the prevailing effects of more sophisticated society and decidedly due to native independence, which allowed all to do "pretty much as they darned pleased.") He lived with his mother on the Brown farm (*destroyed by fire in 1966) helping her to run the place and also "hired out" to do odd jobs for the older families in the area such as the Angells, Hopkins,

Millards, Tafts, and Wilsons.

Mother and son were somehow related to Izola and Ogarita, who both lived with and visited them now and then. (*In the beginning, Miss Hopkins was not aware of their actual relationship.) Alonzo was apparently good natured and quite sociable. In his later life, members of the above families were much concerned with his welfare and " kept an eye on him."

Source: *Norma Izola [Angell] Hopkins (1889-1984).*

Miss Hopkins had in her possession a fading photograph of Alonzo and Mrs. Brown on "their place," which she had obtained from her mother. The picture was enclosed in a folded paper with Mrs. Norma Hopkins' handwriting across it reading, "Picture of Mrs. Brown and her son, Alonzo Mills, also her home." The house is a three storied, clapboard federal with central chimney and much in need of repairs and paint. Alonzo appears near the front door with hat in hand. One would guess him to be in his early thirties at this time. His nice looking face sprouts a close-trimmed beard. His hair and beard appear quite dark. Mrs. Brown, a diminutive person but of formidable face, is standing at the edge of the house dressed in a country cotton frock. Her hair is pulled severely back.

Source: *Brandon Patterson (1907-) resides on East Wallum Lake Road (Wallum Pond Road). His paternal grandmother was Hulda [Millard] Patterson and his paternal great grandfather was Samuel Millard. The Millards owned the abutting farm to that of Alonzo and Mrs. Brown.*

As a young boy, Brandon Patterson would see Alonzo Mills walking past his home on his way down to the village to shop. According to Mr. Patterson, Alonzo was short of stature, stout, and had a full gray beard. He mentions the fact that Alonzo was soft spoken, and that he would stop and talk to everyone as he went along. His mother, who was seldom seen, lived on the so-called Brown Farm with Alonzo. The Millards and the Browns share the burial grounds in between the two sizable farmsteads.

Source: *This One Mad Act by Izola Forrester.*

Miss Forrester places Alonzo Abram Standish Mills on the Booth family tree as being the half-brother of Izola Martha Booth with Abram Standish Mills as their mutual father. Izola and Ogarita and young Izola (*Miss Forrester) live with Alonzo and his mother on and off between theater engagements. Miss Forrester writes that she was born on the Mills farm in Pascoag. (*There seems to be some confusion in her mind as to whom the farm actually belongs . . more on this later.) She mentions throughout the book the letters sent and received between Alonzo and Izola relating to family matters. Betsey B. Benchley is also living on the farm. She is either the mother of Caroline, whose maiden name was Jenkens, or of Abram Mills. The author notes that the men in the family, who are seldom seen or heard from, except Alonzo, are clearly dominated by these women.

Miss Forrester recalls with fondness the old farm, the abundance of visiting relatives, and her adventures as a child. Trunks stored in the garret are filled with either the colorful theater costumes belonging to Izola or with the exotic apparel of her great, great grandmother, Izola Maria (Mary) Mendoza.

Source: *"Burrillville, The Best Town There Is" by Frank H. Potter (1939) (*A collection of tales poking fun at the "individuals" who lived in Burrillville down through the years. Mr. Potter was the editor-in-chief of the Pascoag Herald.)*

Mr. Potter writes: Alonzo Mills, who lived on the Wallum Pond Road a little beyond Wilson's Reservoir, frequently made long trips on foot, sometimes trundling a wheel barrow ahead of him and at other times without the barrow. It is said that he claimed to be able to make better time with it than he could without it. This he explained by saying that when he had the wheelbarrow he had something to follow as a sort of pace setter, -- the faster the wheel turned the faster was he compelled to travel to keep up with it. (*Yankee humor may by funny . . . but not to those who have to grow up with it. We include this to point out that Alonzo, though a character and man-about-town, is accepted . . . or he would not have been a subject of joshing . . . "they" do that to the people they like.)

Source: *Pascoag Herald dated February 28, 1913.*

Fifty years ago yesterday, Alonzo A. S. Mills, moved onto the farm that Mr. Mills now owns and lives on, one and one half miles north of Bridgeton, moving from their home in North Providence. Mr. Mills' stepfather, Edward M. Brown, bought the farm of Andrew Luther of Burrillville. The farm formerly belonged to the late Joseph Brown of this town. (*Until we discovered this little piece, we did not know whether the family was native to the soil . . . so to speak. This places Alonzo, his mother and stepfather in Bridgeton as early as 1863. It also gives Izola and Ogarita a better excuse to flee here other than just going to the "end of the world" by blind chance. We also note that Providence and North Providence appear to be the origins of some of this family with whom we have become so involved. We have not been able to locate any other Mills in the area at this time excepting one John E. Mills, age 45, occupation laborer, listed in the Burrillville Militia Enrollment dates 1861-62-63. We have not established a relationship to date between John E. Mills and Alonzo, or between Edward M. Brown and the Joseph Brown mentioned above.

Source: *Pascoag Herald dated February 12, 1886. "A Burrillville Puff" by Alonzo A. Mills written in 1872. The editor of the Herald states, "The following was recently 'discovered,' and shows how badly the writer felt when he wrote such a glorious puff." (* If you are of Yankee extraction, you would know that the words fire, air and there all rhyme.)*

On the old Huntsville and Wallum pond stream,
Stood an old shoddy mill of fame and esteem:
Together with a saw and grist mill to frown
Took up the attention of Burrillville town.
On the 10th of last June, the mill caught a fire
And how like the Devil it raged through the air
A burning up lumber and so on until,
It raised the old harry with the Wilson's old mill
From the mill went the fire into James Wilson's barn
Trying to burn up his hay and cause great alarm.
And also to the roof of his house went the fire
To try to raise cane with the women folks there.
But as help was quite plenty and wells all about,
They stuck to the buildings, till they put the fire out . . .

(*Other than a nice slice of the time period—fires are frequent and fatal to both man and buildings, but neighbors band together in time of need—Alonzo is having some fun with the Wilson family. But, he winds up his poem with some rather harsh commentaries on those who inhabit this hamlet.)

The people of Burrillville, are busy as bees
Trying to raise the Devil, and kick up a breeze,

They'll lie, and they'll cheat, and nig you if they can,
Its very hard to find an honest upright man.
For as Mr. Russell said, they're scarcer than gold
And plaguey nigh all of them, I think Purgatory'l hold.
But very few of them will rise, any higher
Than did the flames of the shoddy mill fire.
Look out for the store-keepers, and keep your eyes open,
Though they're all very kind and very soft spoken.
As for the mill owners they make the poorest cloth
The half of its shoddy—Well I've said enough.
And as for the farming in Burrillville town
I'm sure it won't fit us for fame or renown
And as for Burrillville people, should they
their own business mind
There would be less trouble, I'm sure amongst mankind. . .

(*Shoddy is cloth manufactured from second hand yarns, and Alonzo implies so are the people in the locale. What is the business that the townspeople (in 1872) should not be looking into? Does this have anything to do with Ogarita and/or Izola? We note that it was not published until 1886 after they have left for Canterbury, CT.)

Source: *Pascoag Herald dated April 24, 1885. (*No matter, by this date Alonzo and family are back to being a part of the community again.)*

Many of the numerous friends of Caroline E. (H) Brown, from Laurel Ridge and vicinity, assembled at her home, about 1 1/2 miles west of Laurel Ridge . . . to associate together and commemorate the birthday of Mrs. Brown. (Newspaper note: The age is withheld on the account of her age.) . . . Alonzo was a little indisposed at first, but before supper he became convalescent and relished both the time and the meal. The first class of people were there, the first class time, and the first class supper . . . All went home in good season, and all wishing Mrs. Brown might live to enjoy many more years of health and prosperity to receive many friends in like manner. (*This does not indicate that she was a recluse as earlier suggested . . . at least not at this time.)

(*These newsy daily papers are obviously a wonderful source of information but we are aware that newspapers are not infallible especially in spelling proper names and exact dates. The life of Alonzo and his family—no mention of his half-sister or niece—is relatively easy to follow as their comings and goings are scattered throughout the pages of the *Herald.* The *Burrillville Gazette*, later to be consolidated with the *Burrillville News* and finally sold to the *Pascoag Herald*, was started in 1880. Izola and Ogarita moved to Canterbury in 1882. Lest the reader think that the information was easy to come by, it was necessary to go through this material page by page. Apparently, no one had ever indexed or previously used these particular copies.)

Source: *Burrillville Historical and Preservation Society's Archives. The Daily Records of Alonzo Abram Standish Mills. (*Not in their original form but rather 26 typewritten pages. A curious collection of births, deaths, marriages and events of local and worldwide interest. For the most part, it is an alphabetized listing of surnames of local families, relatives of Alonzo and famous historical figures . . . some obviously taken from the Herald but not all, with a portion of the material missing, specifically "L through Z" with the exception of two pages of "S." These have been on file for about a decade, but we did not at first connect them to our elusive Booths. The following are selections relating to Alonzo himself. It is not known whether the misspellings, etc. are the work of Alonzo or the transcriber of this material.)*

Electric Cars commenced running between Pascoag and Harrisville and Woonsocket, and around the square of Bridgeton and Pascoag today (noon-time) Saturday Nov. 1st, 1902 - I., (Alonzo A. S. Mills) rode from Main Street Pascoag to Inman & Brooks store, at Bridgeton, this evening—(Nov. 1st) in the Electric Car. (*When he gives us specific facts such as the above, we want to make him an honorary member of the Burrillville Historical & Preservation Society.)

Gifford, George and Earle and George Joslin and myself—Alonzo A. S. Mills went from Bridgeton, R. I. to the city of Providence and back today, Sat. Oct. 27, 1906 by Electric Cars by the way of Woonsocket, R. I. (*George Joslin bought Alonzo's farm from him in 1916, and George Gifford's family had two of Alonzo's daily journals. At one time, both the Gifford and Joslin families lived near the Brown farm.)

I.S.M.M.S.D.T.M.G. Wed. March 13, 1907. (*He can be cryptic.)

Names and ages of inmates at the Burrillville R. I. Town Asylum, during the months of January, February, and March, 1905: Jeremiah Mowry age 80 years, James Taylor 79 years, Session Cooper 75 years, Winsor Ballou 75 years, Willis Sherman 71 years,

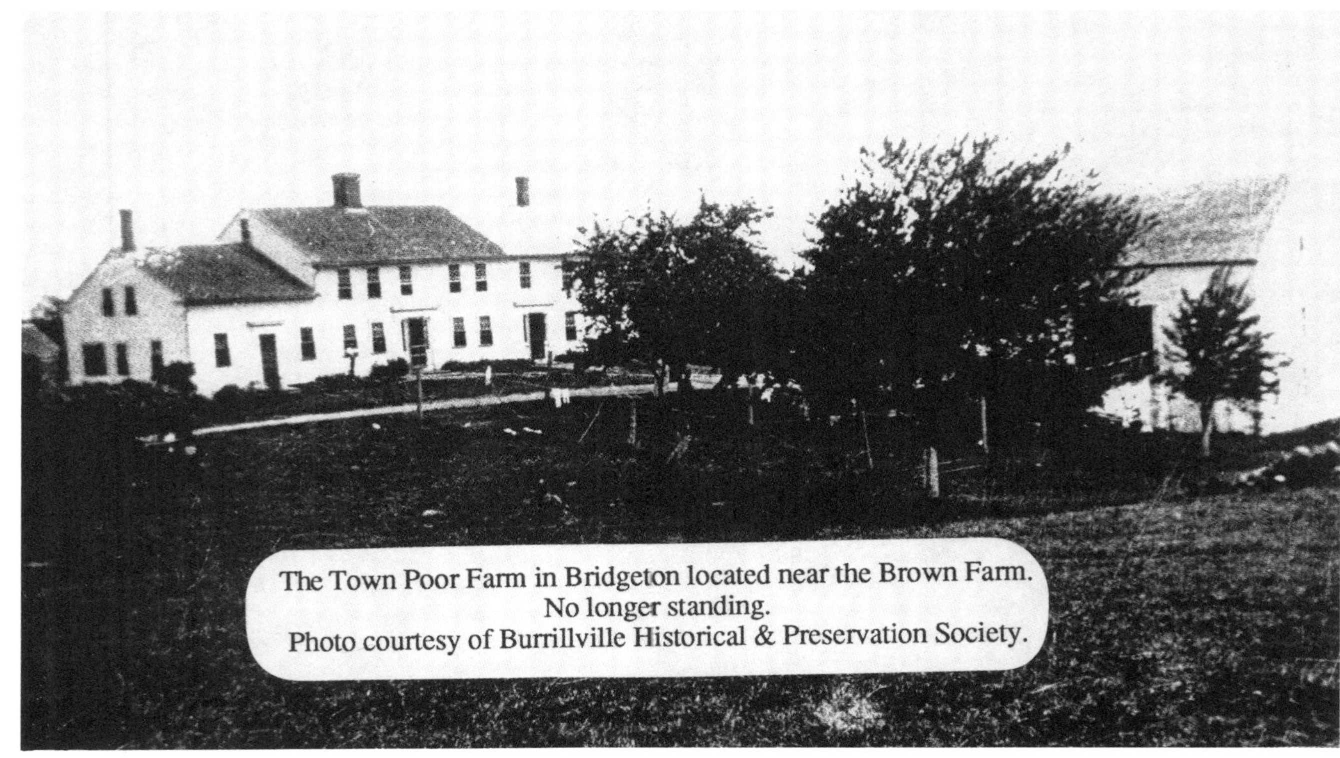

The Town Poor Farm in Bridgeton located near the Brown Farm.
No longer standing.
Photo courtesy of Burrillville Historical & Preservation Society.

Robert Iverson 66 years, Alonzo A. S. Mills 57 years, Fenner Inman 54 years, Edwin Logee 53 years, Michael Black 51 years, Mary Delia Lunn 38 years, Viola Lunn 4 years. (*What is Alonzo doing here? The Town Asylum was located on the Town Farm Road not too far from the Brown Farm.)

Source: *Burrillville and North Smithfield Directory (1910) p. 24.*

Mills, Alonzo farmer h (home) Wallum Pond rd. P (Pascoag) (*Alonzo is back on his farm and living alone. We return to his daily records where he gives us, a few items down, some information that we, perhaps, do not wish to read. We caution the reader not to jump to conclusions the way that we did.)

News: Burrillville, RI., Sunday Jan. 7, 1894. I (Alonzo A. Mills) called on Mr. William R. Wilson, at the home of Mr. Luther C. Angell and Mr. John Ramford (*Stamford?) Burrillville, today on business.

News: Monday Jan. 8, 1894. I (A.S.Mills) commenced cutting wood today for Mr. Smith Angell, Burrillville, RI, by the cord. (*Mr. Wilson, Ogarita's first husband, continues to "look after" Alonzo's welfare.)

Bates, Edwin S. born April 10, 1853. (*Izola's last husband and indeed much younger than she.)

Bates, Mr. Francis L. died in Pascoag Sat. Jan 20, 1883 in his 31st year. (*Brother to Edwin S. Bates? Are they from Pascoag?)

Benchley, Betsey B. died Mar. 12, 1878 (*Here is the great great grandmother, who died the year Miss Forrester [Izola Louise Wallingford] was born.)

Bellows, Mr. Charles S. of Boston U.S.N. and Martha L. Mills of Pawtucket, Rhode Island, were married in Boston, Mass. by the Rev. Streeter on Monday, July 30, 1855. (*We encountered Mr. Bellows in Ogarita's marriage to Wilson, but we thought Martha Izola married him after Booth and not before. The "of Pawtucket" suggests that Martha is from that area. In 1855 she is not living in the South with the D'Arcys . . . at least not on July 30th.)

Brown, Mrs. Caroline H. sold an Ox Sled Tongue to Mr. William R. Wilson Burrillville, Monday, Jan 20, 1896. (*Caroline conducts her own business independent of her husband.)

Brown, Mr. Edward M. Burrillville sold his off ox to Mr. Samuel Spring a butcher in Pascoag for beef, Sat. Dec. 6, 1873. The ox weighed dressed 926 pounds at $8.50 per hundred. (*Business as usual for Mr. and Mrs. Brown; their daily happenings in sharp contrast to those of John Wilkes Booth or Izola Martha in the 1860s.

Bellows, Charles Still son of Charles S. and Martha L. Bellows was born in Boston Mass. Thurs. May 16, 1861 Moon 7 days old. (*Ogarita not listed anywhere. Miss Forrester does mention the Bellows of Boston, but not as her uncle. Martha still in the North in '61? Our two strangers from the South are becoming more like city cousins from the North. We send out for verification or negation to the appropriate city or town. After having been on this project for over two years, we have learned to let our fingers do the walking. Note to the veteran historical or genealogical researcher: We have not included "our failure to find" in the obvious sources one would turn to immediately such as: tax reports, military listings, local genealogical charts, town directories, and vital statistics records.)

Battle of Ball's Bluff Va. Oct. 21, 1861.

Battle of Fredericktown Mo. Oct. 21, 1861. (*Alonzo keeps us abreast of the war news, weather, fires and other calamities both home and abroad. His historical dates correspond with the newspaper dates and not necessarily with the actual day of the event.)

Children of Reuben R. and Izola Merrifield South Canterbury Conn. Arthur Sydnez Merrifield Ogarita Dell. Merrifield. Richard Forrester Merrifield Dorothy Florence Merrifield. (*Wasn't too difficult to ascertain that this is Miss Forrester [Izola Louise Wallingford], who is still living in Canterbury and has married Reuben R. No date given. Remember the name Dell.)

Clutts Mrs. Beatrice R. South Canterbury. (*Beatrice Rosalie Henderson, half sister to Izola Louise Forrester.)

Children of Charles E. and Beatrice Rosalie Clutts of South Canterbury, Conn. Charles Edward Clutts Ogarita Mary Clutts (*Family given names are continued . . . the beat goes on. No dates. Alonzo does not have any time sequence; he also takes a great deal of liberty with his alphabet.)

Destructive fire in Boston Mass. Mon. Feb. 24, 1862. (*Disastrous fires were much a part of the nineteenth century scenario, and Alonzo mentions a good many of these.)

Kershaw, James Henry and Miss Mary Foss Pattison were married at the Laurel Hill M. E. Church Pascoag by the Rev. John Oldham assisted by the Rev. C. D. Foss DD on Wed. Sept. 17, 1879. (*The Kershaws were from England, and there is either a strong friendship and/or a relationship between them and Caroline Brown. We think "Pattison" might read Patterson. The Methodist Episcopal Church on Laurel Hill was put to good use by the Mills, Browns,

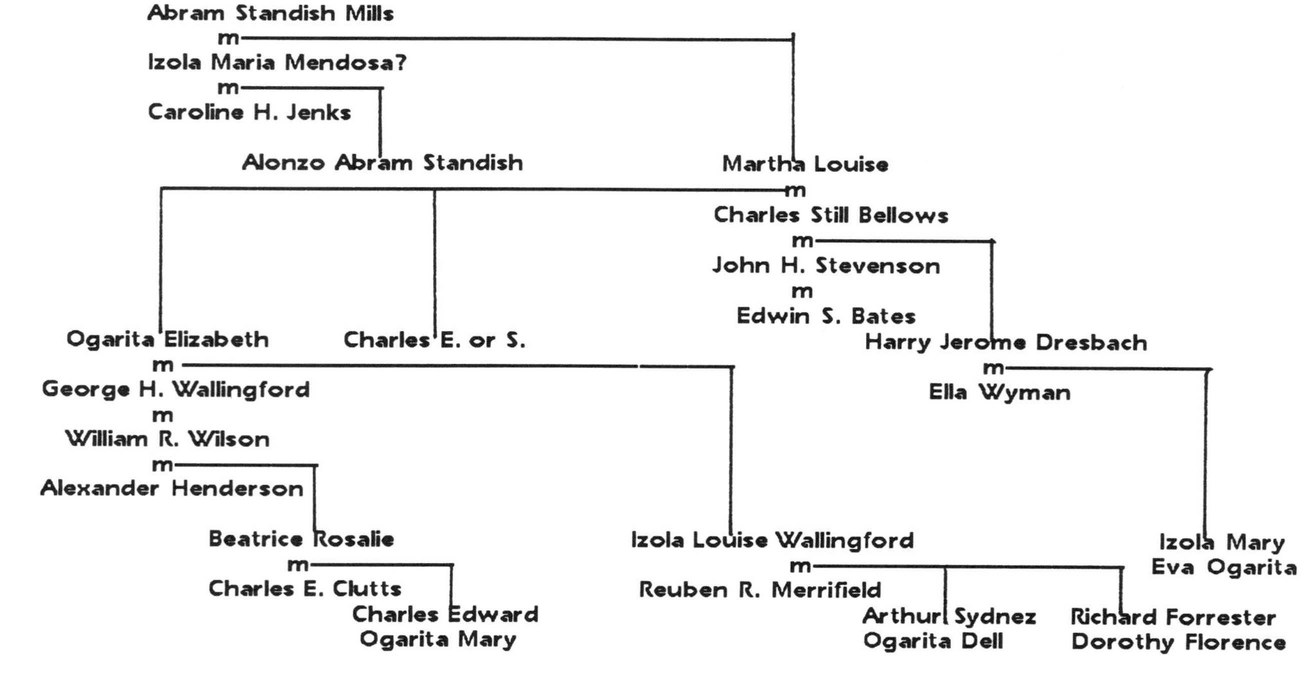
Family Tree by Alonzo A. S. Mills and the Authors
Abram Standish Mills
m
Izola Maria Mendosa?
m
Caroline H. Jenks
Alonzo Abram Standish
Martha Louise
m
Charles Still Bellows
m
John H. Stevenson
m
Edwin S. Bates
Ogarita Elizabeth
Charles E. or S.
Harry Jerome Dresbach
m
George H. Wallingford
m
William R. Wilson
m
Alexander Henderson
m
Ella Wyman
Beatrice Rosalie
m
Charles E. Clutts
Charles Edward
Ogarita Mary
Izola Louise Wallingford
m
Reuben R. Merrifield
Arthur Sydnez
Ogarita Dell
Richard Forrester
Dorothy Florence
Izola Mary
Eva Ogarita

Wilsons, and a great many other families located in this area.)

(*Easy to see that these daily records are a genealogist's dream or nightmare as the case may be. These records continue on with family names and places that we have read concerning our Booths, but the given names and the dates do not correspond. . . they could be relatives but we cannot verify them as yet. At this writing we have found the missing letters "L-Z" and more of Alonzo's "writings" and erased the mystery surrounding their absence. But we do need to continue with the findings in a chronological order and therefore return to Ogarita Rosalie, whom we have somewhat neglected.)

Chapter/File 6

OGARITA (ROSALIE) ELIZABETH

The birth of Ogarita's daughter Izola Louise Wallingford in 1878 and her marriage to William R. Wilson in 1879 have been previously documented. We have yet to find any evidence of George H. Wallingford or, according to Miss Forrester's family tree, George W. Hills who was Ogarita's first husband. Ogarita was considered an attractive girl and shared with her mother a certain "bearing" that demanded attention, a valuable quality for an actress. According to her peers in Burrillville, she was more popular and less formidable than her mother, Izola Martha "Booth". The memory of Ogarita still floats around the northwest corner of Burrillville as well as her "adopted" middle name, Rosalie.

Source: *This One Mad Act by Izola Forrester. (*Page numbers given are for pages in this book.)*

Miss Forrester places Ogarita Rosalie on the Booth Family Tree as the daughter of Izola Martha Mills and John Wilkes Booth. According to this account, she was named for the leading character in an old play of the 1850s, *Ogarita* or *The Sea of Ice,* and her middle name, Rosalie, for her father's favorite sister (page 19). Ogarita divorced her first husband Hills (?) who was living in England (page 45). Alexander Henderson, her second husband, was a stage manager and musical director. Because they were in different road companies, they were often separated. Ogarita died at the age of thirty-two in April, 1892, in Binghamton, New York, where she was appearing with a road company. An article from the *New York World* dated April 15, 1892, informs us that Rita Booth (*a stage name used by Ogarita) was a clever character actress and was said to have been the daughter of Wilkes Booth. (*JWB is often referred to

Ogarita (Rosalie) Elizabeth Bellows Booth
In costume for "The Danites"

this way rather than using his first name.) People who had known Booth stated that Ogarita bore a striking resemblance to him. She was buried on a hill overlooking a valley in Binghamton (pages 81, 82). Shortly thereafter, her daughter, Izola Louise Wallingford (Hills?) was adopted by George Forrester in Chicago. Miss Forrester does not clearly explain—to our satisfaction—the reason for her adoption.

Young Izola found in her grandmother's trunk pictures of Ogarita and Booth inscribed with "Ogarita B. . ." or "O.R.B. from her father, J. W. B. October 23rd." There were also letters from Aunt Rosalie, one with a plea to leave young Ogarita in the convent in Baltimore until Izola firmed up her plans after returning from the West Coast. (*She took her daughter and her nurse, Aunt Sarah, to Boston in 1869.) Many of Ogarita's playbills show that she made her first appearances under the name of Ogarita Wilkes. She played in *Oliver Twist* in Providence in 1877, and the Artful Dodger was played by a young actress named Minnie Maddern. Three or four years later she played in Boston as Rita Booth in *The Two Orphans* (pages 101, 102, 103).

From her mother's trunk also came programs from Sacramento and San Francisco plus the theatrical notices of Junius Brutus Booth, Jr. (*What is their relationship with John Wilkes' older brother, who lived in California until 1864?) There were also carte de visits of Junius Booth along with his old collar of rose point and various pictures and portraits of the Booth family (pages 101-106). Miss Forrester relates of the many descendants of Martha and John, some of whom share the wide ox-eyes, dramatic inclinations and flair for the romantic described in the family as the Booth-look and style (page 438).

(*The author pictures her mother throughout her book as a lovely, talented, gentle woman, who led a bewildering life on the road with a variety of theatrical figures, and who was a woman somewhat confused and tormented by the claim that she was the daughter of Wilkes Booth. Ogarita evolves from her daughter's portrayal as a rather tragic figure. It is noted that dates and names do not always coincide with other recorded data. It would appear that Ogarita lived in Pascoag on and off from the 1870s until 1881 or 1882 when Izola moved to Canterbury. Evidently, she did not spend much time with her husband, William R. Wilson, on Wilson's Hill in Pascoag.)

Charles Bellows, Ogarita's brother, is never mentioned. In fact the Bellows are referred to as distant relatives living in Boston. Harry Stevenson, her younger half brother, lives with them in Canterbury. Names are confused a good deal of the time, such as

Albert or Alexander Henderson, not to mention the variety of names used by both the mother and daughter as stage actresses and in their real life.

Even given the consideration that Ogarita is continually on tour (*like Booth himself), her relatively short life is a maze of activity and relationships. We did forget to mention that Ogarita also had a son, Charles Henderson, who died when a baby. Her two surviving children were Izola Louise and Beatrice Rosalie Henderson.)

Source: *The Reincarnation of John Wilkes Booth. A Study in Hypnotic Regression by Dell Leonardi. The Devin-Adair Company (Old Greenwich, Connecticut, 1975). (*If you are into reincarnation and parapsychology, read this interesting account of Booth's return to the 20th century.)*

Reincarnated Booth said that he used a false name for his marriage to Izola, something like James Brayton, and that they were married in Baltimore in 1859. Dell Leonardi in the book adds that Booth told her he met Izola in Baltimore in 1859. A letter from Mrs. Elijah Rogers to a friend (*Mrs. Rogers was a neighbor of the Booth family when they lived on the farm in Harford County) seems to establish the fact that Izola bore a daughter and a son, Alonso, fathered by Booth, who saw his daughter once shortly after her birth (pages 51-68). (*This is the first time we have heard of a son named Alonso. What is his relationship with our Alonzo?)

(*We noted that Dell is the middle name of one of the Booth's descendants, Ogarita Dell Merrifield, living in South Canterbury when Alonzo Mills was recording his "history" in Pascoag, and this book was published in Old Greenwich, Connecticut. Of course this may be only one of the many coincidences which keep surfacing, and something else we need to explore. We wrote to the author in care of the Devon-Adair publishing company, but to date have not received a reply.)

Source: *The Mad Booths of Maryland by Stanley Kimmel, Bobbs-Merrill Company (Indianapolis-1940).*

(*Mr. Kimmel in this edition devoted a few lines to Miss Forrester's *This One Mad Act* and Izola's claim to the Booth name. He expressed doubts about the marriage in Cos Cob on January 9, 1859, as John Wilkes Booth was then a member of the stock company at the Richmond Theatre and would not have had the time to travel to Connecticut at the height of the theatrical season. He did mention the fact that Booth traveled to Baltimore, Maryland, in April of that year to attend the wedding of his sister Asia to the actor, John Sleeper Clarke. No definite statement was made regarding Ogarita's status. While reading further material, we discovered in a cross reference that another edition had been published where Kimmel provided more information on "our" Booths.)

Source: *The Mad Booths of Maryland by Stanley Kimmel, Second Revised and Enlarged Edition with 83 Illustrations. Dover Publications Inc. (New York, 1969).*

(*If we thought that Izola Martha's claim was fading due to any of the previous information, then consider Kimmel's Supplement I, pages 387 through 390.) In this edition he includes a wife, Izola, a daughter Ogarita, and a son named Alonso as John Wilkes Booth's common-law family. He bases his belief on a letter written by Mrs. Elijah Rogers to Dr. W. Stump Forwood (*Where do they get these names?) dated August 16, 1886. Mrs. Rogers writes that John had two children, a beautiful girl "Ogretia" and a son "Alonso", who looked like Mr. Richard Booth, the father of Junius Senior. According to this letter, she didn't know "Izalia's" maiden name, and John was not married to her. She also related that Booth would give two oil wells to Rosalie so that she could take care of his children. The Booth family paid no attention to them excepting Rosalie who sent them money every spring and fall. After John's death, "Izalia" took the children to Illinois. In 1886 both the children are married. The letter of which the contents are stated is courtesy of the Library of Congress.

(*With JWB's propensity for women, it is not impossible that he had these children of whom Mrs. Rogers writes. But, are they our Ogarita and Alonzo—who could also be Charles Bellows, Harry Stevenson or Alonzo Abram Standish Mills? All of whom lived in Pascoag, Rhode Island, at one time. The letter is open to interpretation. Were the wife and children living near the Booths and Mrs. Rogers before Booth's death? How else would Mrs. Rogers have known them, and how else could the Booths have paid no attention to them? If the common-law family did live near Tudor Hall, Booth fathered these children at a tender age. The Booths all left the farm in the late 1850s. (*Miss Forrester has Izola living in Maryland between 1865 and 1868.) Where were they when Rosalie was sending them money? Why is Mrs. Rogers writing this information to Dr. Forwood? Had he requested it, and why in

1886?)

This letter from Mrs. Elijah (Elizabeth) Rogers concerns us. We wrote to author Kimmel care of Dover Publications and asked why he placed so much faith in Mrs. Rogers' letter and the circumstances surrounding it. Unfortunately, the letter was returned with the chilling "deceased" written across it. We will continue to seek out information regarding her letter.

It would be appropriate to return to Miss Forrester's *This One Mad Act* (pp. 152-154) to relate a visit she made to Tudor Hall in Harford County. At the time, a Mrs. Ella V. Mahoney was the owner and escorted Miss Forrester through the Booth family home. Miss Forrester's guide mentions another visit to the area by a woman with two children (*a girl of about thirteen and a much younger boy), who introduced themselves as the family of John Wilkes Booth to Mrs. Elizabeth Rogers, who was neighbor to the Booth family when they resided at Tudor Hall. Mrs. Mahoney spoke of pictures she had seen in Mrs. Rogers possession, one of the woman and the other of the girl. (*This visit was probably after 1925 according to the time frame in Miss Forrester's book.) Unfortunately, Mrs. Rogers had died and the photos had disappeared by the time Miss Forrester arrived. The woman with the children also told Booth's neighbor that she hoped her daughter would follow in the footsteps of her father. . . on stage.

The above contradicts Kimmel's letter from Mrs. Rogers to Dr. Forwood where Mrs. Rogers knew the common-law family of John Wilkes Booth and therefore needed no introduction. Unless Mrs. Rogers is writing of what she was told and not what she actually knew. In the year 1872, Ogarita would have been thirteen years old and Harry Stevenson about two years of age. Martha Mills by that time had married John H. Stevenson and was living in Boston.

Mr. Kimmel has more surprises in store for us when he writes of Richard Merrifield, Miss Forrester's son, and the great-grandson of John Wilkes Booth. In the summer of 1953, Mr. Kimmel and Mr. Merrifield visit Joe Mudd, who lives in his grandfather Dr. Sam Mudd's house. (*Dr. Mudd had set Booth's leg in this house after the assassination, and had been sentenced to Dry Tortugas for doing so . . . he was later pardoned as were the others who had been sent there for aiding Booth.) Joe Mudd agreed to take them over the escape route traveled by Booth and Herold only after Merrifield's association with Booth was revealed. In October of 1953, an article about this visit appeared in *Yankee* magazine published in Dublin, New Hampshire and written by Richard

Merrifield, who was then its editor. Mr. Merrifield writes of the romance between Izola and Booth as recorded in his mother's book. He adds that Beatrice (Rosalie Henderson) Booth Colony now directs a summer theater in New Hampshire. He tells of residing in Canterbury, where his great-grandmother lies buried at Canterbury Plains. (pp. 388-389).

Included is a letter to Mr. Kimmel from Miss Gail Merrifield, who is listed as the custodian of the John Wilkes Booth family archives, and who also is Richard Merrifield's daughter. (*Miss Merrifield's letter provides us with interesting information; some of which we have unearthed ourselves, and some that only confounds us further.) Izola Martha Mills D'Arcy's real name is Martha Lizola Mills, who was born September 11, 1837. She was married in Boston to Charles Still Bellows in 1855, probably married to Booth in 1859, then married in Boston to John H. Stevenson in 1871, and finally in Pascoag to Edwin Sylvanus Bates in 1881. Miss Merrifield agrees that Martha Lizola was not married in Cos Cob but wherever Reverend Peleg Weaver was minister at the time . . . she is searching for this information.

Miss Merrifield further adds that Martha had at least four children. A boy born out of wedlock in 1852 who died in 1856, possibly the son of George Sheppard. Ogarita Booth born in 1859 and her brother Charles Still born in 1861, both of whom have the last name of Bellows on their birth certificates. . . and probably Booth's children. In 1871, she has another son, Harry Stevenson, whose father was John H. Stevenson. (*Miss Merrifield does not state where they were born although she had their birth certificates.) She also agrees that Ogarita's name was not Ogarita Rosalie but Ogarita Elizabeth. A picture of her great grandmother taken in 1888 while she was engaged at the People's Theater in Minneapolis, Minnesota., shows the first time that Ogarita had openly worn the brooch with her father's (*Booth's) picture on it. Miss Merrifield suggests to Mr. Kimmel that the reasons for wearing the brooch at this time were: Ogarita's mother had died the year before, that she (Ogarita) was in desperate financial circumstances, and that she had begun to sell stories of her family relationships with John Wilkes Booth (pp. 389 and 390).

Source: *Official copy of Certificate of Birth, filed January 1860, File Number 312 issued from State of Rhode Island Records Department, Providence. (*As verification of vital statistics are received, we will insert the information in the appropriate section.)*

Name of Child: "Oganita" Elizabeth Bellows. Female, born October 23, 1859 at 13 Abbotts' Lane in Providence, Rhode Island. Father's name: Charles S. Bellows born in Boston, Massachusetts. His occupation is listed as a Mariner. Mother's Maiden name: Martha L. ———, born Greenfield, Connecticut, and usual residence not given. Both Father's and Mother's ages also not given.

(*Spelling of Ogarita's first name may be a recorder's error. We have her birth as being in Providence on her marriage record at the Burrillville Town Hall. This is contrary to Miss Forrester's writings as well as Ogarita's statements to the newspapers, both of which have her being born in Virginia. Still this does not prove that Ogarita was not the child of Booth, but it does begin to narrow down the odds. We wonder why Martha's maiden name is not recorded. Greenfield, CT is not just over the border of Rhode Island. It is closer to Southport in Fairfield County, not far from the New York border. The town clerk there tells us that it is actually called Greenfield Hills, a residential area today.)

Source: *The Commonwealth of Massachusetts, Copy of Record of Birth, Office of the Secretary of State. Date of original record 1861.*

Name of child: Charles E. Bellows, male, born May 16, 1861, in Cambridge, Massachusetts. Father's name listed as Charles S. Bellows residing in Cambridge, MA. Born in Roxbury, MA. Occupation listed as a Mariner. Mother's maiden name: Martha L.———, residing in Cambridge, MA. Her birthplace listed as Stanford, Connecticut. Occupation not given.

(*It is apparent that Martha is living in New England in 1859, and in 1861 has two children fathered by a Charles S. Bellows from the Boston area of Massachusetts. Is Charles S. Bellows a name used by Booth or a separate and distinct individual? There is no Stanford, CT. It is Stamford and close to Cos Cob in location. We turn to another writer who dispels erroneous thinking, which is not exactly the same thing as revealing the truth.)

Source: *The Great American Myth by George S. Bryan, Carrick & Evans, Inc. (New York, 1940).*

(*George S. Bryan is the well known dispeller of the myths that grew around the assassination of President Lincoln including the figure of John Wilkes Booth and the various conspiracies that his act engendered. With a combination of cold water, cool logic and exacting documentation, the author dispenses with the themes and theories that have been so patiently woven since 1865. Miss Forrester's *This One Mad Act* also comes in for some harsh and brutal criticism, mainly due to her glaring inconsistencies and the exaggerated romancing of her family's history. Other critics—including we two historical detectives—have pointed out similar flaws but not to the degree with which Bryan chastises Miss Forrester's account. Unfortunately, we find it necessary to agree with much of what he has to say, as we have already noted the discrepancies without the far flung documentation he has done.)

Myth-buster Bryan had devoted eleven pages to *This One Mad Act*, and we cannot relate the contents of them all. But, we would like to point out an object lesson in attempting to prove or disprove truths via documentation that confounds us—and which makes us wonder if "truth" about the past can indeed be frozen into focus on the printed page. Bryan has proven that Edwin Booth did not have a home in Cos Cob when Izola and John were allegedly married in 1859. Edwin did not own any property there until 1871 (page 370). Reverend Peleg Weaver was also not in Cos Cob at that time. He became pastor at the Methodist Protestant Church there in 1871 (pp. 369, 370). The author Bryan was also able to speak with Asia Booth Sleeper Clarke's son, who had been interviewed by Miss Forrester regarding events in the Booth family. Clarke protested the way that she "garbled" his account in her writings (pp. 371,372). Of course none of this "proves" that Izola and Booth were never married or that Ogarita was not his daughter, rather, it merely disproves Miss Forrester's account of it.

Ogarita comes in for a similar operation under Bryan's scalpel. Several newspapers had written articles about the actress, Rita Booth, and her associations with John Wilkes Booth. In 1890 Mrs. Booth-Henderson is quoted in the paper saying that she, alone, is the daughter of Booth and that he did not escape. (*There are others who are claiming to be his daughter then as well.) She claims she had seen his body several times before his burial, that she was an only child with two half-brothers, and that she was born in Virginia, etc. (p. 364). (*Like daughter, like mother, her "press statements" are filled with inconsistencies.)

Rita Booth is a member of the Boston Comic Opera Company in 1890 with her husband serving as its director. She was also a leading lady with George C. Miln, the preacher-actor, and later with Grace Hawthorne (p.364). (*We read here as we have from several other sources that she did not want to become a leading actress because she did not seek the notoriety her father's name would bring. Why then does she go by the name of Rita Booth and tell all the newspapers and theater associates of her claim? The impression is that she is cashing in on her alleged last name. We recall the death of her mother, Izola, in 1887 and note the lateness of informing the newspapers of her connection with Booth. Yet, we feel a twinge of guilt in damning her for doing so. All that we have read concerning Ogarita Elizabeth so far paints a picture of a woman, almost always without her husband(s), lugging two or three children with her as she attempts to make a living as an actress touring with road companies. It is difficult not to be more concerned about some historical individuals more than others. We propose the following defense of her actions by saying there just might be some threads of truth in her statements, she needed the attention these statements would bring [she had no press agent], and reporters often do garble what is said . . . even what is written! But, there is more from George S. Bryan.)

There are many others who sought the benefits that might proceed from being the wife or daughter of John Wilkes Booth. Bryan quotes a piece found in the *New York Tribune* in 1885 from the "widow" apparently from Boston. Edwin Booth writes to a friend and reveals that the family has been blackmailed before by various women claiming to be Booth's wife. He suspects that this "widow" in the newspaper is the same one who "got hold of poor Rose and robbed her of all the money she had." Edwin has received an intimation of such from a Boston lawyer a few months previous to the publication, which has the woman declaring that Booth "although not generally known" left a wife and two children, a daughter and a son, and that the family had lived in seclusion under a false name for twenty years (pp. 362 and 363). (*We recommend the reading of *The Great American Myth* for its interest in the Burrillville Booths as well as the author's ability to dispel all the myths generated by Booth's "one mad act.")

Source: *A Child Actress of the 80's by Izola Forrester from the Saturday Evening Post . . . Contributed to the authors by the daughters of Izola Forrester. More on these ladies later.*

While Ogarita sat sewing under the apple tree on the Brown Farm in Pascoag, she taught her young child, Izola, all the lines of Ophelia, Rosalind, Portia and Juliet. Miss Forrester relates many of the plays and places that she and her mother had been in together from *Richard III* to *Uncle Tom's Cabin* with Ogarita as Eliza and young Izola as the child. In 1884, when the author was about six, her mother returned to Pascoag and informed her that she had a stepfather, a professional director of light opera who was now directing Gilbert and Sullivan operas in Chicago at the Chicago Museum. Miss Forrester tells of the many adventures of being on stage as a child actress and also relates the happy times spent on the Brown farm surrounded and visited by relatives such as cousin Maria Angell, Aunt Amy from North Providence and cousin Eugene (*Bellows?) from Boston.

(*Maria Angell apparently lived in the area as she rescued young Izola from danger several times. She is described as a tall spare woman of strict discipline . . . a no-nonsense lady. This Maria might be Maria [Angell] Wood, only child of Enoch Angell, who owned property in the Wallum Lake district. This information was found in Harry Lee Barnes' book, *The Wallum Pond Estates.* Reprinted by the Rhode Island Historical Society with additions and illustrations in 1922. Maria could also be a child or grandchild of Lydia Angell of North Providence. The Burrillville Angells originally came from North Providence to settle in this northwestern corner of Rhode Island. They are cousins to the North Providence Angells.)

A lengthy and fine portrait is drawn of a great-great-grandmother, Betsey Benchley Mills, who seldom left her room on the Brown farm and spent the day alternately reading the Bible and knitting stockings for the whole family. Great grandmother was a Quaker, and the mother of Capt. Abram Standish Mills. Young Izola would venture in to see this fragile ninety-year-old porcelain lady, who kept sugared delights up her sleeves for the young members of the family.

Grandmother Martha, who grows angry if she is not called by the name "Izola," is also living on the farm but obviously as a guest. It is Caroline Brown, her step-mother, who does all the household chores, and apparently humors all the prima donnas around her. Grandmother Izola takes young Izola to the stone-wall enclosed burial grounds not too distant from the house. She points out one small stone bearing the inscription "Mary Mills," who, she declares, is her mother, Izola Maria Mendoza. Yankee prejudice prevented putting her real name on the stone.

(*This like all Miss Forrester writes is delightful to read, but some of the facts do not blend in overly well. We have searched the Brown/Millard cemetery many times looking for Mary Mills as well as others who are supposedly buried there. If Abram Mills' first wife is buried there as Miss Forrester says, it would have been in 1837, long before Alonzo, whose mother and stepfather bought the farm in Pascoag.

(*Another question is who's mother is Betsey B. Benchley?

We had understood that she was Caroline's mother whose maiden name was Jenkins. The assumption we made—no one should ever do that in research—is that Betsey married a Benchley. The family relationships amongst our Burrillville Booths and the Burrillville Mills, Browns and Benchleys do not focus into a clear and well-defined picture. Something does not fit the data that is found. Why? Local genealogists come to a similar conclusion. To complicate matters further, Grandma Betsey died in 1878, the year Miss Forrester was born. Was there another grandmother living with the Browns and Alonzo of whom Miss Forrester is writing? Of course, writing memories from childhood can be tricky. Do we recall what we actually saw or is it combined with what we were told? We need to take a rest from the heady world of the seemingly more exciting and romantic eighteen hundreds as they have been described by others. We will return to the more exacting information devoid of sentiment and romanticism as recorded by Alonzo A. S. Mills in his daily journals.)

Chapter/File 7

WHO IS ALONZO?

For the past several years we have been furthering our search by talking with people, most of them born and/or living in the Bridgeton area, who either knew or had heard of Alonzo Abram Standish Mills. When first inquiring of Alonzo, we were either met with silence or a smile, even though we are both native to the soil. If we did manage to get them talking, before too long the name of John Wilkes Booth surfaced into the conversation. We discovered that there are several local theories and/or beliefs concerning the relationship between Alonzo and Booth. (1) John Wilkes Booth "hid out" on the Brown farm for some time after the assassination of President Lincoln. (2) Alonzo was the son of John Wilkes Booth. (3) Alonzo was actually John Wilkes Booth, who submerged his personality into the figure known as the son of Caroline H. Brown. (4) John Wilkes Booth visited his daughter and/or wife at the Wilson homestead either before or after the assassination. The latter is the most widely acclaimed and would thereby make Alonzo the brother-in-law of John Wilkes Booth.

(*It was relatively easy for us to dispel most of these local myths. First, we knew that according to Burrillville records Alonzo was born in 1847 and died in 1917. He would have been around 16 years old when he arrived on the Brown farm in 1863 with his mother and stepfather, Edward M. Brown. Alonzo's young age would also explain why he was not included on the Burrillville Militia listing in 1864. He was too old to have been the son of Booth and too young to have been Booth himself. As we have grown to know and like the sociable eccentric, our shared feeling is that Alonzo would have done little to discourage these stories and would certainly have enjoyed the attention they caused.

Whether or not Booth was ever in hiding on the ninety-two

acre Brown farm and/or visited his wife and/or daughter here depends a great deal upon one's acceptance of "Izola's" relationship with him and the accounts of this as perpetuated by her family . . . not to mention the belief that Booth survived the Garrett Farm episode. We have yet to fully establish when "Izola" and Ogarita "Rosalie" actually came to live amongst these people in the northwesterly corner of Rhode Island. Knowing these natives fairly well—at least the present generations—we have trouble accepting the fact they would recognize the ladies' claim without some kind of substantiating evidence. There is always the possibility we have underestimated the persuasive capabilities of Izola and Ogarita, and overestimated the skeptical and independent thinking of those who settled in these hinterlands.

The facts indicate that those who lived on the Brown farm did not come from afar but rather from the nearby communities of Pawtucket, North Providence, Providence and Boston. Although the direct line to the older families in Bridgeton has not yet been found, we suspect that "our" Browns and Mills have stronger stuff than water relating them to the Wilsons, Angells, Rosses, et al. One has to recall that Rhode Island is the smallest state, and that Roger Williams settled here with only a handful of families, whose descendants dominated this state up to the turn of the century. A closer study of Alonzo and his family needs to be done in order to capture our local Booths and to either verify or throw doubts upon their claim to fame.

Source: *Burrillville Town Records Deaths (1901-1928) Vol. 2 p. 57.*

Alonzo Mills died March 3, 1917, age 70 at the State Alms House. He was born in Pawtucket, Rhode Island, the son of Abraham (*not Abram?) and Caroline Mills. Father's birthplace listed as Rhode Island. (*not Southport, CT?) None listed for Caroline Mills. Attending physician Harry A. Jones and undertaker John F. Armstrong. Condition "M" for married. (*It would be interesting to know who provided this information to the Town Clerk. Usually a relative gives the information to the physician, undertaker or clergyman. As far as we know, Alonzo left no immediate family living in Burrillville. He and his mother were both affiliated with the Laurel Hill Methodist Episcopal Church. If the information came from this source, more faith could be put into it. But, we repeat, one ought not hang a tale on statistics—vital or otherwise—from only one source. It is interesting they list Abraham (Abram?) as having been born in Rhode Island.)

(*It saddens us to read that A.A.S.M. died at the State Alms House, but this was not an uncommon happening during that time period. [The overseer of the poor was responsible for those who were ill or otherwise incapable of taking care of themselves as well as the destitute. Families were crucial to survival, and even distant kin could find succor at a relative's door.] We are startled to read of his marriage. The "M" condition rules out his having been divorced and precludes his having been a widower. Nothing we had read or heard prepared us for his having been married. Quite the contrary, we were given to understand that he was so completely dominated by his diminutive mother and grandmother that he never even considered matrimony.)

Source: *Burrillville Town Records Marriages (1846-1900) Vol. 1A p. 34.*

Alonzo Mills married Miss Sarah A. Symmonds on May 17, 1871. Both listed as residents of Burrillville. She was 18 and he was 24. First marriage for both. His parents listed as Abraham A. Mills and Caroline Mills. Hers listed as Thomas and Emily Symmonds. Alonzo's birthplace as well as Sarah's listed as Providence. Alonzo's occupation as farmer. Minister's name: Rev. Jabez Pack of the Methodist Episcopal Church. (*To date we have not found another shred of evidence that Alonzo had a wife while living on the Brown farm. Nor has any record of Sarah Symmonds or her family been discovered. We put our faith in Rev. Pack and believe the marriage took place, but we cannot fathom whatever happened to the young bride, Sarah [Symmonds] Mills.)

Source: *Burrillville Historical and Preservation Society Archives.*

Cemetery #2 Brown Millard Lot: East Wallum Lake Road. Fieldstone walls with two iron pipe gates. Twenty-nine fieldstone graves, three which are facing north. Family names readable are Brown, Millard, Stanfield, and Curtis. "Alozo A. S. Mills 1847-1917" is the brief inscription on the gray, polished granite monument that stands out amongst the simpler slate, soapstone and fieldstone head and foot markers. Alonzo was the last burial in this family lot.

This is the same spot where "Izola" brought her granddaughter, Izola, to point out the small stone that read "Mary Mills," who was the wife of Abram Mills and Miss Forrester's great, great grandmother. As noted previously, a stone with this marking has not been found here. It would be interesting to know who chose

Alonzo's stone and the inscription with his first name misspelled. It seems important to interject a point of history which may or may not have some bearing on our case of the elusive Burrillville Booths. Miss Forrester noted that her great, great grandmother, Betsey Beasley Benchley was a Quaker lady, who lived on the Brown farm with Alonzo and Caroline. Many of the Brown families of Rhode Island espoused the Quaker faith. A great many of the early settlers in this area were also Quakers. The first house of worship was the Friends' Meeting House built in 1791. It is our understanding that the early Quakers believed inscribing the names of the deceased on gravestones—even the monuments themselves—was flirting with idolatry. This thinking dismays both historian and genealogist who, after locating a family gravesite, find it to be in a Quaker cemetery with neat little graves without a name, or a hint of one, on the carefully arranged, ordinary fieldstones. In other cases, economy and not religion was the culprit.

Source: *Pascoag Herald dated March 9, 1917.*

Alonzo A. S. Mills, who sustained a stroke of paralysis two weeks ago, died Sunday aged 70 years. He was born in Pawtucket and removed here with his mother, with whom he resided until her death about ten years ago. (*No mention of wife, Sarah.) Their home was on Wallum Pond Road next to the Stanfield farm and was one of the most pleasantly situated residences in town. (*It still is, and only in the past few years has the original ninety-two acres been divided into house lots.) Mr. Mills had a unique personality. For more than a half century he kept a daily record of his most minute transactions, of the people whom he met, of the conversation engaged in and with these were interspersed local happenings and events. (*From all accounts, he was well known for his continual "writings." Alonzo has a rather long obituary, which we will return to later as it tells us more about his relationships with his sister's grandchildren, Izola Louise Wallingford and Beatrice Rosalie Henderson.)

Source: *Joyce Remington (1953 -) president of the Burrillville Historical and Preservation Society, Miss Remington related the following about the origins of the society's typed pages from two of Alonzo's daily journals.*

Gay Evans, who lives in the old Harris house on Lapham Farm Road, was helping a Mr. George Bligh clean out his old home (*formerly belonging to Charles Gifford) located in the rear of her house. The elderly gentleman, who was the son-in-law of Charles Gifford, told her to pick out anything she wanted for helping him. She chose Alonzo's daily journals, which had intrigued her from the beginning and which she hoped would contain some information about her home and the people who had lived there. The Gifford family had previously lived in the Bligh house and also the Harris farmstead. (*George Gifford, Charles' brother, was a friend of Alonzo Mills, which might explain why the journals were there in the first place.)

Mrs. Evans' son was also enthused with the journals and took them to school for Show and Tell. They were inadvertently left in the teachers' room while the teacher who borrowed them went out on recess duty. When she returned, the journals had disappeared never to be located again. Fortunately, Mrs. Evans and her friend, Barbara Shaw, had become so involved with the contents that they had typed those twenty-four pages which were subsequently presented to the local historical society. The suggestion was made that we talk to Mrs. Shaw, as she had also become interested in Alonzo and his mother, Caroline.

Source: *Barbara Shaw, resident of Burrillville. Has a keen interest in the geography and history of our town. Has a collection of local Indian and early settlers' artifacts.*

Mrs. Shaw was also curious about Alonzo and his family. She had done some of her own tracking long before we two took up the scent. It seems that the family who once lived on the Brown Farm in Bridgeton were much a topic of conversation then—as well as today. Caroline Brown was buried in Burrillville Historical Cemetery #2 in an unmarked grave (*contrary to state vital statistics). Alonzo Mills boarded as a hired hand with the Gifford family at various times. (*We suspect Alonzo is related to the Gifford family in some way. Mrs. Shaw's information that Alonzo boarded with them explains the finding of his journals in the Gifford home.) Mrs. Shaw generously allowed us to xerox Alonzo's missing pages of "S" and "L-Z" that she had written out by hand before his two journals vanished. (*We were more than delighted to get them. After reading these, the only question was how to limit the interesting notations and at the same time point out the family relationships which are coming into clearer focus.)

Source: *Alonzo Abram Standish Mills' Daily Records. Both Mrs.*

Evans and Mrs. Shaw agreed that they had written or typed all of the information from both journals, copies of which are now in our possession.

Lincoln, Abraham 16th President of the United States was assassinated by John Wilkes Booth at Washington, DC Friday, April 14, 1865. (*This may or may not be a simple recording of the tragic occurrence. He has noted many Civil War events along with international news such as, "Queen Victoria married to Prince Albert of Saxe Cobergon Mon. February 19,1840.")

Luther, Andrew (of Bridgeton, RI) was born in (or near) Saundersville in the town of Scituate RI October 18, 1833. (*Mr. Luther worked at the Hopkins Machine Works located on Laurel Ridge. He owned and lived at the Brown farm for a short period of time before selling it to Edward M. Brown in 1863.)

Merrifield, Mrs. Izola South Canterbury, Conn.

Merrifield, Mrs. Izola F. Baltic, Conn.

Merrifield, Mrs. Izola F., 463 West 23rd St. New York City.

Merrifield, Mrs. Reuben R. South Canterbury, Conn.

(*A listing of Izola Louise Wallingford's [Miss Forrester] whereabouts is kept by her great uncle Alonzo. Unfortunately, no dates. From her writings we know that she also lived in Chicago and California as well as New York and Connecticut.)

Merry, (?) Samuel died in Pawtucket, RI Wed. February 11, 1874 in his 61st year. (*Pawtucket looms larger and larger in the daily records and other data. Could this read Merryfield? At the Canterbury Town Hall, we found no Merrifields in the General Index of Births, Deaths and Marriages. We did find two Merryfields. A Lucius and Lucy Merryfield born respectively in 1870 and 1869.

Millard, Samuel W. and grandson Frank Patterson and myself (Alonzo A. S. Mills) went to East Douglas, Mass. today Monday, January 22, 1894 with my (A.A.S.Mills) horse and wagon for the aforesaid Mr. Millard to transact some business there. (*One of the many "minute transactions" recorded for future generations and/or historians. Frank Patterson was Brandon Patterson's father and Shirley [Patterson] Greene's great grandfather, both of whom were quoted sources in Chapter/file 1.)

Mills, Mr. Abram A. and Miss Caroline H. Jencks, both of Providence, RI were married in Providence, RI by the Rev. Benjamin Taylor on Thursday, May 14, 1846. (*This has to be verified by other vital statistics).

(*To date we have found no flaws in our eccentric's accounting of human activities. With the day, month and year—even the moon phase—it is not difficult to verify his data. Miss Forrester has the name listed as Caroline Jenkins, but this family name was spelled—as were others—in a variety of ways by those who possessed it. With this marriage Caroline becomes stepmother to "Izola" Martha Louise Mills. The "of Providence" probably means that they were living in that city at the time of their marriage.)

Mills, Abram Amherst, was born in Southport, Conn. Fairfield County, Tuesday, March 4, 1820 on the new of the moon. (*Here "our failure to find" becomes a source of frustration. This is also the first time that we have seen Abram or Abraham's full middle name of Amherst. The State of Connecticut Department of Health Services, Vital Records Unit informed us that the state office only has records since July 1, 1897 and to contact the Town Hall where the event occurred. The Town of Fairfield, Connecticut's assistant registrar of vital statistics wrote that, "I find no Standish, Mills or Amherst in our Arnold copy index." Standish was Abram Mills' mother's maiden name, who was also supposed to have lived in the Fairfield County area. From the Fairfield Historical Society we learned that: "There was nothing in any of the published resources of our library under those names. However, I found the enclosed information in our file of miscellaneous genealogical material. You will note that it was contributed by the same man, but at different dates." This historical society and in particular volunteer Laura B. MacKenzie should be commended for the thorough research that is done for a nominal fee. If only all researchers would be so thorough.)

***Source:** Genealogical sheet of Abraham Mills prepared by David F. Putnam Jr. Bountiful, Utah Dated April 16, 1979. Donated to the Fairfield Historical Society in 1987 in two parts: Source One and Source Two.*

Abraham Mills (occupation: sailor) born in 1820 in Southport, CT died 19 Oct. 1847 in Pawtucket, RI. (*These were obtained from Source One which was indicated as "Pawtucket, R.I. death recorded in Vol. 9 of Vital Records of R. I. Lists father as Joseph, mother as Sarah, birthplace as Southport, CT.)

Married first about 1838-1839 in Spain. Second wife Caroline Jenkins (?). Father's name John or Joseph (?) Mills. Mother's Maiden name as Sarah Standish(?) Wife's Maiden name Izola Maria Mendoza from Spain died Sept., 1839 on board ship, off Martha's Vineyard. Children, Izola Martha Mills born 11 Sept. 1839 aboard ship. Died 9 Nov. 1887 in Canterbury, Ct. Married to:

"several marriages." Family records indicate that Abraham's parents were buried in Southport, that he had a sister Fanny who married Henry D'Arcy. (*Question marks indicated are from the record as presented.) All from Source Two which reads "Family records of Izola Martha Mills, and her granddaughter Izola Forrester. Part of these records were published in the book *This One Mad Act* by Izola Forrester. A copy of the manuscript and additional notes from the book are in the possession of my mother, Mrs. David F. Putnam of Keene NH." (*We are disappointed in Source Two as it is the material from *This One Mad Act* and not verified by recorded vital statistics. Written on the sheet was also the notation that the family would be very grateful for information on Abraham's ancestry. Does this mean that in 1979 the descendants of "Izola," Ogarita, and Miss Forrester had not been able to verify Abram Mills and Izola Maria Mendoza's marriage or their birth dates and places?)

Source: *State of Connecticut, Connecticut State Library, Hartford.*

A preliminary search of the following indexes were made: (1) Barbour Collection (vital records of Connecticut towns to 1850). (2) Connecticut Church Records. (3) Family Bible Records. (4) U. S. Census for Connecticut, 1790-1850 (excluding New London County, 1790). (*The librarian searched for Abraham/Abram Amherst Mills born in Southport and Martha Louise Mills born in Stamford or Greenfield Hill but found no information.)

Source: *Genealogical Chart on Abraham Mills donated to Fairfield Historical Society from David Putnam, Jr. of Centerville, Utah in 1987.*

This contains basically the same data as found in the first chart (1979) with the following exceptions: Caroline's maiden name is now spelled "Jencks", her birth as 17 April 1820 and her death as 26 January 1907 at Howard, Rhode Island. (*Actually this is the Howard State Insane Asylum located in Cranston, Rhode Island. More on this subject will be dealt with in the chapter/file on Caroline H. Brown.) Mr. Putnam also has a new Source Three which is: "Letters from Alonzo A. S. Mills to Izola Page." (*Miss Forrester [Mrs. Merrifield] has presumably remarried.) From Source Three comes the information that Caroline's father was Warren Jencks, and that she was buried in the Joseph Brown Cemetery on the Mills farm in Pascoag. Also, that Abraham Mills was buried in Pawtucket Cemetery, Pawtucket, RI . . . this verified by the Vital Records of RI.

The data supplied by Source Two is the same as found in the 1979 genealogical chart researched by "Izola Hills Forrester Merrifield Page" . . . part of which is reported in her book, *This One Mad Act.*

There are two charts provided in the 1987 donated data. In the second one, Source Three is "Seamans certificate, RI, 1844, age 25" referring to Abraham Mills. The material in the three charts concerning Abraham and his marriage to a lady from Spain, Izola Maria Mendoza, and the birth of "Izola" Martha Mills on 11 September 1839 off the coast of Martha's Vineyard, in Stamford in 1837 or in Greenfield (*Hill?) for the same date has never been verified by the descendants of Abraham. (*Apparently they have hit the same brick wall we have regarding these happenings. We are fully aware of the difficulties one may encounter to prove ancestry as suggested by past generations. It is obvious that the offspring of Martha L. Mills have been searching for their roots for nearly a century. Nonetheless, we will continue to scratch and find by our own particular methods, and under the watchful eye of the ever helpful "Uncle" Alonzo.)

Source: *Alonzo A. S. Mills' Daily Records courtesy of Barbara Shaw.*

Mills, A. A. S. bought a sleigh Saturday, Jan. 21, 1893 of Mr. William Carter, Bridgeton, RI for four dollars cash.

News: Burrillville, RI, Sunday, Oct. 18, 1874 - Mrs. Caroline H. Brown bought a horse, harness and buggy today of Mr. Andrew Luther. (*Alonzo and his mother are either in or out of the money. There is no order of events in the time frame only the arrangement of his loose alphabetical order, which can be maddening.)

Mills, A. A. S. worked ten hours today, Wednesday June 30, 1880 for his sister Mrs. Martha L. Stevenson hoeing at 75 cents per day and board. (Settled.) (*Martha—her brother never refers to her as Izola—is probably living in the Bridgeton/Pascoag area as Mrs. Stevenson. What the "settled" in parenthesis means is questionable. Does it mean that the debt was paid? Or, that Martha is settled in after moving and subsequently is not on the Brown Farm? There appears to be a close relationship between Alonzo and his half sister, Martha.)

Mills, Mr. Abram Amherst, of Providence and Pawtucket, RI died in Albany, NY. Tuesday Oct. 19, 1847, age 27 years, 7 mos. and 5 days. (*Nothing comes easy from this family. There is much contradictory material concerning Abram or Abraham. "Of Providence and Pawtucket" could read that he lived at one time in both of these cities. If these dates are correct, he would have been rather young in 1837 or 1839 when Miss Forrester has him as the owner and captain of a schooner in the China trade . . . not impossible in that time period but not probable either. Seaman Records list him as just that: a seaman, a sailor. Alonzo would understandably have little recollection of a father who died when he was about five months old. Other than Alonzo, men just don't seem to last long in this family. We read that Abram was buried in Pawtucket from several sources—we have not been able to find the lot or the burial site from the Pawtucket Cemetery Files—and that he died in Albany, NY. Miss Forrester has him buried in Southport with his parents, and David Putnam has his death occurring in Pawtucket. We tend to believe more of what Alonzo has written as his track record is rather good. We also realize that in recording the events and dates he did not actually live through, he had to rely on what was told to him or what he himself had read from other sources . . . perhaps family Bibles.)

Morse, Bro. George M., a pioneer cotton manufacturer of Putnam, Conn. died in Putnam of pneumonia at his home, Thursday February 13, 1913 age 82 years. He was president of the National Society of Habness(?) and had labored as an evangelist through the New England states. He was head of the Douglas Mass. Camp Meeting Assoc., and was well known as a religious worker at the annual gatherings. (*Some of which were held less than five miles from Bridgeton. Many early New England "capitalists" also knew the need of spiritual values. We note Brother Morse for several reasons. His activities, as do those of many others, take place in this triangle where the three states coincide. And, Martha was involved with the temperance movement and served as a preacher, although we do not know to what extent. Chas. Morse was a preacher at the Methodist Episcopal Church on Laurel Hill Avenue (1862-63). This handsome structure, which is no longer standing, was built in one of the waves of evangelistic fervor during the eighteen hundreds . . . which was also cause for the revival meetings held in nearby East Douglas, Massachusetts. All was in response to the rather wicked ways of that century, though rather pale by our present times. Not far from the campgrounds and a nearby Mormon chapel, in fact nearly back to back, was the notorious area known as Round Top in Burrillville with three houses of ill repute at one intersection doing a healthy business as directed by Shang Bailey, a capitalist with no spiritual values. He later saw the light and became a well known regional evangelist himself. More knowledge of Martha's participation in this evangelistic fervor is needed, which leads us to search for more information concerning this segment of her life. We also recall that Ogarita was the leading lady with George C. Miln, the preacher-actor, whose touring company was fairly well known. According to Miss Forrester, Martha held prayer meetings at Terrace Hall in Canterbury.)

News: Burrillville, RI Friday September 18, 1872 about ten o'clock am today Mr. James Monroe Wilson (*Of "A Burrillville Puff" fame) got caught in the shafting under the saw, grist and shoddy mills on the farm of the Wilson Bros. in Burrillville and was carried around a number of times by the belt, which bruised and jammed him terribly. (*Yankee Anglo-Saxon words were so indicative of the actual thing or experience to be expressed. Jammed is one of them. No one ever said that life was easy in the 19th century. This was the same year that the Wilson shoddy mill burned "down to the ground.")

Morton, Miss Maud, South Canterbury, Conn.

Newton, Miss Alma, South Canterbury, Conn. (*Some more relatives from Martha's final residence?)

Patterson, Allen, died at his late residence at Laurel Ridge, Pascoag, RI Monday, January 10, 1881 (of diphtheria) age 28 years, 11 mos. and — days.

Patterson Etta, Daughter of Allen and Jane Patterson was born in Burrillville, RI Sat. August 23, 1873. (*The Allens, Pattersons, Millards appear to be interrelated. We know that J. C. Allen and Samuel T. Patterson were both ministers at the M. E. Church, the former in 1869; the latter from 1881-1883 and again from 1887-1888. Whether they are related to Alonzo and his family or just share the common interests of their farms abutting and belonging to the same congregation is a tantalizing question. There is also the temptation to change the "B" of Sarah Standish Mills Batterson [Abram's mother's second marriage name] to "P" as in Patterson, but no back-up data is found for this stretch of the imagination. No Batterson appears in Alonzo's records that we have found, and Sarah would have been his grandmother. In support of Alonzo's records, the Fairfield Historical Society has also found no records of Battersons/Pattersons in their files.)

Smith, Mr. Columbus, South Canterbury, Conn. (*We have found these one liners from Canterbury usually to be relatives of Martha and Ogarita. We have not seen this name before and no date listed as is also usual for the above relationship.)

Stevenson, Irene Caroline, daughter of John H. and Martha L. Stevenson died in Boston, Mass. Fri. February 6, 1874 age 3 mos. and 14 days. (*This kind of information could only come from family and not from the newspapers. It seems as though John H. Stevenson was a little more than a gentleman of the Knights of the Golden Circle aiding the wife of John Wilkes Booth. This would be their second child since Harry Jerome Dresbach was also born in Boston either in January of 1870 or 1871.)

Stevenson, Mr. John H. of Cleveland, Ohio and Mrs. Martha L. Bellows of Boston, Mass. were married in Baltimore, Md. by the Rev. Mr. Bowers on Tuesday March 2, 1869 (*Mr. Stevenson is full of surprises. We thought he was a gentleman from Maryland. There was a family of Stephensons, previously from England, who lived in Burrillville during this time period, latter-day-colonists. We wonder what became of Charles S. Bellows, USN. *This One Mad Act* has Izola in California in the spring of 1869 returning to Baltimore in the late fall when she returns to Boston, "leaving the South for good." Another curious entry from Miss Forrester: while going through her grandmother's trunks, she finds a clipping from a Baltimore paper dated around September 1868 stating that Martha D'Arcy had died in Baltimore. She was as curious as we were, and thought that perhaps her grandmother had put it in the newspaper before she went to California to meet Booth, so those who knew of Booth's marriage to "Izola" Martha Mills D'Arcy would be put off the trail. The California episode grows dimmer and dimmer in our minds.)

(*There are many more gold nuggets in these twenty-two handwritten pages transcribed from Alonzo's lost journals. Some of which we have yet to recognize as valuable until another clue from another source surfaces. There are no Wallingfords listed in the "Ws" much to our disappointment. Many little insights into the lives of those who lived through this time period are told by Alonzo, such as the large fires throughout the New England states. One of these in September of 1881 has him writing, "It was so smoky which caused the day to be quite dark, so dark that the mills throughout the town of Burrillville, RI, had to stop work as the help could not see neither by the light of day nor by the lamps in the mills for to attend to their work, neither could people see plainly to work at out-of-doors labor." The friendly eccentric on the Brown/Mills farm writes of the births, the marriages and the deaths of those who live around him and of those who are related to him from other places. Alonzo Mills' history is local and regional, but it reflects the life of many of those who lived through the nineteenth and into the twentieth century.)

Chance, fate, or whatever you choose to call it, appears to be kind to us throughout our quest to discover just who the elusive Booths of Burrillville actually are and how they fit into the pattern of the Burrillville Mills, Browns, Wilsons, et al. While one of us was

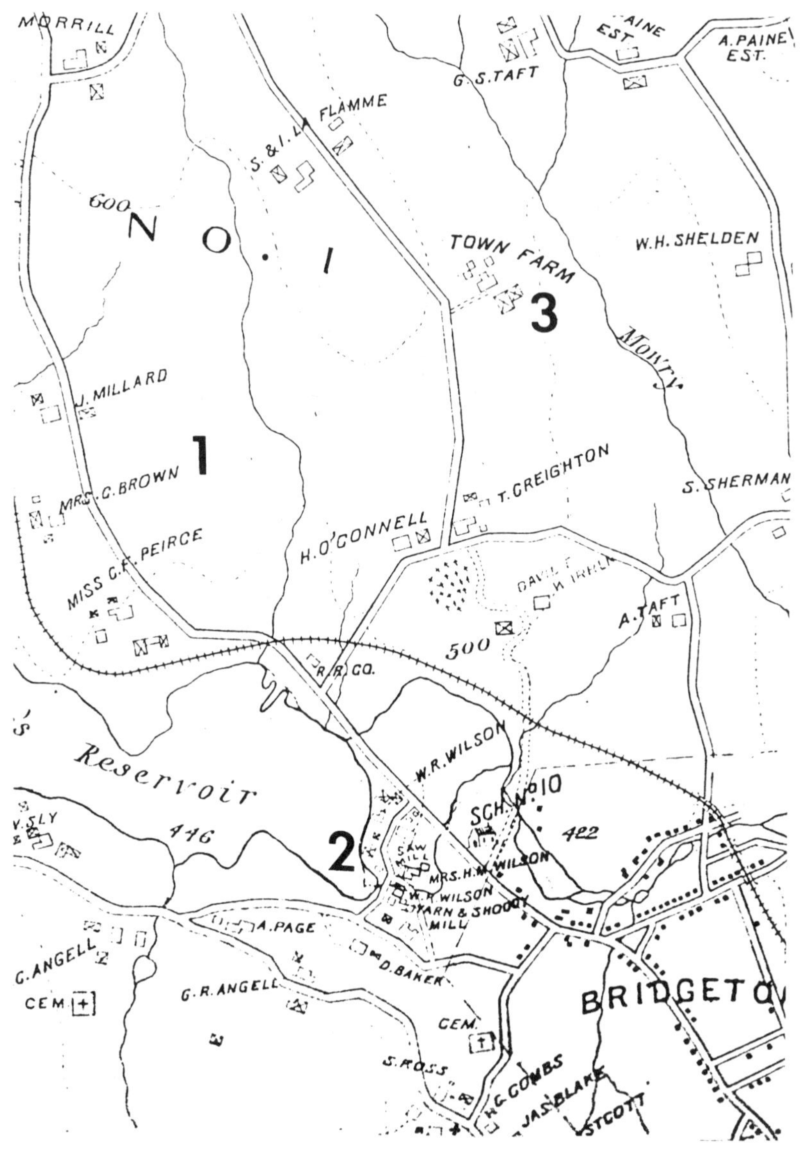

Map of Bridgeton - 1895 Everts & Richard
1. Brown Farm
2. Wilson's Complex
3. Town Farm

serving as Burrillville Town Clerk, two ladies from New Hampshire ventured into the Town Hall seeking genealogical information on their family. They were shown how to glean this material from the Town records . . . and that was that. Until a year and a half later, a letter arrived from these very same two requesting information on anyone in the area with the name of "Izola." We have already hinted about them as the source of Miss Forrester's article in the *Saturday Evening Post*. The next chapter/file is devoted to them.

Chapter/File 8

TWO LADIES FROM NEW HAMPSHIRE

The two ladies from New Hampshire, Mrs. David F. Putnam and Mrs. John H. Colony Jr., are two of the daughters of author Izola Forrester and the granddaughters of Ogarita "Rosalie." A letter dated January 13, 1989 from Mrs. Rosamond Putnam inquiring about the "origins of the name Izola in the area of Pascoag during the last century" and "any references to persons bearing that name, past or present" was received by us. We knew of three "Izolas" locally: Nora Izola [Angell] Hopkins, Izola [Carpenter] Sherman and Vesta Izola [Carpenter] Dunn, who is presently on the Board of Trustees for the Pascoag Public Library, named after her aunt, Izola [Carpenter] Sherman. Reputedly, the latter was named after "Izola" Martha Louise Mills.

Letters and information were exchanged between us, i.e., a copy of Alonzo's twenty-four typed pages, a copy of the BH&PS Cemetery #2 and various odds and ends relating to the Wilsons, Browns, etc. We also forwarded a section of the deed to the Brown farm which states that the descendants of those buried in the family plot would possess the land rights of the cemetery forever. (*Old deeds quite often have this stipulation written into them, and it was a wise precaution on the part of those who wanted to keep their family gravesites in family hands without legal hassle.)

The sisters in turn sent us copies of letters from Alonzo written to members of their family. Their contents cleared up some mysteries such as the final resting place of Alonzo's mother Caroline. Vital statistics in this instance are incorrectt. More on this later. We also received a copy of Miss Forrester's book along with Eleanor Ruggles' *Prince of Players*. The latter depicts a more flattering portrait of the Booth family members and their outstanding thespian talents. "Ros" Putnam (*whose facial structure hints of Ogarita, her grandmother) and "Peggy" (*who "looks more like their mother") are the daughters of Miss Forrester and her second husband, Mr. Mann Page. The Merrifields including Richard (see chapter/file 6) are their half brothers and sisters by Izola's first husband. Gayle Merrifield, their niece, has done extensive research attempting to verify the family history and specifically the relationship between "Izola Martha" and Booth, the origins of Maria Mendoza, Abram or Abraham Mills, and his parents Sarah Standish Mills and John/Joseph Mills.

Obviously, Mrs. Putnam and Mrs. Colony have worked along similar lines for many years. At the moment, they are transcribing their great grandmother's letters and diaries. Keeping on the theme of relatives, Ogarita's half sister, Beatrice Rosalie [Henderson] Clutts Colony, originated and directed a summer theater in Keene, New Hampshire where Ros now lives and, a few miles away, Peggy resides. Beatrice Rosalie is also the Mrs. Alfred Taylor Colony mentioned in Miss Forrester's *This One Mad Act* in whose home the full length portrait of John Wilkes Booth was displayed. Peggy married a Colony as well, all of which does get confusing. This is only one of the reasons why we refer to their mother, Izola Louise [Wallingford or Hills according to the sisters] Forrester Merrifield Page as Miss Forrester or young Zola.

In April of 1989, the two sisters from New Hampshire visited us for an interesting afternoon. (*There is also a third sister, Izola, named after her mother.) The two attractive, slim 'n' trim—even with eleven children born between them—and "with it" gals bowled us over with the amount of research their family has actually done to verify (*or discredit) that their great grandmother was the wife of John Wilkes Booth and Ogarita his child. We also learned they knew of Mrs. Shinsel (see Chapter/file 1). It is quite likely whatever Mrs. S. gleaned from the folks and records in Burrillville are now a part of their family archives. We learn that Mrs. Shinsel will not be answering our letter as she has passed away. We have lost many of our resource people this way. We shared much crucial knowledge as well as interesting bits and pieces of information. It took us several weeks to assimilate what had been learned in that one afternoon.

Their family has corresponded and exchanged information with well-known authorities on John Wilkes Booth including James O. Hall, one of the authors of our recommended readings, *Retribution.* We noted a letter from Gayle Merrifield to her dad, Richard, that Mr. Hall was in possession of a certificate of marriage for "Isola" and Booth. He later thought it a forgery or maybe a joke.

We would like to know more about this forged marriage certificate, but this is all the information the sisters had for us. Gayle is co-producer of the Shakespeare Festival Theatre in New York with her husband, Joseph Papp. They are most likely the family who visited Izola Bates' grave in Canterbury. (*It would appear that the progeny of Izola and Ogarita Rosalie still favor the stage as the place to be.)

Ros and Peggy told us they knew of Ogarita's marriage to William R. Wilson and that they are in possession of the divorce papers which accused Ogarita of smoking and frequenting a certain tavern in the town. Grounds for divorce in the good old days. As we had previously guessed, Ogarita had not stayed over long on the "Wilson Place," two or three years at the most.

While we broke bread over lunch, they verified that Izola and Ogarita were indeed actresses and possess the playbills and other memorabilia to support that claim. Charles was mentioned as being Ogarita's younger brother. (*Why Miss Forrester chose to eliminate her uncle Charles from the family history is a sensitive question . . . especially when Ogarita had named her short-lived son after either him or—according to vital statistics—her father, Charles Still Bellows. In any case, it was not a particularly prudent thing to do as it throws much doubt onto her family history, in particular Izola's stay in the Shenandoah Valley as Booth's wife between 1859 to 1865, when in 1861 she was actually in Boston giving birth to Charles Bellows.)

The sisters admit that Fanny D'Arcy is an enigma and that they have not been able to verify her existence. We suspect they are also experiencing the same difficulties we are with Abraham (Abram), Maria Mendoza and Sarah Standish Mills. The genealogical charts (see Chapter/file 7) and sources of David Putnam, who is Rosamond's son, indicate the same problem.

We all skirted around John Wilkes Booth and whether or not the ladies were one hundred percent sure Booth was their great grandfather. Leading Booth authorities have told them that unless they could procure some definitive documentation, it would be impossible to prove. There were plans to have a monument erected on their great grandmother's grave in Canterbury, but there seems to be some disagreement over just what name to use for the inscription. This suggests there might be differences of opinion as to whether or not they are descendants of the Booths of Maryland. We needed to constantly remind ourselves that these two sisters were the children of Miss Forrester and that Ogarita was their grandmother. Unfortunately, it was difficult to be quite as honest as we would have liked to have been regarding our findings and still be as gracious to them as they were to us. We realized we were on sensitive ground. In a way the whole afternoon was as Peggy wrote later a bit "magical." We still cannot quite find the right words to describe our own feelings about actually being with the children of those whom we have been researching (*actually tracking) for so many years now. It was as if we knew them . . . not deja vu exactly but akin to that slightly eerie though not unpleasant sensation.

After lunch, we drove the approximately quarter mile to visit Alonzo's gravesite. As private driveways are used to get to the site, we had previously phoned the owners for their permission to explore Cemetery No. 2. It is a courteous and wise thing to do for those who haunt family graves looking for their roots. Fortunately, the Brown/Millard burial lot is off the beaten path thus it has not been vandalized by humans, but nature has done its steady and progressive job to eradicate what man has done. The stone walls and the pipe gates are still intact, though woodchucks have nested in the area. The agile sisters quickly arrived at their great uncle's polished granite stone. They, too, wondered who had placed it there and when? We suggested that Alonzo's friends and neighbors might have "seen to" his burial and placement of the monument as well. They knew, via Alonzo's letters, that Caroline Brown rested here too, but we were not able to identify her spot. We were bold enough to mention that Miss Forrester wrote about Maria (Mary) Mendoza Mills being buried here as well, but they were also confused about the contrary information regarding Maria's final resting place.

Our visitors were impressed with the "pleasantly situated" stretch of land once owned by their relatives. The ninety-two acres are on higher ground. In the eighteen hundreds with much of the surrounding land in pastures or fields, the Browns would have had a sweeping view of the villages below them. We point out that Clear River runs through this acreage and into Wilson's Reservoir somewhat southeast of the Brown farm. As the actual home was destroyed by fire in 1966 and others have built in the area, we could only suggest where the house and outbuildings had been located. Later, an aerial overview dated before the fire was sent to them which delineated the complex of home, barns, orchards, fields and the like. Mrs. Colony and Mrs. Putnam were understandably moved as they stood on the ground where their own mother was taught her lines from Shakespeare while their grandmother, Ogarita, sewed under the apple tree. Miss Forrester had written lovingly of this place many times. Silence prevailed as we made our way back to the car.

We then drove "down the road a piece" to the "Wilson Place." There is little left of the once busy grist, saw and shoddy mills though the foundations which distinguish each are still noticeable. We cross over a dam, of more recent construction, and walk up the dirt road that was once lined with trees which shaded three of the homes belonging to the Ross/Wilson family. Neither William R. Wilson's larger multifamily dwelling nor his nephew Herbert T. Wilson's charming Italianate house (*built in 1885 after a trip to Europe) are standing. The smaller original Ross homestead cannot even be recalled by the old timers. Two well worn steps which would have taken us into the ell of William Wilson's home is all that is left. There are several stone lined wells, but we cannot locate them today as the land is being prepared for development. We step back and leave the two sisters contemplating the picture of their grandmother living here with Mr. Wilson and his two unmarried sisters, Almira and Sarah.

There was no time to visit the Wilson cemetery, and it was probably just as well. Upon a recent trip there we found it in deplorable condition. But, they promised to return to visit us to see other spots they have only read or heard about. On our return trip, we detour through Ross Village where Mrs. Shinsel had interviewed Florence Taft and her sister Nora Hopkins with Miss Hazel Rosalie Hopkins in attendance nearly twenty-four years earlier.

Before departing, they show us a picture of Alonzo and his cousin Eugene Allan. (*Eugene, born 1850, is probably the son of Dexter and Rosanna/Rozanna Allan of Pawtucket.) Alonzo, who appears to be a mustachioed dandy in the style of his day, just might suggest a similarity to John Wilkes Booth. We accept an invitation to New Hampshire to view the materials in their family archives. Because we are all individually off to the seven winds during the summer months, a tentative date is set for September and farewells are said. A very pleasant meeting by all parties concerned.

Later, we wrote them regarding our book—which we had mentioned during lunch—and about its particular style and content. We admitted to doubts about Izola and Booth's marriage with the data on hand, though the jury is still out on Ogarita being his child. It cannot be solidly disproved . . . more later. One final word on that April visit, Peggy read a letter from Alonzo to her mother where he mentions Betsey Benchley. We asked just whose mother was she, Caroline's or her first husband's, Abraham Mills? Again, they agreed with us to the contrary data and to the confusion it brings. We turn now to the mysterious Betsey Benchley to see whether or not her true identity can be established and her double identity resolved.

The "Wilson Place" was one of the Ross homesteads at the Wilson complex - 1750 - 1815 - no longer standing.
From the Frank Potter Collection of Old Houses in Burrillville.
Photo courtesy of the Burrillville Historical & Preservation Society.

Chapter/File 9

BETSEY B. BENCHLEY

Our search for Betsey leads us to examine available documentation in order to verify her existence and her relationship to the Mills/Brown family. It is important to find out whether she is the mother of Caroline H. Brown or the mother of Abram A. Mills. Her placement on the family tree would help us determine the origin of the Mills family, and would also resolve a few other thorny problems regarding the family relationships amongst our Burrillville Booths.

Source: *Burrillville Town Records. Deaths - Vol. lA (1846-1900) p.86*

Betsey B. Benchley died March 11, 1878 in Burrillville, age 86 years. She was born in Providence, Rhode Island of American parents, Arnold and Elizabeth Benchley. According to these records, she died a widow. (*Her listing as a widow is confusing as her daughter's maiden name was Jenks/Jenkins. Apparently, Betsey used her maiden name.)

Source: *Alonzo's Daily Records.*

Benchley, Betsey B. died March 11, 1878. (*She is the mother of Caroline H. Brown and grandmother to Alonzo, who lived with them on the Brown Farm in Bridgeton in 1878. What her middle initial stands for, we do not know. Miss Forrester is the only source identifying the "B" as Beasley.)

Benchley, Arnold died January 19, 1823 aged 72. (*There is little doubt that Arnold is the father of Betsey B. and that Benchley is her maiden name, or else she married another Benchley.)

Benchley, Mrs. Deborah died January 21, 1832 aged 51.

(Listed again in Alonzo's records as:)

Allen, Mrs. Deborah (Benchley) died in Central Falls, Rhode Island. January 21, 1832 aged 51 years. (*Another Benchley girl who used her maiden name? She is likely the sister of Betsey B. and thereby the great aunt of Alonzo and possibly Martha . . . although she died before either one of them was born.)

(*The New Hampshire sisters showed us a photograph of Eugene Allen and Alonzo Standish Mills identified as half-cousins. Eugene is either Eugene Allen, grandson of Deborah, or Eugene Allan Bellows. If his last name is Bellows, then half-cousin would be accurate. If it is Allen, then Alonzo and Eugene would have been full cousins as Deborah is Betsey B.'s sister. The Allens figure prominently in the Mills, Brown and Jenks families.)

Benchley, Betsey T. daughter of Nathan and Betsey Benchley was born October 21, 1815. (*Another Betsey. We assume that Nathan is Betsey B.'s and Deborah's brother. Genealogy is tricky business at its best and especially so when families such as the Benchleys—not to mention the descendants of Izola Martha Mills—insist on carrying on the tradition of retaining family first names and surnames through many generations.)

Benchley, Mrs. Elizabeth wife of Arnold Benchley died in North Providence Sunday, April 11, 1835. (*The mother of Betsey, Deborah, and Nathan. We find ourselves in the cities located in Providence County and not in the local countryside.)

Source: *Elizabeth J. Johnson. Genealogist and research person who works out of the Spaulding House Research Library, Pawtucket, RI. (*After we heard that Betsey and her daughter Caroline [Jenks] Mills Brown along with Caroline's first husband, Abram Mills were buried in Mineral Spring Cemetery in Pawtucket, we decided to call Mrs. Johnson, who knew this area "like the back of her hand." She was most generous with her knowledge. We received the following letter from her dated March 30, 1989.*

". . . I have checked "all over the place" for proofs of Betsey B. Benchley, Abraham A. Mills and Caroline H. Jenks/Mills/Brown being buried in Mineral Spring Cemetery here in Pawtucket all to no avail. Recorded deeds for Mineral Spring Cemetery don't begin until the mid 1840's. The only Bensley deed is for John dated October 26, 1848 . . . Have talked again with my old friend Georgia Collins (*A descendant of the Benchley/Allen family) and she still states that Caroline Mills is in the Brown/Millard Cemetery. "After all why would I have taken you there if she weren't there!" Could it be that

Betsey, Abraham & Caroline are buried without a marker to show no evidence of their being somewhere? (*Another undercover agent of ours found similar "none findings" at the small building in Oak Grove Cemetery where the records of the Mineral Spring burials are housed . . . kept helter skelter in small boxes. That of course does not prove that Betsey, Caroline and Abraham are not buried there in unmarked graves. Note that the spelling of Benchley has many variations such as Bensley, not unlike the various spellings of Shakespeare.)

(*Just a reminder that Miss Forrester has Abraham (Abram) buried somewhere in Connecticut with his parents Sarah and John (or Joseph) Mills along with Izola Martha's mother, Maria (Mary) Mendoza. She also has Maria Mendoza Mills buried in Cemetery No. 2, the Brown/Millard lot in Burrillville. David Putnam lists Abraham's death in Pawtucket, but Alonzo has his father's death occurring in Albany, New York. We are now reasonably certain that Betsey B. is the mother of Caroline, grandmother to Alonzo, and could not possibly have been the mother of Abram Mills, who was Caroline's first husband. If Betsey B. were Abram's mother, then Caroline would have been married to her own brother. After communicating with Mrs. Johnson, we get the feeling that she has been over this ground many times before with others who have been seeking similar information. We now return briefly to Miss Forrester's accounts of her “great-great grandmother”.)

***Source:** Miss Forrester's writings.*

In her *Saturday Evening Post* article entitled "Child Actress of the 1890s," she wrote about a great-great-grandmother, Betsy Benchley Mills, who was the mother of Abram Standish Mills. This Betsy lived on the Mills (*Brown) farm in Pascoag and ruled the roost from her bedroom. The ninety-five year old Quaker lady, dressed in dove-gray silk with long satin streamers to her little lace cap, sat in her high-backed winged armchair with an old pink and gray parrot named Jolly Roger for company. Grandmother passed away seated in that very chair in 1883 when Miss Forrester was five years old.

From *This One Mad Act* Miss Forrester writes of a great-great-grandmother Betsy Beasley Benchley reigning from her winged armchair in her bedroom. She was also a ninety-five year old Quaker lady who also lived on the Brown farm, but dressed in gray alpaca gowns and snow-white muslin caps with lavender streamers (p. 45) She also writes that Harry (Stevenson) her uncle is living on the Pascoag farm with them. (*In 1883 Harry would have been around thirteen years of age. This is the first time we had encountered Harry living with Caroline and Alonzo on the farm.)

On page 170, she refers to Betsy as "another great-great-grandmother of Providence" who had entertained Col. Washington and his staff while he was in that city. On this page she also clearly defines the mother of Abram Mills as being Sarah Standish Mills who later married a Mr. John Batterson of Greenfield, Connecticut (page 181). (*It would appear that Miss Forrester has made some heavy use of poetic license and blended both "great-great" grandmothers into one fine portrait for her *Saturday Evening Post* story. Of course this is no crime, but it has led to despair for those researching her family with the conflicting identities of Sarah and Betsey B. We know all too well that Betsey died in 1878, the year Miss Forrester was born. Could there have been another grandmother who lived to ninety-five and died around 1883 who also had lived with the Browns? We find no evidence of it at this writing. It is interesting that Alonzo's wife was also named Sarah. It is clear from *This One Mad Act* that Miss Forrester knew the difference between the two grandmothers. It is also curious that Alonzo has never referred to Sarah Standish Mills, who was also his grandmother, in his exacting daily journals.)

Source: *The New England Historical and Genealogical Register. Volume CXII: April 1988. Whole Number 566. "The Benchley-Bensley Family" (continued) Roger D. Joslyn. page 177. (*Mrs. Johnson, the genealogist previously noted, and Brian Taft of Burrillville both sent us copies of this publication. Brian, grandson of Florence Adeline [Angell] Taft, has been researching the genealogies of local families for several years. More on Mr. Taft's contributions later. Roger Joslyn has done an indepth and painstaking tracking of the descendants of Arnold and Elizabeth Benchley. We find additional pertinent information each time we review his research in the above publication.)*

Betsey B. was born ca. 27 Jan. 1792 in Smithfield. She died of old age in Burrillville, RI 12 March 1878. (*Rhode Island Deaths, Vital Statistics are again incorrect, probably miscopied from Town records.) A Miss Betsey Benchley lived in Providence in 1826 and in North Providence from 1844-1845. She remained in North Providence in 1850 living with her daughter, Caroline Mills, who married Edward M. Brown. Betsey quite probably moved to Burrillville (in 1863) with them as she appears on the Town census in

1865 and remained there until her death. All records show Betsey's surname as Benchley, and no married record found though her death lists her as a widow . She may have married Warren Jenks born in 1792 possibly of Smithfield and listed as a yeoman. (*Independent farmer, small landholder.)

Warren and Betsey had a daughter Caroline born in North Providence or Smithfield in ca. 1819. After 1820 Warren Jenks disappeared from Rhode Island records. Relatives claimed that Caroline was first cousin to Dexter Brown Allen (*The Allens again!), who was evidently the son of Betsey's sister Deborah. (*All of the above works in well with family data provided by Alonzo. None of the information proves that Betsey or Deborah were ever married to the fathers of their children. Marriages by parsons sometimes never made it into town hall listings of vital statistics. The above outline of a lifestyle reads much like Izola's and Ogarita's with missing and mysterious husbands. This is a stripped down version of Mr. Joslyn's exact documentation. Many names he mentions find their way into Burrillville as well as into Alonzo's journals, and it does get complicated. People marry first, second and third cousins and names become hopelessly entangled. Only someone with Roger Joslyn's dedication would even attempt to sort it all out.)

(*The Benchleys were a spicy family. We hastily add that if any one of us collected all of our family data we might appear likewise. It is one of the reasons we concentrate on the genealogy of others and not on our own.)

Arnold Benchley (1751-1823) of Smithfield, RI. married Elizabeth Tucker (ca.1755 - 1837) also of Smithfield who bore him at least ten children. (*Betsey, Deborah and Nathan among them.) Corporal Arnold Benchley was tried for mutiny and found guilty in Tiverton, RI on 2 February 1779 along with Major Beriah Bump and Sergeant William Smith. They were to be executed nine days later. The revolt was caused by their dissatisfaction with the remuneration for their services in Captain William Whipple's Company, Colonel John Topham's Regiment, in which Arnold Benchley enlisted on the 9 June 1778. All were reprieved and pardoned thanks to a Baptist minister, Peleg Burroughs, who pleaded their case as family men who were needed to support their kin. Arnold later moved his family to North Providence where he hired out his children to the now famous Slater Spinning Mill in Pawtucket. (*The textile industry in the United States started with this Slater Mill.) This enabled the family to receive company housing and benefits. Almy and Brown—as in Moses Brown—hired mostly Quaker children from seven to fourteen to work from 5:30 am to 7:30 pm. Arnold was still arguing about wages but this time about those of his children. He was in debt with George Jenk's stores and Thomas Arnold's flour mill as well as with Slater and others. Also, Arnold and his brother Samuel signed a petition in 1804 concerning an act to repeal the 1778 Act preventing the draining of the seines in Providence River. (*In other words Arnold B. is a typical Rhode Islander, independent and contrary.) It is recorded that North Providence voted to have the Benchley family removed back to Smithfield from whence they came as they were liable to be chargeable. It gets hazy here but he took his time moving back to Smithfield.

(*A history note: Towns had the power to vote to accept or to remove individuals and families to or from their communities. This may seem harsh to our twentieth century sentiments, but it is necessary to view past actions within their own time frame. Men and women worked from dawn to dusk to provide for their families on the notoriously rocky soil in New England. Life on the farms in Burrillville in the 1800s was mainly sustenance living. This is another reason why the early textile industry was welcomed with wide open arms in the small village in Burrillville as well as in the rest of the state. Drifters, especially those with large families, were a considerable drain on a nearly cashless society. Families felt a strong obligation to care for any relatives, "adopted" children of those less fortunate and boarded hired hands not to mention the occasional school teacher. The Benchley family in later years is a good example of this way of thinking when we find Ogarita, Charles Bellows and Harry Stevenson living with Alonzo and Caroline along with grandmother Betsey. Being sent to the Town Farm was the last resort. In Burrillville, wards of the town lived reasonably well, received adequate medical care, even earned money for their upkeep by selling produce from the sizable farm, all according to the annual reports for this period.)

In 1844, Arnold's children applied for a pension based on his service in the American Revolution. Our Betsey "Benckley" was entitled to her share of $58.33 per year. Obviously, Mr. Benchley had served more than his one year with Capt. Whipple. From this claim we learn the living children of Arnold are: the eldest William; Stephen of Smithfield; Sally (Sarah) Bly widow, of Cumberland; Anna Babcock, widow; Betsey Benchley; and Lydia Angell, widow of North Providence; Amy Benchley of Providence and Nathan Benchley of Windham, Connecticut. (*Same county in Connecticut where Izola Martha lived.) Lewis Salisbury of Providence was their attorney and Paris Hill, Agent for paying Revolutionary War pensions. (*Please notice all the familiar family names associated with Izola Martha, Ogarita Rosalie and Alonzo Mills. It is easy to jump to conclusions with all these local Anglo-Saxon names which keep reappearing, but it is difficult to pin down a definite relationship. It was very common practice for people to marry their near relatives. Consider Lydia Benchley who married her first cousin Christopher B. (possibly Brown) Angell of Smithfield in June 16, 1820 and is listed as a widow in North Providence in 1844. Christopher was Captain of the United Volunteers in the 2nd Regiment of Militia in 1825 through 1827. In 1850 Lydia is living in North Providence with her son "Frederic" and her sister Sally Bly . Frederick, a character in his own right, married Louisa R. Pierce of Providence, Mary Mook of Fall River and others until he was finally arrested in Fall River, Massachusetts for polygamy. A Caroline Pierce lived on the Stanfield farm abutting Caroline Brown's property in the Bridgeton area.)

(*We relate all of this to offer the complexity of attempting to document anyone in the 1800s in Rhode Island even when records are fairly ample. Also, our main personalities are a part of this family. We have a strong sense that Martha Mills is related to the Benchley family in other ways than just being the step-daughter of Caroline Jenks/Mills/Brown. Hazel Hopkins and others suggest that photographs of "Izola" Martha and Ogarita "Rosalie" favor family members from the older families around this area. It has been suggested that Ogarita in particular looks like an Angell . . . no pun intended. We are wary of using photography as a means of identification as Miss Forrester "as well as others" have done to claim blood lines. Much has been made of Ogarita and Harry Stevenson's resemblance to Booth. But through our eyes, neither one possess the very distinctive features of the Booths. "Studio made" photographs of the Booth family made for an idolizing public tend to soften their characteristics. The informal pictures of the Booth brothers reveal them. Basically, we are saying it is necessary to explore the relationships of those close to Martha and her family, including her husbands, if we want to resolve her claim of having married Booth. We turn to Caroline, Alonzo's mother and Martha Izola's stepmother, who is another product of Rhode Island and is a strong personality in her own right.)

Chapter/File 10

CAROLINE H. & EDWARD M. BROWN

While researching Caroline's life, we often visualize her standing beside the Brown farm in Burrillville with her son Alonzo near the front door as pictured in the photograph in our possession. She is diminutive of size but even at this distance one can see the strong jaw and the indomitable will that makes its way into the expression on her face. There is a sizable amount of documentation on this little lady, who was "Izola" Martha's step-mother. She and Edward, her husband, can also be reasonably tracked. Miss Forrester was correct when she wrote that husbands were just not prominent beings in this matriarchal family. We are now locating and receiving more selective data on individual family members, and it is relatively easy to outline Caroline's life with only a few hidden spots to tantalize us.

Source: *The New England Historical and Genealogical Register, Volume CXII: April 1988. Whole Number 566 - pps. 184-185. The Benchley-Bensley Family by Roger D. Joslyn.*

Caroline H. Jenks was born circa 1819 in North Providence or Smithfield. (*Alonzo's more definitive information aids us greatly in our verification of facts. He writes that his mother was born in North Providence on Saturday, April 17, 1819. Moon 23 days old.) As was noted in the previous chapter/file, her parents quite probably were Betsey B. Benchley and Warren Jenks.

Her first marriage was to Abraham A. Mills, a mariner who was born in Southport, Connecticut 14 March 1820. He was the son of Joseph and Sarah———— Mills. (*From Alonzo's missing pages we read that Mr. Abram—whose son always insists on using Abram—Amherst Mills was born in Southport, CT in Fairfield

County on Tuesday, March 14, 1820, on the new moon. These are both in accord with David Putnam's charts on the Mills family, but he, as did Roger D. Joslyn, obtained his data from Pawtucket Death records and the Seaman's Protection Register. To our knowledge no one has discovered any verification of the above in Fairfield County. Many have tried over the years to do so. This does not confirm nor deny Abraham's birth there. It just proves that he is not recorded in available statistics. Caroline married Abraham A. Mills in Providence 14 May 1846.

Source: *James N. Arnold's Rhode Island Vital Records, Providence Deaths p. 131. Located at the Rhode Island Historical Society Library in Providence.*

Abraham A. Mills of Providence, son of Joseph of Standford, Connecticut and Caroline H. Jenckes of Providence, daughter of Warren of Smithfield, married by Reverend Benjamin Taylor, May 14, 1846. Mothers names are not given here, and Abraham still listed as the son of Joseph but of Standford . . . and not Southport. (*Martha Louise Mills' vital statistics are curiously the same. The place of her birth changes, but they both remain faithful to the state of Connecticut.)

Source: *Arnold's Pawtucket Vital Records 1-21 Births p. 405*

Mills, __________, son of Abram and Caroline born 13 April 1847. (*We assume that this is our Alonzo as it is his birth date and his parents. The Mills are living in Pawtucket in 1847, and Pawtucket is the residence of Martha Mills as recorded by her brother, Alonzo, in her marriage to Charles S. Bellows in 1855. Pawtucket, North Providence and Providence comprise another triangle of activity amongst this family. We admit this switching back and forth from Abram to Abraham does bother us. We also wonder about the lack of a first name for this child born in 1847. There is something mysterious about the relationships amongst these people, as suggested by Miss Elizabeth Johnson, genealogist, in her letter regarding the burials of Abraham, Caroline and Betsey in Chapter/file 7. Local genealogists have also expressed the same concern.)

Source: *Arnold's Pawtucket Vital Records Deaths p. 446*

Abraham A. Mills died 19 October 1847 (in Pawtucket) 27

years, 7 months and 5 days. Son of Joseph and Sarah. He was born in Southport, Connecticut. (*This coincides with Joslyn's account except that he has Mr. Mills' death in Albany, New York, either on the 18th or the 19th of October. Alonzo writes that his father, Abram, died in Albany on Tuesday 19 October 1847. It was a brief marriage for Abraham and Caroline Mills. Martha would have been about ten years old when her father died and Alonzo five months. Miss Forrester lists Abraham as the captain of a schooner when he married Izola Maria Mendoza of Cordova, Spain. If the above dates are correct, the captain would have been sixteen years of age at the time of his first marriage! Why is Abraham, a mariner, living in Albany in 1847? From Joslyn's study, we note that Abraham had one son, though he is not named and no mention made of a daughter. David Putnam has our sailor buried in Pawtucket as do others. If so, his body would have had to have been shipped from Albany to Pawtucket for burial.)

Source: *The New England Historical and Genealogical Register. The Benchley-Bensley Family by Roger D. Joslyn.*

In 1850 the widow Caroline is living with her mother, Betsey Benchley, in North Providence. No mention is made of Alonzo or Martha living with them. Caroline married Edward M. Brown in Pawtucket, second marriage for both, in September 15, 1857. We cannot find his first marriage, but Alonzo writes, "a daughter, Emily, was born to Edward M. Brown on July 6, 1837." He is listed as a mason, farmer and trader born in North Providence (*as was Caroline) 26 October 1801. Edward was the son of Morris and Amelia Permillian [Bucklin] Brown of North Providence. (*Oddly enough Alonzo does not make notation of his mother's marriage to Edward in the journals we have found. But, he does record another marriage of Edward M. Brown formerly of Woonsocket, Rhode Island (*the closest city to Burrillville) now of Camp Seco, Calaveras County, California to Miss Hannah Fawcett of San Francisco, January 22, 1857, married by Rev. Dr. Ver Mehr. This was found in another set of Alonzo's journals, the discovery and contents of which will be examined in the next chapter/file. This is not Edward's first wife because her name was Sarah. We checked with the California State Library and found in their Newspaper Collection - Microfilm on page 3 column 1 of the *San Francisco Bulletin* the announcement of this marriage. We made further queries regarding Edward's jaunt to California along with the reputed one of Izola Martha and John H. Stevenson but came up with a zero.

What became of Hannah Fawcett of San Francisco, we do not know.

One of Edward's occupations is a trader. Could this mean that he was also at sea and went around the Horn in the 1850s seeking his own fortune? A Burrillville resident recalled that his grandmother, who came to the United States from England after the Civil War and lived in Bridgeton, often spoke about a sea captain who lived on the Brown farm who returned to sea now and then. Edward was living in Bridgeton at that time period, but this could also have been Charles S. Bellows, husband to Martha, who was at sea most of the time. There seems to be an abundance of seafarers in this local lore. The above might also explain the pink and gray parrot in Grandmother Benchley's room on the farm. If we had not read of this marriage in California in Alonzo's journal, we would have passed it off as the coincidence of another stranger sharing the same name. Still, it is interesting to have at least one verified Californian connection mentioned by Alonzo. We should add that the inhabitants of the villages in Burrillville were not immune to the lure of the gold rush in California. Familiar family names were to be found in the various "camps" on the west coast. The Burrillville Historical and Preservation Society has a photograph of two such men with their pack mules in California from the Ross and Angell Villages of Burrillville.

Source: *Packet from Roger D. Joslyn, Certified Genealogist, New Windsor, New York. (*We wrote to Mr. Joslyn asking if he had any other information on Alonzo, Caroline, Edward and Martha. He kindly and promptly sent us all the substantial material that he had including genealogical charts, probate records, federal census and even a list Edward M. Brown's debt as a minor in 1821.)*

From Mr. Joslyn we learned that Edward's parents were Morris Brown and his second wife Amelia Bucklin. Morris's first wife was Amelia's sister Permelia Bucklin. The elder Mr. Brown died in his early fifties. His minor son Edward contracted some debts which were paid from the estate of Morris Brown by his guardian, William Morris. Edward must have been a bit of a dandy as his debts involve clothes, stockings, and shoes made for him. (*All the men in the extended Mills family appear to be dandies in their youth. Is this what attracts the matriarchal ladies?) In 1820 he has siblings Sylvester and John B. Brown and Mary D. Mason. (*Sylvester Brown also lived in Burrillville at one time.) Browns, Sylvesters, and Angells were sizable landholders in the Wallum Lake, Buck Hill area with interchangeable names and intermarriages. Mrs. Amelia

Brown left the majority of her holdings and monies to her two sons, Edward and John, "because they furnished her with part of the money to buy a certain farm 18 1/2 acres east of the highway leading to Providence, RI."

(*We learn that Edward is indeed related to the George Brown who purchased the 92 acres in 1792 and to Joseph Brown who sold to Andrew Luther who then sold them to Edward in 1863. The Browns are cousins, all related to Chad Brown of Providence, and are also well known in North Providence, Pawtucket and Burrillville. Land is important, even this rocky soil in northwestern Rhode Island, and a good deal of it was divided up by Roger Williams and Company whose ancestors were still living on it in the late 1800s up to the mid 1900s as well. Mr. Joslyn didn't reply to our question whether he was related to the George and Lena Joslin who purchased that by now famous 92 acres for $10.00 from Alonzo in 1916 shortly before his death at the Alms House in Cranston.)

Edward probably married Sarah N. Hawkins in 1822, both of them residing in Seekonk, Massachusetts at that time. (*His individual personality escapes us. The data is there, but the essence is not. Edward was in his fifties in 1857 when he married Caroline, and we hear nothing of his daughter Emily. Could she be the mother of Alonzo's wife, Sarah Symmonds, whose mother's name is Emily? That is a long shot but the time frame makes it possible. Alonzo records that Edward M. Brown married a Hannah Fawcett in California in the early part of 1857. Apparently Mr. Joslyn had no information on this.) While checking through Alonzo May's unpublished manuscript, *History of the American Theater 1750-1904,* on microfilm courtesy of the Maryland Historical Society, we found a David Fawcett and an Emma Fawcett, his daughter, both stage personalities, mostly in the west. The Fawcett family name appears in theatrical enterprises both in England and America. Alonzo Mills only mentions Hannah Fawcett once.

(*We have questioned Miss Forrester's suggestion that the Brown farm was known as the Mills farm in the 1830s, with Mary Mills buried there in 1837. From old records in the Glocester Town Hall [Burrillville was part of this town until 1806], we came across a deed to George Brown for 92 acres purchased from old familiar names (*Esten, Angell and Ross among them) in our area in 1792. We surmise the federal home was built before 1800. The Browns lived on the farm up through the 1850s. Andrew Luther bought the house during the early 1860s. All of which tends to negate the Mills family (*other than Alonzo) owing this property. Continuing our search in the Burrillville Town Hall deed books, we found an odd set

The Brown Farm in Bridgeton - 1795 circa to 1966
Caroline H. Brown and her son, Alonzo A. S. Mills.
Probably taken in late 1870s or early 1880s.
Photo courtesy of Miss Hazel Rosalie Hopkins.

of circumstances which we cannot explain.)

Source: *Town of Burrillville, Deed Books 17 and 20.*

Edward M. Brown of North Providence bought 92 acres from Andrew and Phebe Luther on January 30, 1863 for the sum of $1,500. (*A goodly sum in 1863 during the Civil war. The discovery in the *Pascoag Herald* files of Edward's purchase of these same acres in 1863 has been previously noted.)

Edward M. Brown sold to William R. Wilson for the sum of one dollar 92 acres of land on the 8th of April 1875. (*This is four years before William's marriage to Ogarita. Martha was married to John H. Stevenson at this time and probably living in Boston. This transfer could be for a debt or as a retainer for whatever . . . but read on.)

William R. Wilson sold the same property above to Caroline H. Brown for one dollar on September 1, 1877. (*Edward died August 18, 1877. They certainly put trust in Mr. Wilson's integrity. Perhaps the property was entrusted to him to prevent the attachment of a lien for Edward's debts, and after his death returned to Caroline. Ownership of land and property in the 1800s meant that roots were established and a family inheritance was assured from generation to generation. Along with the many responsibilities, the right to vote and hold elected office in local or state government was also a privilege of the landowner. Possession of land separated the propertied from the laboring class, though each of them labored equally . . . but to continue on with the deeds.)

Alonzo A. S. Mills sold said property on August 9, 1916 for ten dollars to Lena and George Joslin. (*We know that George and Alonzo were friends and quite possibly relatives, but we cannot explain the sale of 92 acres of land and a sizable home for this scanty amount. There are things going on here that we cannot explain but they do spark our interest. We sense that this has more to do with family than across-the-board economics. The deed states the cemetery plot will be retained by the Joseph Brown heirs "by them forever." There doesn't seem to be any substance to an early Mills family ever owning this property.)

(*The above 92 acres does have an interesting history, and some of it is hidden by historical veils of secrecy. We hear of sea captains who come and go, of the possibility that Booth "hid out" here after the assassination of President Lincoln, of the elusive Martha and Ogarita living with Caroline now and then—not to mention Martha's two sons, Charles and Harry—and that Miss

Forrester was born on the Brown Farm with the unidentified George Wallingford as her father. Then there is this curious fellow Alonzo who hires out as a hand, chops wood, writes poetry and records daily in his now famous journals, and who has a young wife who unaccountably disappears from any records. In fact Sarah A. Mills is never mentioned in the local lore involving this extended family, even with their intricate relationships with prominent family names in Burrillville as well as a great many other towns and cities in Rhode Island, Massachusetts and Connecticut. There is a seemingly tolerant Caroline who manages the farm and cares for all of those who come and go at intervals. Much of the above information remained in the minds of those who lived during and soon after their time period and was carried on in oral history by the generations who followed. With or without the Booth connection, this is a fascinating family. Like Booth, himself, their burial sites appear shrouded in mystery.

(*We have the obvious affiliation with the Methodist Episcopal Church with all of their social activities covered by the *Pascoag Herald* in the local section. Miss Forrester mentioned a steady flow of visitors and guests from Boston, North Providence and Pawtucket. The Brown farm was not seldom seen but the place to be. It is time to return to the more mundane world of records and other documentation which only hint at all the activity on those 92 acres from 1863 through today. Strangers are still coming to look for this particular spot in Burrillville, RI.)

***Source**: Town of Burrillville Mortgage Records Book 22 pp. 88-89*

Caroline H. Brown took out a $3,000 mortgage from Clark Walling on a wood lot in October 26, 1880 and paid it off by 1882. (*Walling was another early family name in Burrillville around the village of Harrisville . . . and it is Walling and not Wallingford!) Witnessed by William R. Wilson. (*Old faithful.) Reserved all rights to her husband, Edward M. Brown, the Clear River Saw Mill's water privileges called Esten Angell's saw mill and privilege. (*Strange that Edward is included here as he died in 1877. Perhaps she may have borrowed money previously and this line was in the contract? We wonder why Caroline needed to borrow this large amount in 1880. We do know that Martha was living in Pascoag but quite probably in her own home and not on the Brown farm, as her brother Alonzo worked and boarded with her in 1880-1881. Was Caroline again aiding her step-daughter? Martha was known as Mrs. John H. Stevenson at this time, though she had to be divorced from him as she married Edwin S. Bates in 1881. The hardworking

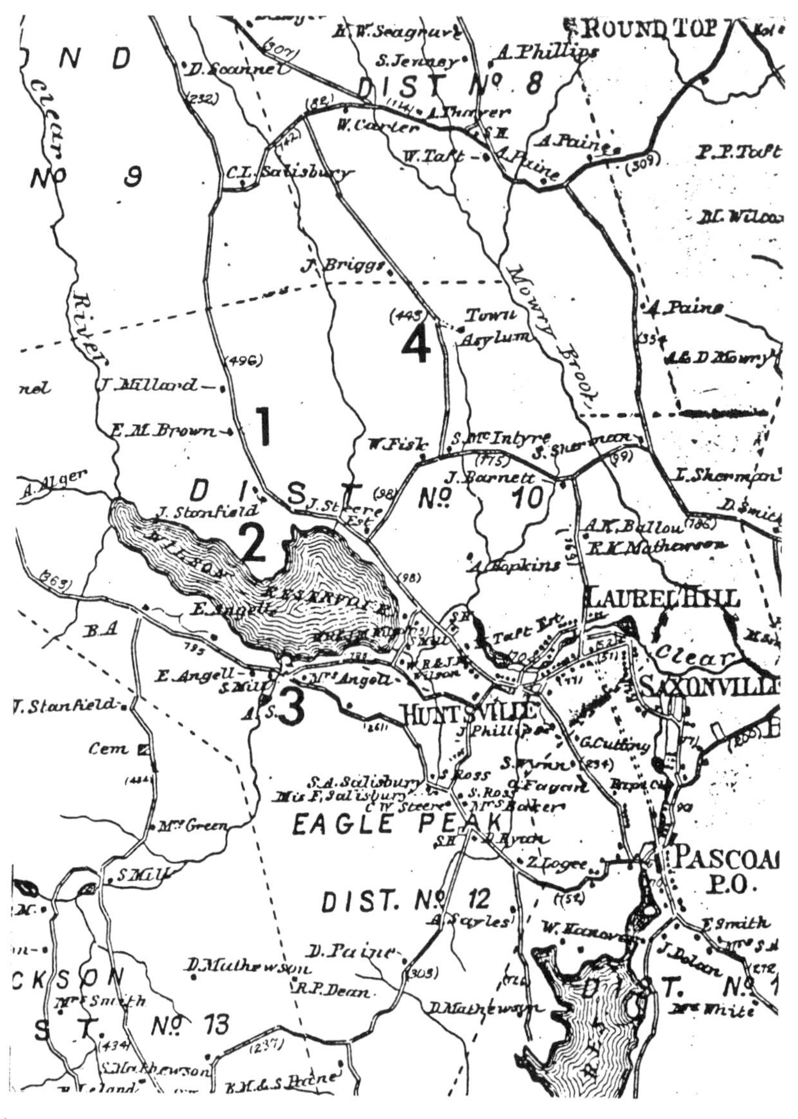

Map of Bridgeton and surrounding area
Beers Atlas - 1870
1. E. M. Brown
2. Stanfield Farm
3. Angell Village
4. Town Poor Farm

Caroline pays off her debts promptly, suggesting that the farm was a productive and profitable one, but trouble lies ahead for Alonzo and his mother.)

Source: *Pascoag Herald dated April 1, 1904. Report on Burrillville Probate Court Meeting.*

The next probate matter to be considered was the petition of Gilbert S. Taft, Overseer of the Poor, for the appointment of a guardian of the person and estate of Caroline H. Brown, a person of full age. This matter came up at the last regular meeting . . . at that time it was deemed best for the Overseer of the Poor to apply for the appointment of a guardian. Mrs. Brown is a woman of advanced years and, with her son, lives on a farm which she owns near Wilson's reservoir; she is 89 years of age (*Incorrect). Edward F. Lovejoy spoke in behalf of Mrs. Brown, having been requested to do so by her. He said that he had known her for many years and that he believed that she was as capable of managing her affairs now as she had ever been. She was much opposed to having a guardian appointed, he said, and it really seemed too bad to do so as she was now in the evening of life and had always cared for herself and property during the long years of her residence. (*How sensible this all sounds compared to what would be said today under similar circumstances.) If there had been any difference between her and her son, there seemed to be none now. It was believed they could get along without the intervention of a guardian. The matter was continued until the next regular meeting when it will very likely be dismissed if there seems to be no greater occasion for the appointment than now. (*According to the next *Pascoag Herald*, it was dismissed. Evidently there was a problem between Caroline and Alonzo. Caroline was 85 and Alonzo 56 . . . not too difficult to fill in the story line here. Alonzo you will recall was placed on the Town Farm in the early months of 1907. Why he is not able to care for himself, we do not know. Perhaps he was ill.)

Source: *New England Historical and Genealogical Register. The Benchley-Bensley Family by Roger D. Joslyn.*

Caroline H. Brown died 28 Jan 1907 aged 87 years in Cranston, R. I. of senile dementia and arteriosclerosis and was buried in Mineral Spring Avenue, Pawtucket, Rhode Island. (*Along with her first husband and mother Betsey we assumed. Please note that our feisty lady has outlived the younger Martha, Ogarita and William

Wilson by quite a few years. Caroline does not make her departure from this story easily. We previously mentioned speaking with genealogist Betty Johnson concerning Caroline's burial place which she insisted was in the Brown/Millard lot despite the "official documentation." Burrillville records also have her buried in Mineral Spring Cemetery. Georgia Collins, descendant of the Benchley family, pointed out Caroline's grave located on the Brown farm to Miss Johnson several years ago. In getting to the truth of the matter in our own inimitable way, we found out that Caroline was indeed removed from the Howard Asylum in Cranston to a vault at the Mineral Spring Cemetery, Pawtucket, in preparation to being placed beside her first husband and mother.)

Source: *Town of Burrillville Probate Court Records September 18, 1908*

Gilbert S. Taft, administrator, inventory of said late Caroline H. Brown amounting to $41.25 after bills. Probate Court Judge John McCabe adjourned with all unfinished inventory received and accepted.

Probate Package 31-319 of Caroline H. Brown. (*A folder containing folded paper bills and receipts contains the probate records of Caroline H. Brown. It is not necessary to relate them all, because the amounts were so meager, but we did find what we were looking for.) Cemetery Department, Pawtucket, Rhode Island, May 2, 1907. Varnum Steere to the city of Pawtucket tomb rent of Caroline M. Brown $4.00 dated May 2, 1907. (*The "M" probably stands for Mills, and we still wonder what her "H" actually stood for . . . could it have been Hannah?)

May 2, 1907 paid to Varnum Steere for body of Caroline H. Brown being removed from Pawtucket to Pascoag, coffin box cost was $12.00. (*All paid for out of his mother's estate by Alonzo S. Mills. One interesting bill to Alexander T. Ritchie of Buffalo, NY September 17, 1908 for eleven dollars and 13 cents. Ritchie. This will tantalize us for months to come. We do know that there were Ritchie's living in this tri-state corner at one time. The only outstanding bill was to Henry J. Bruce, M.D. for $50.00. Caroline must have been seriously ill for some time.)

Source: *Pascoag Herald dated May 10, 1907.*

The body of Mrs. Caroline H. Brown was removed from the tomb in Pawtucket to the home farm north of Bridgeton for interment by Undertaker Varnum Steere last week. (*She waited patiently for nearly five months for mortals to discover their error. It was Alonzo himself who tells us the rather sad story in the following source.)

Source: *Letter dated Jan. 22, 1911, Pascoag, RI from Alonzo to "My dear niece: —"Izola."— Given to us by the two ladies from New Hampshire, Mrs. Colony and Mrs. Putnam.*

. . .How glad and thankful I were, yesterday, when I received a letter at the Pascoag Post Office from you. I little expected that I should ever hear from any of my sister Martha's children, or grandchildren again. May the Lord bless you Izola, I would be so glad to see you, and your sister Beatrice, and your uncles Harry Stevenson and Charley Bellows. I am so overpowered with gladness this morning to hear from you . . . I am not married and are living alone in my farm home. (*We do not know how to interpret this, either Sarah has died or they have been divorced although he is still listed as married in his death notice.) My mother died four years ago the 26th of this month (*January) at the Howard, RI. Insane Asylum. She became strictly insane during the summer and fall of 1906 and refused to let anyone take care of her, or any physician doctor her; and the Burrillville Town Council and Doctors found they had got to carry her to the Insane Asylum . . . she was carried there November 15, 1906, and died January 26th 1907. . . I went to the Asylum to see her Jan. 13, 1907, and found her in very poor health, and failing fast . My mother is buried in the old "Joseph Brown" Cemetery on my farm. (*It is now the Mills Farm!) After my father Mills's death, in October 1847, mother bought a grave-lot in Pawtucket Cemetery, and had father buried there, and also my grandmother Benchley, but, at the time she bought the lot, neglected to have the lot put on record, and after mother's death, I found I could not hold or own the lot, and so therefore had to have mother buried in the Brown Cemetery on my farm. My sister Martha, (your grandmother), always thought mother owned the grave lot in Pawtucket.

(*Sounds as though he would have preferred to bury his mother in the Mineral Spring Cemetery rather than the "so-called" Joseph Brown Cemetery so she would have been with her first husband, Abraham. Caroline must have told Alonzo about his father being buried there, but he would have known himself when and where grandmother Betsey Benchley was placed to rest as she died in 1878. These facts suggest that Martha was living with Caroline and her father, Abram, in 1847 when he died, contrary to Miss

Forrester's having Martha whisked away by Fanny D'Arcy and brought up in the South.

We are convinced that Caroline rests in peace with her son on the Brown/Millard lot in Bridgeton. We are also inclined to believe—despite vital statistics records—that Alonzo's father and grandmother are, or were, buried in the Mineral Spring Cemetery. Caroline deserved a better ending then this after holding the family unit together by caring for and tolerating all those who landed on her farm . . . but even in death the indomitable Caroline keeps everyone busy and still has some of us guessing as to where she actually rests. This misunderstanding of who was buried where and when adds to the mystery of the elusive Booths and the families from whence they came. Because of the closeness and familiarity amongst Caroline, Alonzo, and Martha, we tend to accept the fact that Caroline raised Martha at least from the time she married Abram. It doesn't seem possible that Martha was unknown to them until she landed on the Brown farm after 1865 with Ogarita [and Charles] in hand . . . according to local lore.)

(*Alonzo continues to tell us some more interesting news in his letter to Izola Merrifield. Apparently his nieces and nephews have neglected him for decades until this 1911 exchange of letters.) "The administrator (Gilbert S. Taft) and the Town Council, that had charge of settling mother's farm property, talked of having an auction and selling the farm, (as there were at that time a few farm debts). . . but as there are a large amount of handsome growing pine timber and wood on the farm, that can be sold in a few years for a high price; they concluded that I had better keep the farm. Lawyer Edward Lovejoy, of Pascoag, (an old friend of mother's and to me) advised me to keep the farm, and hire money enough to repair my house, (which was in a bad condition to live in) and settle what few farm debts that there were that time, and let some one take a mortgage of the amount of money hired. So Mr. Jesse H. Ross, of this town, (a friend of mine) took a mortgage . . . which amounts to one thousand dollars, running on interest, at six per cent. If I can keep the farm four or five years longer, I can sell timber and wood enough to clear me from debt, and take care of me the rest of my life . . . I have been offered twelve hundred dollars for the timber and wood on the farm, and can get three thousand dollars for the farm, but the farm is agrowing more valuable every day . . .The Providence & Springfield Railroad, that runs from Providence to Pascoag and Southbridge, Massachusetts, crosses my farm cutting the farm in two parts, and now there is a talk of putting another railroad (The Grand Trunk Railroad) through my farm. (*Unfortunately for Alonzo as well as many others he did not reap any windfall for selling the right of way although Caroline probably did when the New York Springfield Railroad Company purchased the land in 1892 or 1893. The train went through their farm in 1894. The gentleman who had the capital for the Grand Trunk Line or Air Line, Charles Melville Hayes, went down with the Titanic in 1912.)

But to return to Caroline H. Brown whose life began to read like that of a character from William Faulkner's mythical Yoknapatawpha County (Northern version). From Alonzo's missing pages we read, "News: Burrillville, R. I., Friday, May 3, 1907 - Undertaker Varnum Steere brought the body of my (Alonzo A. Mills) mother (Mrs. Caroline H. Brown) to my (AASM) farm in the latter part of the forenoon today for burial in the late Joseph Brown Cemetery on the aforesaid farm. A number of the neighbors together with Mr. Gilbert S. Taft and Mrs. Frances Kershaw (*An old friend of Caroline's from Laurel Ridge) gathered at the grave and Rev. Walter Ella and Rev. Mr. Beele of Bridgeton, RI, took charge of the burial service." He also records that on May 2, 1907 Mrs. Caroline H. Brown (late of Burrillville) was brought to Pascoag today from Oak Hill Cemetery, Pawtucket, RI—this is a mistake also found in the *Pascoag Herald* as Oakhill Cemetery is in Woonsocket—by undertaker Varnum Steere of Pascoag, the body having been in the tomb at the aforesaid cemetery since January last." (*Oak Grove Cemetery is where all the records are kept for the Pawtucket Cemeteries including the Mineral Spring one.)

We really did not want to leave Caroline with this last entry. We do tend to get involved with the individuals whose lives we are trying to put into some kind of focus by revealing their truths and foibles. Alonzo's mother and Martha's stepmother—if indeed that is their true relationship—was colorful yet diligent, feisty yet pragmatic, who we chose not to leave in an unmarked grave. Believe this or not, just in the last few weeks the Griffin family from Pascoag donated copies of the *Burrillville Gazette* from 1880 on to the Pascoag Public Library. In the following edition, we found something which we believe captures the essence and spirit of Caroline H. [Jenks] Mills Brown.

Source: *Burrillville Gazette October 10, 1890*

The last and best excursion was to be from Pleasant View House to Mrs. Caroline H. Brown's two miles west of Laurel Ridge. Mrs. Brown came after the band about 8 o'clock a.m. The band was carried in the golden chariot (so-called). When the chariot was about to start there were seven of Eve's fair daughters, all seated and numbered, and started from the front gate of Pleasant View House. The line of travel was up Inman Street to Salisbury Street, up Salisbury Street to Highland Street to Brown Avenue, to the mansion of Mrs. Caroline Brown. The time of march was about two hours and forty minutes. Upon arriving at the mansion, Mr. Mills (*Mr. Mills being Alonzo) took the horse to the stable to give him rest from his fatiguing labors, preparatory for the return trip.

The forenoon was spent in singing of hymns and reading of the Scriptures, and solemn prayer for the good of all Christians and the conversion of the worldly to Christianity . . . at 12 o'clock a blessing was invoked by Mr. Mills (it being his daily habit), and the delicacies of the season were on the table, and the band did the dinner ample justice. The afternoon was spent same as the forenoon (only more so). Supper was served at 5 p.m. A teapot Brittania two feet long with wooden handles graced the table, the teapot being over 80 years old. A child who was present was rocked to sleep in a cradle over 100 years old. The chariot was brought up to the door and one hour after tea, all ready for the return trip, Mrs. Brown carrying the band home. Mrs. Brown has been in feeble health a number of years, but being of a hardy enduring race, she retains her strength and vitality to a remarkable degree . . . a perfect success socially, religiously, morally, with a prospect of being repeated in the near future, and we hope that Mrs. Brown will live to enjoy many more of the same kind of social entertainments, as that is her nature and her nature helps to make these meetings pleasant and agreeable.

(*We believe that this newspaper article gives a more fitting end to the file on Caroline. It does show that Alonzo and his mother were no strangers to the people living in this local area and in fact were part of the social life evolving in the 1890s. In our next chapter/file, we take you to our discovery of a new journal in Alonzo's own handwriting which continues to fill in more of the gaps in this interesting family tree.)

Chapter/File 11

ALONZO'S DAILY RECORDS

In Chapter/file 7, we quoted Alonzo's obituary in the *Pascoag Herald* as follows: For more than a half century he (*Alonzo) kept a daily record of his most minute transactions of the people whom he met, of the conversation engaged in and these were interspersed with local happenings and events, etc. We knew that in the twenty-six pages belonging to the Burrillville Historical and Preservation Society and the missing pages from Barbara Shaw we had nowhere near a half century of transactions, conversations and happenings of the writings of Alonzo. Local lore also has Alonzo writing in his journals on a daily basis.

Word was sent out we were looking for any of these writings by Alonzo either in journal form or whatever. Admittedly, we often seem to be using Miss Marple's methods in pursuing knowledge of our local "Booths." Strangely enough, the method is quite successful. "By indirections find directions out." This is not to say we slight the more orthodox manners of research which are needed for verification and supportive data.

Joyce Remington, president of the Burrillville Historical & Preservation Society, was introduced several chapter/files ago. Miss Remington is co-owner of an antique shop in nearby Chepachet, Rhode Island, an avid collector of material on Burrillville and also does extensive work on the genealogies of local families. She has dug up facts for us at the Rhode Island Historical Society Library.

She attended an auction on the Lovejoy Farm in Bridgeton, located three roads over from Wallum Pond Road and Alonzo's farm. We have introduced this family before as it was Reverend Lovejoy who officiated at the marriage of several family members, and Edward Lovejoy, the lawyer, who was friend to both Caroliné and Alonzo for many years. As Joyce tells it another dealer suggested to her that she check out a box of books with some Burrillville material in it. Under normal circumstances the lot would have been sold intact, but when several others showed interest in this item, the auctioneer decided to sell it separately. Our president persevered and brought back an "original" Alonzo A. S. Mills daily journal for us to study. We wonder at the strange ways his "histories" keep getting into our hands.

To say we trembled with anticipation may sound over dramatic, but it is also not far from the truth. The journal is a middle sized Victorian ledger book in excellent condition. Someone, perhaps Alonzo himself, had covered this cache with a rough cotton fabric and secured the corners with long accurate stitches of heavy thread. There are 334 pages and all of them filled with the now familiar handwriting of our favorite eccentric. A quick glance told us he had changed his method of recording from the alphabetic format to a curious system of headings of the month and the day . . . but not the year. If you were listed and had been born on say January 1st, your birth would be under the first column on page one with the year added. It is a painstaking method, and we suspect this was the final accounting of the information he had gathered. Entries seldom go beyond the late 1880s and there are none for 1900. Because each page in this journal is basically filled, there is the probability other journals are out there waiting to be discovered. He begins:

Jan. 1, 1863 A.D. Thursday. Battle of Galveston.

Jan. 1, 1875 A.D. Died, In East Providence, Dr. Peleg Clarke, in the 91st year of his age. Friday.

Jan. 1, 1873 A.D. Died, in Pascoag, RI., Mrs. Elizabeth B. Brown, widow of the late Martin Brown, in the 62nd year of her age. (*We assume these are members of the Benchley/Mills/Brown family.)

We note the different color of ink on each page ranging from black to blue to purple which leads us to believe he wrote these entries at different times. Alonzo's handwriting is studied, pleasing to the eye and legible. There are places when his penmanship changes, expressing his mood at that time of either being hurried, out of humor, or under stress. There are interesting large "X's" throughout the journal. These were probably not done by Alonzo. They are placed beside names which have a familiarity to us and quite possibly denote relatives of the Mills, Browns, et al.

Toward the end of this journal is an accounting of the hours and the pay received by the hired hands who worked for Caroline as well as those of Alonzo when he hired out to local families. Caroline hired Silas Lewis, Everett Carpenter, and Hosea Hopkins for haying and hoeing on her farm. For a day's work the hired hand received 75 cents for hoeing and $1.50 for haying. Interestingly, Miss Forrester mentions Hosea Hopkins in her *Saturday Evening Post* article. Great grandmother Caroline hitched up the horses and drove up to the Buck Hill area to purchase a stock of baskets from him. Miss Forrester says that Hosea is a basket maker with a peg leg with which he cracks nuts for her. But, according to Caroline's bookkeeping accounts in 1879, he was able to hay and hoe with ease. We doubt the story of Hosea having a peg leg. Miss Forrester would have been about a year old when Alonzo and Caroline kept their exacting records. Silas Lewis, who also lived in the Buck Hill area, was from a colored family, one of the few living in the northwest corner of Burrillville. Alonzo hired out for hoeing, haying and cutting wood to William Wilson, Andrew Luther, John Stanfield, and even did work for the Town Farm, all in 1879. His basic pay seemed to have been $1.00 a day even when he helped lay the stone foundation for Mr. Wilson's shingle mill.

When Alonzo traveled to Providence in 1875, he listed the goods he bought and their prices. Among these is an inordinate amount of money spent on pens, ink, foolscap and stationery. It appears he takes his writing quite seriously. In addition, we learn from the *Pascoag Herald* that he also has a collection of first editions of several publications. After his niece, Mrs. Merrifield, contacts him in 1911, a curious story evolves from his letters to her (*in our possession) and bits and pieces found in the *Pascoag Herald* . . . but more on this at the end of this file.

After feasting our eyes on his journal, we did not want this treasure to vanish so we xeroxed copies of it . . . a three hour task. That way we felt assured his writings would be kept for posterity and not disappear as did the original small journals. This led to staying up to wee hours in the morning reading, with Alonzo teasing us by dropping a small bomb in our lap every twenty pages or so. There is still much to discover in his writings. Scanning the material in our individual ways, one of us decided the best way to present the information found would be to pull out the specific family names and hope for the best. We begin with the name Mills:

Jan. 16, 1877 A.D. died, in Chepachet, R. I., Lucida B., wife of John A. Mills and daughter of Susan B. and the late Arnold A. M. Steere of Glocester in the 23rd year of her age. (*This is probably Lucinda. We checked the Glocester vital records and verified it. We noted a John E. Mills in Burrillville age 45 listed in the Burrillville Militia, laborer. John A. could have been the son of John E. We have yet to tie either one of them into our Mills.)

April 13, 1847 A.D. Born in Pawtucket, Mass., (lately Pawtucket, R. I.) Alonzo A. S. son of Abram A. and Caroline H. Mills. Tuesday. (*Our historian is correct. Boundary disputes were not settled until the 1860s by the Supreme Court. Even though Alonzo's first name is missing from Arnold's historical records, there is little to dispute that Alonzo is who he says he is and that he was born in Pawtucket. But, Martha's story is another and a more complex one. We shall return to Martha and her brother's history on her one milestone at a time.)

May 17, 1871 A.D. Wednesday, Married, in Pascoag, R. I. at the residence of Mr. Smith Wheelock, by Rev. Jabez Pack, Methodist minister at Laurel Hill Pascoag, Mr. Alonzo A. S. Mills, to Miss Sarah A. Simmons, both of Pascoag. (*His own marriage is recorded without fanfare or any special indication. We see that the Burrillville Vital Statistics record led us astray as his bride is recorded as a Sarah A. Symmonds. Her mother and father, Thomas and Emily, came from Providence though she is listed as a Burrillville resident. We hurried back to local records and found a Sarah Simmons where we did not think she would be found . . . in the annual tax reports.)

Source: *1873 Burrillville Tax Book*
Mills, Sarah A. . . . . Personal 17,000 taxes 102.00
Brown, Edward M. . . . . . .Real Estate 1400 Personal 400 tax 10.80

Source: *1874 Burrillville Tax Book*
Mills, Sarah A. . . . . Personal 14,000 taxes 84.00

(*Alonzo's bride in 1873 is a wealthy lady by anyone's standards. This is a greater sum than the local mill owners paid for their personal property. Edward Brown, who owned the farm at this time, only paid a tax bill of $10.80. Sarah was eighteen when Alonzo married her. In 1873, she possibly came of age (twenty-one) or was left an inheritance. After these two entries, the elusive Sarah vanishes again. What happened to the $3000 spent between the years 1873 and 1874? She did not appear in the 1871 or 1872 tax bills and disappears again in the 1875 and 1876 lists. Also, the Burrillville Census of June 1875 lists Edward, Caroline, Betsey, and Alonzo as living on the Brown/Mills Farm. No Sarah. Alonzo does not record her birth nor her death. He does record his marriage again on page 254 in a clear and steady hand, the only changes being the additions of Jabez Pack, as pastor of the Laurel Hill M. E. Church, and that both bride and groom are from Burrillville. There is one more notation in Alonzo's journal on Sarah as a co-author of a poem dedicated to Mrs. Almira Howard.)

Source: *Return to Alonzo's Daily Records.*

June 22, 1870 A.D. Wednesday. Died in Pawtucket R. I. Mrs. Almira E. Howard wife of Hiram L. Howard, and daughter of the late Benjamin and Lydia Angell of North Providence, RI. aged 67 years. (*Lydia was one of the Benchley girls, sister to Betsey Benchley and thus great aunt to Alonzo. It is a six stanza poem and "Composed by Alonzo A. S. and Sarah A. Mills, Pascoag, R. I." We thought at first this might be the elusive grandmother, Sarah Standish Mills Batterson, until we read of Alonzo's wife, Sarah A. [Simmons] Mills. Sarah is living on the Brown farm at this time, but is not yet married to Alonzo. We wonder why this aunt merits Alonzo's and Sarah's attention. This eulogy to Almira suggests a meeting of their minds and a gentleness of feeling between them. Perhaps Alonzo copied it into this journal after their marriage the following year. All of which confounds us further. Why and when did Sarah disappear from his life, and why is he still listed as a married man on his death certificate? A lady with that kind of money would have been noticeable in Burrillville in the 1870s. A search for her parents in Providence led us to the State of Rhode Island Archives and in the 1852-1853 *Providence Business Directory* we did find three Thomas Simmons, one a jeweler, one the owner of a hat store in the Arcade in Providence, and the other a harness maker. We are checking city census to see whether she can be tied in with any of the three assuming their residence is Providence as indicated in Burrillville Vital statistics.)

July 30, 1855 A.D. Monday Married in Boston Mass., by Rev. Streeter. Mr. Charles S. Bellows of Boston Mass. U. S. N. to Miss Martha L. Mills of Pawtucket, R. I. (*This is identical to the notation in the original twenty-six pages which leads us to believe that this ledger contains a culmination of his work. Easy to see that Alonzo's entries of the birth, death and marriages of his family members made our pursuit of the elusive Burrillville "Booths" relatively simple when checking for recorded vital statistics. The following verification had been received earlier, but we thought it best to insert it at this time.)

Source: *Commonwealth of Massachusetts. Archives Division.*

Charles S. Bellows and Martha L. Mills married in Boston, Mass. July 30, 1855 by Rev. S. Streeter, Boston. Groom is age 28, born in Boston of Elijah and _____ Bellows, mariner, first marriage, and resides in Boston. Bride is age 23, born in Stanford, Ct. of Abraham and _______Mills, no occupation, and resides in Boston. (*If Martha has given her correct age, she would have been born in 1832 and not the 1837 she records elsewhere. Charles S. Bellows appears to be a man in his own right and not a shadow of John Wilkes Booth. It would seem unlikely that Booth fathered both Ogarita (1859) and Charles (1861) during Martha's stay in Boston. This is probably the main reason why Miss Forrester omitted her Uncle Charles from the family tree entirely, as his arrival spoils her story of Martha living in the South in that time frame. Still we cannot ignore the fact that Martha was living in Boston when Booth was on stage at the Boston Museum or visiting his brother's home in Dorchester. If Charles were at sea a good deal of the time and if Martha were on stage as her family claims, then the possibility exists that she did meet and become infatuated with the handsome rising stage star.)

Source: *Return to Alonzo's Daily Journals.*

Sept. 11, 1837 A.D. born at Greenfield Co. Conn. Martha L. Mills, daughter of Abram A. & Mary A. Mills. (*Greenfield County is actually Fairfield County today. When we read this we had already seen the various other places Martha claims as her birthplace. She does not appear to know exactly where she was born . . . and note the middle initial "A" in Mary's name . . . no Izola Maria Mendoza here. We both noticed a difference in the handwriting of the above material. It is not in the careful style of Alonzo, but is rather cramped and appears to have been hastily written in contrast to the placid and deliberate style of the ledger's owner. Whoever wrote it appears to have learned penmanship from the same school, but there are too many individual differences for it to be from Alonzo's pen. Strangely there is also a date scratched out beneath the 1837, which brought our attention to the differences between studying a typed transcript and an original writing. We noted this before in vital statistics but not to this degree. One can glean a great deal more from the handwriting on a page than from the cold and sterile sameness of a typewritten page.)

Oct. 23, 1859 A.D. born in Providence, Ogarita E. R. Bellows, daughter of Charles and Martha Bellows of Boston, Mass. (*Alonzo finally records Ogarita's birth. Martha gave birth to Ogarita in Providence at Abbott's Lane though she was still a resident of Boston according to Alonzo. We surmised that Martha returned to relatives to give birth to her daughter, though we do not know exactly with whom she stayed. Caroline was living in North Providence in 1850 and was listed again in 1860, married Mr. Brown in Pawtucket in 1857, and moved to Burrillville in 1863. In 1855, the widow Caroline and her mother Betsey could have been living in Providence, but we do not know. The Pawtucket, North Providence and Providence areas form another triangle within which this family moves about at will. Please note the E. R. in Ogarita's name. Outside of Miss Forrester's writings, this is the first time we have seen the "R" for Rosalie (?) listed. It is possible Alonzo wrote it at her request because Ogarita had been using it for some time.)

May 16, 1861 A.D. Thursday. Born Charles A. Bellows son of Charles S. and Martha L. Bellows of Boston. (*We have seen this before but not with the middle initial "A" . . . for Alonzo? In his first recording he wrote, son, Charles Still Bellows, and not Charles "A". Families were more inclined to name children after relatives in the 1880s, and not always out of affection for the person. Mr. Kimmel lists the second child of "Izola" and Booth as Alonso and the first as Ogarita. It is a mystery why Alonzo changed the middle name "Still" to "A".)

Dec. 16, 1869 A.D. Died in Chelsea Hospital, Mass., Mr. Charles S. Bellows Sr. of the USN age 43 yrs. 10 mos. and 3 days. (*Martha's husband served a long stretch in the Navy at least from 1855 through 1869. If she were still with her husband, Martha would have been in Boston area in 1869 and not in Baltimore as her family claims. With the receipt of this new piece of information we can now send for service records on Mr. Bellows, USN, from the Naval Archives in Washington, DC. Thank you, Alonzo. We now skip over into the Stevenson family to record the following information.)

March 2, 1869 A.D. Tuesday, married in Baltimore, MD. by Rev. Bowers, Mr. John H. (Horatio) Stevenson of Cleveland, Ohio and Mrs. Martha L. Bellows of Boston, Mass.

(*Her husband Charles was still alive in March of 1869. Could they have been divorced? Alonzo's early writings state Stevenson was from Cleveland. If this entry is correct, Martha would have been in Baltimore in 1869 as Miss Forrester writes, but under quite different circumstances. Miss Forrester has Mr. Stevenson limping from a wound he received serving the Confederacy. We wonder whether Ogarita and Charles Jr. are also with them. Miss Forrester writes that Izola D'Arcy (Booth) lived in

Pleasant Valley, Maryland, during this time. While going through *The Seventh Rhode Island Volunteers 1862-1865* by William P. Hopkins, printed by the *Providence Press* in 1903, we saw that Pleasant Valley served as a mustering out point for the Union Army. Is Stevenson mustering out? And from the Union Army and not the Confederacy? Is that why Martha is in Baltimore? We question whether it was Martha who visited Mrs. Elijah Rogers with Ogarita and Charles Jr. in tow. Ogarita would have been about ten and Charles "Alonzo" around seven or eight. None of the Booths were living at Tudor Hall though Mrs. Rogers was living close by at that time.)

(*We sent to Maryland for verification of this marriage but even after repeated letters and phone calls the only reply we have received to date is a note stating that it takes time—a long time, though our check for this service was cashed immediately. It is important to verify this entry with vital statistics. Mrs. Shinsel (Chapter/file 1) spoke of the difficulty of locating these people. We can heartily agree with her. They are the prototype of restless Americans. The mobility of those who lived in the 1800s is amazing, and it wasn't only the theatrical people, the Booths among them, who crisscrossed America by whatever means available. The Benchleys, Mills, Browns, and others in our locale were always on the move.)

Feb. 27, 1871 A.D. Monday, Born, in Boston, Mass. Harry J. D. Stevenson, son of John H. and Martha L. Stevenson. (*Seems little doubt that she married Stevenson in 1869 and that Harry J. D. is Stevenson's son and not the son of John Wilkes Booth. Mention has already been made of Alonzo's earlier recording of John Horatio Stevenson being born on August 31, 1839, and the sad death in Boston Highlands in 1874 of Irene Caroline, daughter of John H. and Martha L. Stevenson aged three months and 14 days. We assume the little girl was named after Caroline H. Brown. The name Irene is a puzzler . . . from Stevenson's family? At this point Sarah A. Mills, the bride of fortune, is on the Brown farm living with Caroline, Alonzo, Edward and Betsey.)

(*When calling the Vital Statistic Records Department in Cleveland, we were told they have no statistics prior to 1849 though some might be available in the records of the individual churches throughout the city. This area of research is put on hold for the time being unless it becomes absolutely necessary in our tracking of this elusive family. During the writing of this particular chapter/file, a Mr. Wilkinson, grandson of John H. Stevenson, came to Burrillville looking for Alonzo and Caroline. Unfortunately, we did not meet

Day of the Month September 11th.

1869 A.D. Saturday. Died in Whitinsville Mass. Mrs Lydia J. Dines. wife of David Dines. and daughter of Jonah and Mary Starr of Burrillville R.I. aged 30 years and 8 months.

1873. A.D. Thursday. Married, In Providence R.I. Mr. Jacob Dunnell, of Pawtucket, to Mary Attimore, daughter of the late Wm A. Robinson.

1875. A.D. Saturday. Died, In Burrillville R.I. Hannah Inman, a very worthy member of the Society of Friends, in the 97th year of her age.

1844 A.D. Wednesday. Died at Portsmouth, England. Capt. Basil Hall, author of books of travels and voyages.

1874. A.D. Friday. Died. In Norwich Ct. John Leffingwell. aged 90 years.

1837 A.D. Born at Greenfield Co. Conn. Martha L. Mills. daughter of Abram A. + Mary A. Mills.

Page 128 from Alonzo's Daily Journals
Please note last entry - 1837
Different handwriting than rest of this material.

him, but did receive an interesting phone call from him which will be related in the following chapter/file. It is amazing how so many family members have by one way or another made contact with us after the knowledge of our writing about Martha and Ogarita *et famille* was given to Mrs. Colony and Mrs. Putnam. Could be coincidence, but they themselves admitted to a family network searching to document Booth's link with their great, grandmother's marriage. Also of late, doors have closed on us which were previously open regarding information pertaining to our quest. Incidentally, the notation on the death of Irene Caroline Stevenson in 1874 is written in the same penmanship as the one used to record Martha's birth. Both are written on the bottom of the page as a last entry. We sense that someone besides Alonzo had access to his journals. This concludes the Bellows and Stevenson entries with the Mills notations saved until later. The following are the only two Wallingford entries listed.)

Nov. 15, 1878 A.D. Friday, Born, in Pascoag, R. I., Izola Bellows Wallingford, daughter of George H. and Ogarita E. Wallingford; on the Wilson Bros' farm, at quarter to four in the morning. (*The Burrillville Town Hall records are the same except her middle name is listed as "Louise." Alonzo seems quite sure of this entry and even lists the exact time of birth. The information which concerns us is that according to him, she was born on the Wilson Brothers' farm and not on the Brown/Mills farm. By that date, Edward would have gone to his reward along with Betsey Benchley, and the Brown farm would have been in Caroline's name. We do have information that the Wilsons had houses for rent within their complex. It has been suggested that Ogarita and Martha lived in one of them in the late 1860s though we have no substantiating data. Of course, Ogarita herself could have been living in one of them with her husband at that time, George H. Wallingford. Miss Forrester may have just assumed she was born on the Brown/Mills farm. Alonzo notes other families either moving in or out of Wilson's rental houses throughout his journal. If Izola had been born on Wilson's farm, he would have said so in his entry. You might think we are splitting hairs here, but we have found these little differences have led to larger quarry. Alonzo aids us again with the following entry of the marriage of Ogarita to William Wilson.)

Oct. 12, 1879 A.D. Sunday. Married. In Burrillville, RI at the residence of the officiating clergyman, Rev. William Fitz, William Ross Wilson to Mrs. Ogarita E. Wallingford (widow of the late George H. Wallingford) both of Burrillville. (*This supports our belief that Ogarita was living or renting from the Wilsons and possibly living with a George H. Wallingford the previous year. We are still drawing a blank in the attempt to document Mr. Wallingford's presence. This would have put Ogarita in close contact with William Wilson and the people of the Ross and Angell villages. In fact it has even been suggested by local lore that she lived in the Wallum Lake or Buck Hill locale with the Angell family, again there is no supporting evidence.)

Alonzo continues to list more Mills who are not familiar to us. We can only assume they are either related or he just decided to put them in his records because of their names. Hattie L. Mills, aged 22 years died in Webster, Mass. August 30, 1872. Corbin Mills died at 57 in 1873 in Thompson, Conn. (*Which is about ten miles from the Brown/Mills Farm.). The Mills are found in just about every cemetery in our tri-state corner. Getting into the Boston area, we read that William Mills died suddenly in Lowell, Mass. of apoplexy on November 6, 1874. This next one does puzzle us. Died in December 1872 in Merinoville, S. A., Luela Mills, daughter of Thomas and Betsey Mills, aged only six years old. Where is S. A.? Could it possibly by South America? There is a Merino Village just over the border from here in the abutting Douglas, Massachusetts area. Last but certainly not least, a Mills recording which we have seen many times before. October 19, 1847 in Albany, N. Y. Mr. Abram A. Mills late of Providence and Pawtucket, R.I. aged 27 years and 7 mos and 5 days. We still have many doubts about the claim of direct relationship to the Mills family of Fairfield County, Connecticut. Checking through the Providence Street Directories, we did find one A. A. Mills (*Abram Amherst?) living at 40 India Street in Providence in 1847-1848 with his occupation listed as "rolling mill." (*Checking with the historic Slater Mill in Pawtucket, we learned that a rolling mill operator worked on machinery which flattened iron.) We have no real evidence that it was our A. A. Mills. The directory would have been completed before Abraham A. Mills death in October of 1847.

There are also a sizable group of Benchleys, Browns, Hopkins, Millards, Rosses, and Salisburys along with the Sayles, Wilsons and Wallings. Even with the magic of a computer, it would take too much time to arrange all the births, deaths and marriages into a reasonable and readable format. We may be letting some important connections go by, but we have to continue on with the leading characters in our drama. It is quite clear that both the city cousins and country cousins are all related by both blood and marriage and that Alonzo, Caroline and Edward were not strangers to those who lived in Burrillville before their arrival in 1863. This may also be true of

"Izola" Martha . . .but we are not sure of this. Alonzo is taking us somewhere and trying to help us out as best he can to see that we stay on track. Genealogists and other historians will be able to find a bonanza of data from these daily recordings. Alonzo's vital statistics will continue to be inserted throughout our investigations whenever connections are made with people involved in our search. It is time to take a break from his journals and continue with Alonzo's obituary and his letters to Miss Forrester, with the *Pascoag Herald* filling in the missing pieces.)

Source: *Pascoag Herald March 9, 1917 (Alonzo's obituary continued.)*

. . . He (*Alonzo) studiously preserved old papers of every sort and had in his possession several first issues of Rhode Island publications. He disposed of the homestead farm several months ago (*in 1916 for ten dollars to George Joslin) and settled up his affairs preparatory to removing to Connecticut to pass the remainder of his days. (*Had he planned to live in Canterbury with his nieces?) He afterwards decided to remain here during the winter and he was seized with illness before he could complete other plans. His nearest relatives were two nieces (*Izola Wallingford Merrifield/Miss Forrester and Beatrice Rosalie Henderson Clutts?) The body was taken in charge by Undertaker J. J. Corrigan from whose rooms in Harrisville the funeral was held Wednesday afternoon. The funeral service was conducted by Rev. W. C. Darby, pastor of the Laurel Hill M. E. Church. Entombment was in Pascoag cemetery. (*Wrong again! In Bridgeton on the Brown/Mills farm.)

Source: *Letters from Alonzo to Mrs. Izola Merrifield (Miss Forrester) donated to the Burrillville Historical and Preservation Society by Mrs. Rosamond Putnam and Mrs. Marjorie Colony in May, 1989.*

In our possession are five letters from Alonzo to his "niece" Izola beginning with the **January 22, 1911** letter which has already been quoted. Alonzo has Box 284 in the "new" post office in Pascoag, which means he walks or drives two miles to pick up his mail. The assumption is that Mrs. Izola Merrifield is living in Canterbury. Mrs. Colony read an additional letter, whose contents brought up the unresolved problem of Betsey Benchley, which was explained in Chapter/file 9. The two daughters of Izola Forrester Merrifield Page were not really sure at that time just whose grandmother she actually was either. In the missing letter, we also learned that Alonzo was joshing young Izola about her married name Merrifield. He said the folks around here were getting a chuckle out of her name and thought it should be Merrymen. Why only part of this letter was read to us, and that part in particular, we do not know. We continue with the letters in hand interspersed with articles on Alonzo from the *Pascoag Herald.*

In **March of 1911** we are informed that Alonzo was confined to his home with a severe attack of the grip and rheumatism and able to be out on Wednesday for the first time. There must have been correspondence between the January and July 30, 1911 letters, as we continue to read in the newspaper that Alonzo A. S. Mills visits relatives in South Canterbury, Connecticut, Wednesday and Thursday of last week. Alonzo had left Burrillville when a forest fire swept through his northwest corner, as he places a card of thanks to his neighbors, friends, and the section hands of the railroad for helping save his dwelling house and other buildings of his farm property from being destroyed by the fires that occurred on the 26th and 27th of April 1911. (*The origins of this fire are unknown, but the wood and coal fired trains often sparked fires through the countryside.) Earlier in 1909 we had read that Alonzo had done expensive repairs to his home and farm, suggesting that his financial problems have been resolved.

July 30, 1911, Alonzo writes to Izola stating he is in good health and sorry to hear she has been ill. He says that because of the terribly hot and dry summer there will probably only be a half crop of anything harvested in the New England states this year. We learn Izola is writing for *The House Wife* as his neighbor, Mrs. William H. Millard, lent a copy to him. He finds her story, "The Mother's Consulting Hours" containing pictures of Izola and her children in it. Alonzo also promises to come to Canterbury (*Obviously, Izola is still in Canterbury in 1911) as soon as there is some rain as he does not want a repeat performance of his last trip when he went to visit his relatives in South Canterbury and his farm was threatened by fire. Alonzo hopes there will be rain enough so it will be safe for him to leave his home for one or two days without worry. (*He was known for his firefighting as he helped to extinguish the Wilson fire and also attempted to save the Stanfield farm which was next his home . . . unfortunately this farm burned to the ground. Because of the lack of water and personnel to fight them, fires were a great worry for the scattered farms in Burrillville as well as a threat to the mills.) He sends his love and respects to her family and children and to Beatrice and her family "when you write to her." (We wonder where Beatrice is living at this time.) "With love and best wishes I remain your uncle, Mr. Alonzo A. S. Mills, Pascoag, RI."

Evidently he is still waiting for it to rain when he writes Izola on **August 20, 1911.** He informs her that Mattie Ross, wife of George Ross, (*Marthae [Hawkes] Ross who named one of her children, Eva Ogarita, after Miss Forrester's mother) wanted to be remembered to Izola and asked her to write to her in Bridgeton. We learned that recent heavy thunder storms helped allay Alonzo's fears of fire and that Izola has had a lawn party in Canterbury. He certainly gets around as he asks her if she got the letter he sent three or four weeks ago from Slatersville, Rhode Island. He speaks of the cranberries on his farm which he will either ship to her or will bring some when he visits in the fall. (*Cranberries were a secondary crop for the people around Wilson's Reservoir. It is also good to hear he has neighbors who look after him.)

Alonzo writes to her again on **September 10, 1911,** saying he hasn't replied to her letter because he has been very busy working for his neighbors. We learn Izola's husband (Mr. Merrifield) has been seriously hurt but not the circumstances, and Alonzo hopes to come and see her before winter sets in. His dahlias and other flowers are in bloom even though it has been raining quite a bit and he wishes he could send some to put on his sister's grave in Canterbury. He writes that the fires which occurred when he visited them in April damaged his vines and fruit trees so the crop is not too good. Alonzo makes note of a flying ship going over his farm. He "never expected to live to see flying ships sailing around." He reminds Izola that the next day (*September 11th) would have been her grandmother Bates' 74th birthday.

From the *Pascoag Herald* of **September 22, 1911**, we read that Alonzo received a call from a gentleman from California last Saturday afternoon. Mr. Mills exhibited a portion of his large collection of curiosities and some of his carefully kept records. This certainly intrigues us. How would anyone from California know of his recordings, and why would they be of interest to him? We do recall that Izola Merrifield lived in California after her marriage to Mr. Page, but this event would predate that time. According to the *Herald*, the very next Tuesday Alonzo leaves on the 7:52 a.m. train for Canterbury to spend several days with relatives. Is there any connection between these two events? We wonder how much of Alonzo's journals Izola Merrifield/Miss Forrester read. To judge by the proven accuracy in his writings and the differences in her "facts," apparently, not too much. Either that or she was very selective in the information she gleaned.

Our last letter jumps into **September of 1912.** His handwriting is still Palmer method, steady and legible. Apparently Izola has moved because now he has to get to the Baltic Depot and from there find someone who can take him to their house. He intends to visit the beginning of the week as he wants to be home over the Sabbath, and intends to stay only two or three days. Alonzo tells her everybody here wants him to work . . . they hardly give him time to eat his victuals he is so busy. The sled he promised Arthur (Izola's son) will be shipped to him either before or after he visits. The *Herald* tells us in the Nov. 22, 1912 edition that Alonzo A. S. Mills returned home last Saturday from a visit of several days with relatives in Baltic, Connecticut. In 1912 Alonzo seems content in his sixty-fifth year with good neighbors and relatives to visit.

We have nothing else until **July of 1914**, when we read that he had been in poor health for several weeks and is slowly improving. Two years go by with nothing in the paper until September 12, 1916, where it notes Alonzo was the guest of George A. Joslin and family and Henry O. Sayles Sunday on a delightful automobile trip through Putnam, Danielson and Brooklyn to Canterbury, Connecticut. In 1916 we know that George and his wife Lena bought the farm from Alonzo for a pittance.

From Alonzo's obituary of **March 9, 1917**, we read he had previously disposed of the homestead farm and settled up his affairs preparatory to removing to Connecticut to pass the remainder of his days. He afterwards decided to remain here during the winter but was seized with illness before he could complete other plans. We read that his nearest relatives were two nieces who "formerly resided in Canterbury." We can't help but wonder if he had planned to live with or near his relatives. He suffered a stroke of paralysis towards the end of February of 1917. Our interest is piqued as to why he sold the farm for so little to Joslin and why his decision to move was stalled. We would like to know who placed the headstone on his burial site on the Brown/Mills farm. Was it his relatives who did it or his kindly neighbors who looked out for his welfare for so many years and considered Alonzo one of them? It is our hope that his two great nieces keep their promise to have the family plot taken care of for Alonzo's and Caroline's sake.

Later, we learn that after his illness incapacitated him beyond his neighbor's care, Alonzo was at the Almshouse for four days before he passed away. The above facts have all been mentioned not only to bring out Alonzo's nature, but to stress the fact that Miss Forrester could have obtained as much information from her uncle as we have. It is curious why she chose to ignore so much of this knowledge concerning the births, deaths, and marriages of her own family. It is disconcerting to say the least. Because she has misled us upon many occasions, we are understandably cross with her over the time lost in chasing wild geese. On the other hand, without the information in her book, we could possibly have been off on another track which might have led us nowhere. It at least gave us starting points in our quest. We cannot help but wonder whether it was Miss Forrester who placed the “X's” beside the maze of family names in Alonzo's original journal. We have sent Alonzo's facts and figures out for verification, and are taking time to digest all the news found in his letters to his niece along with the information concerning him in the *Herald*.

It is time to go back to "Izola" Martha [Mills] D'Arcy Bellows Booth Stevenson Bates and pool all of our varied reports on her. We will study them to see if there is any chance she might have had an affair with John Wilkes Booth and given birth to Ogarita as a result.

Chapter/File 12

THE TRACKING OF MARTHA

Tracking Martha Louise Mills' whereabouts during her five decades on this earth has not been easy, and at this writing, has not yet been completed. She probably fell through the cracks of the census-taking process more than once because of her frequent moves. Martha's use of a variety of names during her lifetime, for what reasons we may never discover, only adds to her allure and elusiveness. We now have in our possession assorted city and state vital records, newspaper articles, and pension records in addition to nine letters written by Martha to her half-brother Alonzo and information supplied by the grandson of Harry J. D. Stevenson.

The statistics on her beginnings, early youth and young adulthood are not only scanty but contradictory as well. The latter part of her life is relatively easy to document as she stays for longer periods in Boston, Burrillville and Canterbury. At this point, we are not totally convinced that Martha L. Mills is the daughter of Abraham/Abram Mills, the stepdaughter of Caroline and half-sister to Alonzo. There is an inherent danger and a distinct disadvantage to our playing detectives investigating historical mysteries. We, like other sleuths, are often mislead, misinterpret clues and jump to conclusions as we progressively record our findings and attempt to fathom their meaning. It is our hope that this will be a source of interest and instruction even though our mistakes will be picked up and our weaknesses shown along the way.

Alonzo writes in his journal that Martha is "of Pawtucket" as well as he. His mother, Caroline, married Abraham Mills in 1846 in Providence. Can we make the assumption that Martha lived with Caroline after this and grew up with her much younger step-brother? They appear to be a close-knit family as revealed by the accounts of their living nearby or together, frequent visiting, the flowing of correspondence between them when apart, and even the family squabbles erupting now and then. We do know that Martha's first surviving child, Ogarita, was born in Providence in 1859. In that year, according to the Rhode Island 1860 census, Caroline, Alonzo and Edward M. Brown are living in North Providence along with Betsey Benchley.

We found written in Alonzo's last journal that Martha L. Mills was born in Greenfield, Connecticut on September 11, 1837. But this entry does not appear to be in his handwriting and looks suspiciously like Martha's penmanship when compared with one of the letters reproduced in Miss Forrester's book, *This One Mad Act.*

The following is a list of Martha's birth year information as gleaned from various vital statistic records.

1832 - Lists her age as 23 and Charles S. Bellows as 28 on marriage records in Boston dated July 1855.

1835 - Her age given as 20 and groom's as 24 on marriage records from Boston copy dated Sept. 16, 1870 on application for widow's pension.

1837 - Her age given as 34 on children's pension application - March 1872.

1837 - Lists her age as 31 and Stevenson's as 28 in first marriage in Baltimore in 1869. Second marriage to Stevenson in Boston 1871, bride is 33 and groom is 31.

1847 - Her age given as 34 and his as 28 in her marriage to Edward S. Bates in Burrillville in September 1881.

Various educated guesses can be made for the reason Martha records different dates for the year of her birth on vital statistic records. There is the possibility she was a minor in 1855 when marrying Charles Bellows and listed her age as 23 so no questions would be asked. In her request for Bellows pension in 1870, the copy of the marriage certificate from the City of Boston Registrar's Office lists her age as 20 and Charles' as 24. Telephone calls to both the state and city records departments suggest there might have been an amendment filed in 1870 to correct the ages. So far, no firm evidence has been received. Bellows died at the age of 42 in 1869. This date would confirm the original age of 28 at his marriage to Martha. As an aside, John Wilkes Booth would have been 17 in this time period.

Because her third husband, Edwin S. Bates, was much younger than she, we can understand Martha fibbing about her age. Family tradition has her born in 1837. Her death in Canterbury in

1887 at age 50 tends to reinforce her birthdate of 1837. We do know that Martha's husband, Edwin Bates, and her daughter, Ogarita, were with her when she died. As stressed previously, the registrars of vital statistics only write down what is presented to them usually with no need for further proof. It is rather important we know when "Izola" Martha was born as it will determine whether certain parts of her life story are plausible or even possible. For example, the Pawtucket Vital Records relate that Martha's father, Abraham, died at the age of 27 in 1847. However, the *Pawtucket Gazette and Chronicle* shows his age at time of death as 25, leaving one son with no mention of a daughter. If Martha were born in 1832, her father would have been 12 years old at the time, and if the correct date is 1837, he would have been 17 years old.

Her actual place of birth is another problem facing us. It is listed on vital records variously as Stanford, Stamford, Stafad, Stonefield, and even Greenfield, although the state is always listed as Connecticut. Some of the above names are probably misspellings, but to muddy up the water even more, her descendants suggest she was born off the coast of Martha's Vineyard. The copy of her death record from the Canterbury Town Hall states her birthplace as Long Island. (*We wonder who put this on her death certificate?) The Connecticut areas she lists as her birth are located across from Long Island Sound. Her death record would have her born in New York and not Connecticut. Since the New York state records do no go back that early, we contacted various communities on Long Island but struck a blank. We had neither a firm place name nor a date to make this task any easier. It is important to place her in the Fairfield County, Connecticut area as this would strengthen the supposition that her father was indeed Abraham A. Mills. No one as yet has been able to unearth any firm evidence that either of them were located in this southwestern section of Connecticut.

Shakespeare said, "What's in a name?" This surely applies in the case of our Martha Louise Mills. She certainly confuses matters by using a variety of names in a variety of places. The name Izola is used either as her first or middle name with a variation of Lizola or just Zola. She used Mills, Booth, Bellows, Wilkes, D'Arcy, Stevenson and Bates at different times as her last name. Orianna Collier, Hero Strong, and Eleanore St. Clare were stage names reputedly used by Martha.

The Canterbury record of her death is the only place we have actually seen Izola used as her official name. Various ladies in this northwestern corner of Rhode Island, born in the late 1890s and early 1900s, also bear that name. Martha has several descendants named in her memory, Izola or Zola, including one of Miss Forrester's daughters. After many letters and phone calls, we finally received from Baltimore records the marriage certificate dated March 2, 1869, of John H. Stevenson and Martha J./I. M. Booth. The middle initial is difficult to read. It is either "I" for Izola or "J" for John. It states that Martha, a widow of 31, marries John age 28, a bartender with the officiating minister, Daniel Bowers. This certificate was not filed until June 13, 1871. By that time the Stevensons are living in Boston, have remarried each other, and have a son named Harry Jerome Stevenson. This is the first time we have seen her use the Booth name on any vital records or anywhere else, with the exception of Miss Forrester's book and the family collection. We wonder whether the "Booth" fact or fancy all began in Baltimore of 1869 and not in Cos Cob in 1859.

Alonzo never refers to his sister as Izola anywhere in his letters to her or in his journals. In fact, his notation of the above marriage simply has John H. Stevenson marrying "Mrs. Martha L. Bellows of Boston." There is the possibility that Martha never told Alonzo, or the rest of the family, that she was the wife or widow of Booth. After reading the "Booth" on her Baltimore marriage certificate, her granddaughter might have based her assumption on the Booth connection, and then wrote the book supporting this belief. We bemoan the fact that Miss Forrester chose to romanticize the family history. Her story line has sent us on many a merry chase. This leads to the awkward position of having to verify whatever she wrote concerning her family's affiliation with the Booth family and to look upon her writings with a grain of skepticism and suspicion . . . unfortunately supported by all too many of our findings.

Source: *This One Mad Act by Izola Forrester.*

Speaking of Miss Forrester's book, we would like to point out that she tells of finding in one of those "famous" trunks a manuscript written by Martha in 1870 which gives a description of her early life. Pages 171-176 of Miss Forrester's book include her grandmother's "autobiography" with its dedication written "By the Authoress, M. I. V. Booth." Martha lists her name here as Martha Izola Violetta Booth, her father's name as A. Alonzo Mills, and her mother's name as Violetta, who died when Martha was a baby. According to this, Martha was adopted at an early age by Mr. and Mrs. Henry Miller, who had six sons. They assumed Martha would marry their son, Henry. While on a tour with the Millers—sans Henry—in 1858, Martha met John Wilkes Booth at a fancy ball in

Richmond, Virginia. She then flees with JWB after her adopted father tells her not to darken his door again. This is the story which Bryan decimates in his book, *The Great American Myth*. Her book reads like a story written in the style of the romantic novels of that time period. We question whether this is what she meant it to be. Miss Forrester discredits her grandmother's story with a story of her own. Her descendants suggest that her publisher/editor encouraged Miss Forrester to enhance the family history.

According to Miss Forrester, her grandmother wrote and published in magazines and newspapers. We do find evidence that she was a correspondent for the *Danielson Transcript*. (*Danielson is a small town in Connecticut close to the northwest border of Rhode Island. It is about fifteen miles from Burrillville.) There was also a piece written for the *Burrillville Gazette* under the name of Mrs. Edwin S. Bates. The names both grandmother and granddaughter use always command attention. We have finally discovered that both splice proper names and place names with little effort in addition to adjusting their facts to improve the story line. There are threads of truths sewn throughout, and it is a difficult task to sort these out and verify them as best we can.

The adopted family name of Miller is interesting. We found a family named Miller living on a farm near the Browns and Wilsons. Martha in a letter to Alonzo writes that the Miller farm is for sale. She asks him to check it out as she has someone who might buy it for her. In the *Danielson Transcript* of 1887, we read in the Canterbury column that a man named L. E. Miller sold his drugstore in Pascoag. Alonzo also records this fact in one of his journals. Her "adopted" name could just as well have been Miller, Millard, Brown, Angell, Benchley or even Bellows with Miss Forrester having the name as D'Arcy. There is a record of two colonial families by the name of Miller and Mills in the *Commemorative Biographical Record of Fairfield County*, J. H. Beers & Co. Chicago, 1899. This information was discovered by Joyce Remington. We have not found our Mills among them. There is the possibility that Miss Forrester also read this text and spliced a few names together. She does admit to much research in Fairfield County.

In the early history of New England, there were not too many surnames to play with, and most of the people were related to each other in some way. It is evident that certain first names were in vogue for a time, and then were replaced by a new wave of popular names. The earlier records show a great many Biblical names. In the mid 1800s, the more exotic names from the Mediterranean areas became popular: Alonzo, Izola, Lucinda, Rosalie, and the like.

Comparison of features of Alonzo A. S. Mills
and his half sister, Martha.
Photo of Izola Martha courtesy of *Norwich Bulletin-Courier*
Alonzo Mills & Eugene Allen - Circa 1870
Photo courtesy of Mrs. Colony and Mrs. Putnam

Alonzo is a relatively common name found in the earlier Burrillville and Providence directories. We also find a great many Marthas, Carolines, Betseys, Sarahs, and even Fannys. These are first names which are involved with our search for the elusive Booths of Burrillville.

To get back to our quest for the real Martha, she seems as unsure of her parents and grandparents names as she does her own birthdate. She lists her father's name on vital statistics as Abraham Mills, Abram A. Bellows in her marriage to Stevenson, and in her last marriage, back to Abraham Mills. She lists her mother's name as Mary A. Mills in 1871 and in 1881 lists Caroline as her mother. Is she providing what people would expect to see or are there some shreds of truth in this? (*Martha's picture in Miss Forrester's book, and the one of Alonzo and his cousin Eugene Allen show distinct family features, in particular the forehead, nose and eyes. Martha and her half-brother Alonzo would certainly pass as brother and sister.) Martha's true age is important here. If she were born in 1832 as listed on her marriage to Bellows, Caroline would have been rather young to have been her mother.

Where the truth lies in this complicated family history, we do not know. After reading Martha's letters to Alonzo and Caroline, we discovered she really didn't know who she was and where she was born. This is not as strange as it may sound if we consider that her mother supposedly died in childbirth and her father died when she was only ten. She obviously was brought up by someone else, but who is the question. These letters have thrown a completely different light on the individual, Martha Mills, and the person known as Izola Booth.

Source: *A collection of transcribed letters received from various sources.*

The first letter containing a bit of knowledge is judged to be dated 1877. These are transcribed letters for the most part and we are dependent on the accuracy of the transcribers. Martha asks Alonzo to send her "the names of our dear father's father and mother . . . she wants the "given name" and "my mother's name before she married father." She insists that "your mother" namely Caroline, "can tell you and can tell also where father was born." Martha continues, "give me all the information you can . . . I have a clue . . . but I must prove we are the children. She signs "in haste and without order . . . your loving sister, Martha." (*Why does she need this information when she is over forty and living in Boston? Has she found someone there who possibly could be of her family? Why does she need to prove that she and Alonzo are the children? Is money involved? We will probably never know.)

From West Canterbury in April 1886, she writes cryptically that "the minister who married my father and mother called on me last Monday. I had a very pleasant talk with him." We wonder if this was a ploy to encourage Caroline to talk. In a letter dated March 8, 1887, six months before Martha's death, she asks again. "Dear Mother (*Caroline), "I wish you would tell me what my mother's name was and where they were married." Unfortunately, we have no knowledge of letters written between these two dates, but it is obvious she has slim knowledge of her parents other than her father, Abraham. Why is Caroline so tight-lipped about this? Either she doesn't know or she is hiding something . . . or shielding someone. We question whether Caroline, who survived everyone except Alonzo, ever told Ogarita what Martha wanted to know. If she did tell Martha's daughter, it would explain the Long Island entry on the death record in Canterbury.

We admit to the heavy veil of secrecy surrounding the beginnings, early youth and young adulthood of the person known as Martha L. Mills. Our first inkling that Martha officially existed came from the marriage record from Massachusetts showing that Charles S. Bellows married Martha L. Mills in Boston on July 30, 1855. He is a mariner, living in and born in Boston, son of Elijah Bellows and Sarah. We learn of their son's birth in May of 1861 in Cambridge, Massachusetts, namely, Charles E. Bellows. We need to keep in mind that Martha declared her father's name as Abraham A. Bellows when marrying Stevenson. The history of the Bellows family in New England is massive, with several genealogical books written on this subject. At that time there were numerous Bellows in Burrillville, Pawtucket and Boston.

Source: *National Archives Military Records*

Again, Alonzo opens up a wealth of material when he writes that Charles S. Bellows was in the United States Navy and died at the Chelsea Naval Hospital. When information was received from the United States National Archives, it contained applications for widow's and children's pension from Martha regarding Bellows' twenty-eight years service time. As usual, much contradictory material was received. This supports our belief that no one ever bothers to read these papers. Martha married Stevenson nine months or so before Charles' death, but he is listed as single on his service death certificate. This pension request was filed from Boston in 1870 when Martha was listed as 33 years old.

From this material we read that Charles was 42 years old in 1869, five feet eight, dark eyes, black hair and a dark complexion (*perhaps from being at sea). This same description could fit John Wilkes Booth, who was approximately the same height, dark eyes, glossy black hair, but with a fair complexion. Fireside psychologists may wish to ponder this comparison. The appearance of our sailor in the hinterlands of Burrillville might very well pass for JWB. Alonzo writes in a poem about the people in Burrillville having a high curiosity into the comings and goings of their neighbors. He tells them to mind their own business.

Martha, in her statement to the pension board, gives the information that Charles joined the Navy when a boy and served until his death . . . never remaining at home over three months at a time. She swears that his last enlistment was in the fall of 1868 in New York. She also gives a list of his tours of duty which include time on the "Merrimac." This makes him an active participant in the Civil War. After verification by the pension board in December of 1871, the widow Martha received $8.00 a month retroactive to December, 1869, and $2 additional for each child. When Martha married Stevenson for the second time in Boston in March of 1871, the pension was suspended. She reapplied for the children's pension in March, 1872 which was approved in May, 1872. We assume Martha married Stevenson again because Bellows was still alive in March, 1869. There is no record of a divorce between Martha and Bellows.

This same packet contained a certified letter from Dr. Dana B. Putnam of Suffolk County, Massachusetts dated September 1871, which states that he was the family physician of Charles Bellows, his wife and children, and in fact had taken care of them for the past three years before Bellow's death. This was music to our ears as we have not been able to place Martha in Boston during the years mentioned, 1866-1869. (*Family tradition has them in Baltimore, Maryland, hiding after the assassination of President Lincoln by Booth.) Of course, this means we need to trust the doctor's word.

It is evident from the pension file that Martha is a sea widow for a good deal of their married life. There is no indication of a divorce, but there must have been a parting of the ways as Bellows is listed as single upon his death as previously stated. When Martha writes to Alonzo from Baltimore in 1869, she signs her name as Martha D'Arcy. No doubt she is hiding her identity for some reason. Miss Forrester, however, has her in Baltimore from 1865 to 1870 with a side trip to California. While in hiding as the wife of John Wilkes Booth, she is living with a family by the name of Stevenson. This whole time frame throws out the Burrillville story that Martha and Ogarita arrived here after the assassination and that Booth visited them here. On the question of whether Ogarita and Charles are the children of Bellows, we have sent for his actual service record to see whether he was in port or out during those crucial times.

This past summer, a gentleman arrived at the Pascoag Public Library seeking information about Alonzo, Caroline and the location of their gravesites. He was told to contact either one of us but was unable to do so at that time. Fortunately, when he returned home to Maryland, he did telephone us. That was our introduction to Mr. Thomas Wilkinson, the grandson of Harry J. D. Stevenson and the great-grandson of John H. Stevenson. He is actively pursuing the history of his family and we welcomed his interest. From Mr. Wilkinson, we learned that John enlisted in Company "E" Second Regiment of the Massachusetts Cavalry in San Francisco, served in the Civil War, and is buried at Arlington Cemetery. Although both the records and Alonzo indicate that Stevenson was from Ohio, one of his descendants thinks otherwise, mainly because of his enlistment in the Massachusetts Cavalry. From his records and phone calls, we learned that Stevenson's descendants believe there is some substance to the Booth story and that Harry J. D. was of Booth's blood. This would mean that Mr. Wilkinson believes in the escape theory and that Martha was united with Booth for a period of time. Harry J. D. Stevenson married Ella Oretta Wyman and had two children named Izola Mary and Eva Ogarita. The latter is Mr. Wilkinson's mother. These names do get carried on with much determination and persistence. There was a local person named Eva Ogarita named by a friend of the original Ogarita, Mattie [Hawkes] Ross.

In searching for the origins of his great-great-grandfather, Abram/Abraham Mills, he has been most generous with his findings and we are reciprocating. Mr. Wilkinson has sent the pension papers of John H. Stevenson and also his marriage record to the widow Booth in Baltimore in 1869. This information was received prior to our long awaited copy from the Maryland State Archives. If they were in hiding as the widow and friend of John Wilkes Booth, why would they sign the marriage certificate as they did? Why do this at a time when the assassination and its aftermath were still in the hearts of those involved . . . and especially in Maryland, home of the Booth family. More will be learned about the new avenue which has opened up through Mr. Wilkinson's generosity in the following chapter/files.

This chapter/file closes with a chronological and geographical chart of Martha L. Mills and her family. The list will fully bring into focus a decidedly New England centered story with only occasional visits to other parts of the country. When our investigation of the local lore started, we sensed the story began here, and perhaps ends here, in the Northeast. Time and facts appear to bear this out.

Chronological and Geographical History according to Official Records.
*exception - taken from family records.
Part One

1801 - RI/North Providence - Birth of Edward M. Brown.
1819 - RI/North Providence - Birth of Caroline H. Jenks.
1820 - CT/Southport - Birth of Abraham A. Mills - March.
1826 - MA/Roxbury - Birth of Charles Still Bellows.
1832/1835/1837/or 1847 - CT/MA./NY- Birth of Martha L. Mills/Bellows.
1839 - OH/Cleveland - Birth of John Horatio Stevenson.
1841 - MA/Boston - Charles S. Bellows enlists in USN.
1846 - RI/Providence - Abraham A. Mills marries Caroline Jenks.
1847 - RI/Pawtucket - Birth of Alonzo A. S. Mills - April.
1847 - NY/Albany - Death of Abraham A. Mills - October.
1850 - RI/North Providence - Caroline living with her mother Betsey Benchley/Bencheley.
1855 - MA//Boston-Charles Bellows marries Martha Mills - July.
1855 - MA/Boston-Charles Bellows reenlists in USN. - August.
1857 - CA/San Francisco-Edward M. Brown marries Hannah Fawcett - January.
1857 - RI/Pawtucket - Edward M. Brown marries Caroline H. Mills - September.
1859 - RI/Providence - Birth of Ogarita E. Bellows - October.
1860 - RI/Providence -Ogarita, 6 mos old and living with a McNamara family.
1860 - RI/North Providence-Caroline, Edward, Betsey and Alonzo in same household.
1861 - MA/Cambridge - Charles E. Bellows born - May.
1863 - RI/Burrillville - Browns, Alonzo and Betsey move to Wallum Pond.
1863 - CA/San Francisco-John H. Stevenson enlists in Co. E 2nd Reg.Mass. Cavalry.

1865 - VA/Fairfax - John H. Stevenson musters out of the service.
1868 - MA/Boston - Charles S. Bellows enlistslast time - August.
1869 - MD/Baltimore-John H. Stevenson marries Martha I.M. Booth - March.
1869 - MA/Chelsea - Death of Charles S. Bellows. - December.
*1869 - MD/Baltimore - Martha writes to Alonzo in Pascoag.
1870 - MD/Baltimore-577 N.Fremont.-Stevenson-conductor Martha - dressmaker.
1870 - MA/Boston-Spring St. Place-Martha Bellows applies for widow's pension.
1871 - MA/Boston - Dr. Dana Putnam states on pension request that he took care of Charles S.Bellows's wife and children from 1866 - 1869.

Chapter/File 13

TRAVELS WITH MARTHA & JHS

Source: *This One Mad Act by Izola Forrester.*

Miss Forrester chose to ignore the presence of Seaman Charles Bellows in her family history although she does mention the Bellows of Boston as being distant relatives of the Mills family. She introduces John H. Stevenson as a Knight of the Golden Circle, a friend or associate of John Wilkes Booth and of Confederate sympathy. It is suggested that Stevenson was wounded in the service of the South and limps as a result. After the assassination, Martha flees from her Shenandoah home with Ogarita and Aunt Sarah to find safety in Baltimore with a family by the name of Stevenson. Here she uses the name Martha Wilkes and/or Izola D'Arcy. Being a true Southern gentlemen, John H. escorts Martha to California to be united with Booth then returns with her to Baltimore. He offers his name to the second child of John Wilkes, Harry Jerome Dresbach, whose birth is in 1870 but not recorded until 1871 in Boston. In the book it is not clear whether Martha and Stevenson were actually married. Miss Forrester has it both ways.

The author recalls, as a young child, she and her grandmother visiting John H. at the Tremont House in Boston, "where she has many friends." Mr. Stevenson is courtly and reserved. During these visits the volatile Martha would become upset, and Stevenson would have to calm her down. The young Zola often wondered what they talked about with such seriousness. (*So do we! This would probably be between 1884 and 1887 when Martha is living with her last husband, Edwin Bates, in Canterbury, Connecticut.) Miss Forrester notes that John H. was always happy to see her mother, Ogarita. He never comes to Canterbury to see them but sends books and magazines for the education of young

Harry Jerome, who—we are told—frequently goes up to Boston to see his reputed father. Stevenson, however, failed to attend Martha's funeral in 1887.

In various parts of her book, Miss Forrester describes John H. Stevenson as being short and slight of size. He is balding with carefully trimmed light chestnut hair, has large meditative gray eyes, and wears a small Vandyke beard and moustache. She speaks of his manicured nails and his dandy mode of dress. "Grandmother never speaks ill of him," except for the fact that he had a fondness for gambling . . . especially in "those gilded palaces of the Gold Coast."

A few years after Martha's death when Harry becomes nineteen, he receives notice from his father to meet him at Delmonico's on Fifth Avenue and Broadway facing Madison Square. Harry is impressed the waiters all seem to know his host rather well. John tells Harry that he is not his son but rather is the son of John Wilkes Booth. Stevenson continues to relate episodes of Martha's stay in the South, their trip to California, etc. Harry is elated with the news that he and Ogarita are full brother and sister. Mr. S. is ill and is heading West to spend the remainder of his life. He advises young Harry, who has a good tenor voice, to stay off the stage, marry a nice girl and live in the country. (*We suspect our Southern gentleman is kissing his responsibilities goodbye with this revelation.) John takes the next train west and dies on board around 1889. Exit our Knight of the Golden Circle and enter the other personality of John H. Stevenson as gleaned from other sources.

Source: *Grandson of Harry J. D. Stevenson.*

Thomas Wilkinson believes that both Martha and John were being circumvent when they gave vital data for various records, possibly because of her association with John Wilkes Booth. (*We repeat . . .why does she use the name, Mrs. Booth, on her marriage in Baltimore to Stevenson?) John Stevenson always lists Cleveland, Ohio, as his place of birth and his parents as being from Cleveland. Although on his death certificate, they are listed as natives of England. (*Interesting that a family by the name of Stephenson/Stevenson lived in Pascoag during the same time period. In 1894, according to the *Burrillville Gazette*, another Martha Stevenson journeyed to England to visit her mother.)

Source: *1870 Baltimore City Directory and Martha's letters to Alonzo.*

The Street Directory indicates that Martha and John are living in Baltimore along with several other families by the name of Stevenson. In a letter from Martha to Alonzo dated September 5, 1869, she says she is stopping with the Stevensons in Baltimore who "endeavor to make her forget all sorrow." (*What sorrow? Certainly not referring to Charles Bellows' death as he was still alive in September.) She neglects to tell her brother of her marriage to John Stevenson since the previous March, although his journal indicates he had knowledge of this fact later on. Alonzo does not indicate that he knew she used the name Booth on the marriage certificate. The tone of her letter suggests that Alonzo was acquainted with this Stevenson family from Baltimore. Possibly they had visited or had lived in our tri-state corner at one time. Another strange fact is that she signed the letter "Martha D'Arcy." We wonder why Alonzo would not have found that rather odd.

Reading between the lines, we discover they are not living a particularly happy life. Martha is sick and tired of cities, Ogarita is not well and "Alonzo" (*little Charlie Bellows) would much rather be with his uncle in the country as "the city is no place for children." She strongly suggests that Alonzo take the children—then about ten and eight years old—to live on the farm in Burrillville. Martha laments to Alonzo that he ought to bless God hourly that he has been kept from all temptation. (*What temptation has put her in this situation? Could it have been Booth or John Stevenson?) Various moods erupt forth in her letter. The city is filled with sickness and death. Martha is busy soothing the sick and laying out the dead, which she sees as her duty, though she tells Alonzo not to look upon her as a nurse. We wonder at her medical qualifications with her frequent caring of the ill, laying out the dead, and operating a maternity hospital in Canterbury in later years.

This is not the "Izola" from the pages of Miss Forrester's book. Martha sprinkles Biblical words and pulpit phraseologies throughout this curious letter. In her unhappiness she dreams that she has gone to heaven and asks God to bring her children there as well. But, the Lord has further work for her to do on this earth. She hopes and prays that her deeds and acts—in fact, her life—be such that her name will be loved and remembered long after she has been laid to rest. (*There is much of the "hollow piety" that author Bryan *The Great American Myth* decries in his criticism of *This One Mad Act*. We refrain from judgment in this case as we do not have the ability to look into anyone's heart.) John Wilkes Booth also had this need to be well thought of in the years to come. In fact he considered returning to Washington, DC in order to clear his name after reading the newspaper accounts of his deed. Booth apparently thought he would be considered a hero by many Southerners— and others—for ridding the nation of President Lincoln.

Martha hopes to go to Boston that fall and wishes Alonzo could spend the upcoming holidays with them. But then again, circumstances may compel her to remain in Baltimore. Is this pertaining to Stevenson's work or promise of work up North? She concludes with love and best to her mother, grandmother, and Mr. Brown. These letters are a good indication of the closeness of the family. They also support the probability that Martha grew up living with Caroline and the Benchley family in Rhode Island.

In the exchange of letters, Martha has discovered that Mr. Brown has a girl living on the farm with them. She warns Alonzo that the girl is there for a purpose and offers him some motherly advice using the old axioms: Never marry for money, never marry to please anyone except yourself, only marry for love, look before you leap, etc. (*Could this girl be Alonzo's future wife, Sarah Simmons? The warning about marrying for money would apply in this case. Has Martha herself felt the price of not taking her own advice? Had she married Bellows, possibly Booth, and Stevenson for all the wrong reasons?)

Source: *1870 Baltimore City Directory.*

We learn that John H. and Martha I. Stevenson are living at 577 North Fremont in Baltimore. He is listed as a "condct" and she as "dressmkr." Their occupations are interesting as we have been unable to actually place Martha either on stage or affiliated with the theater in any way. The only exception is the naming of her daughter, Ogarita, after a theater persona. Referring to Mr. Stevenson's previous occupations as a U. S. Cavalryman, bartender, watchman and detective, it doesn't seem plausible that he would be a musical conductor but rather one associated with transportation. The career in dressmaking does spark a faint hope that Martha might have done costuming as well. Both actresses and actors prized their theatrical apparel which, during that time period, they had to supply themselves. Perhaps Martha, who was forever redoing Ogarita's and young Zola's costumes, sewed a fine seam for the more famous actors and actresses of that day, including the Booths. The theatrical costumes of the Maryland Booths are much a part of their family history.

(*Before leaving Baltimore for Boston, we would like to raise several questions concerning Martha's marriage on March 2,

1869. According to the Baltimore State Archives, this marriage was not filed until the Stevensons were safely in Boston on June 13, 1871. Why wait so long to file? Did Stevenson accept Martha being the wife of Charles Bellows and John Wilkes Booth? There is also the question of whether a divorce had taken place. He must have known about Martha's family and her past as we believe Alonzo knew the Stevensons from Baltimore. It would be interesting to know how and where Martha and John met, and why they were both in Baltimore in 1869. Was Stevenson associated in any way with the Booth family? We have become very skeptical of our contradictory findings and question whether the "Widow Booth" was a salted piece of work. Still, this is our first documentation of Martha as Mrs. Booth. Alonzo never associates his sister's name with any of the Maryland Booths at any time.)

Thanks to Mr. Wilkinson we know something of Stevenson's activity prior to his living in Baltimore. John was a member of Company "E" of the Second Regiment, Massachusetts Cavalry. He enlisted on the 26th of January, 1863, in San Francisco and was mustered out July 20, 1865, at Fairfax Courthouse in Virginia. (*He was indeed a soldier of fortune, and we suspect he was in California looking for gold just like everyone else in the early 1860s.) In March of 1864, he saw action in Muddy Branch, Maryland, where he fell from his horse down an embankment onto rocks thirty feet below. He was treated by the Regiment Surgeon and returned to duty. On a raid near Aldie, Virginia, he was thrown from his horse again and was injured but refused treatment and returned to the fray. This information comes from Stevenson himself on his pension applications. The accidents may explain the limp of which Miss Forrester wrote, but she had him on the wrong side of the Mason-Dixon line and in a uniform of gray and not Union blue. This places John in the South in 1865 but does not account for the intervening four years until 1869. Not surprisingly, he entered and mustered out as a private.

We first learn of their living in Boston when Martha applies for her widow's pension from Bellows in September of 1870 . . . even though she was married to Booth and is now married to Stevenson. A Mr. and Mrs. Joseph Averill of East Cambridge swear to the Assistant Clerk, Edwin A. Wadleigh, that they are acquainted with Mrs. Bellows and her children. They verify that she is who she claims to be and that Ogarita and Charles are also the children of the late Charles Bellows. In February of 1871, Harry Jerome Dresbach Stevenson is born at One Spring Street, Boston. John H., his father, is working as a conductor, but in March he is listed as a watchman.

Martha applies for a minor children's pension in March of 1872. Ogarita and Charles are allotted $15 per month until the age of eighteen under Charles Bellows' pension. On November 23, 1873, Irene Caroline was born at Washington Street. Stevenson is now working as a detective. Alonzo informs us of this baby's death a few months later.

(*The above tells us a great deal about Martha's life during this decade. The birth of Irene erases any doubt of Stevenson and Martha carrying on a platonic affair. John has problems keeping a steady job. He does list himself as a conductor in Boston and Baltimore but apparently only for brief periods. If this pertains to a musical conductor, then like actors and actresses work is sporadic at best. We are still trying to find an association between the Booths and Martha. This is one of the reasons for examining Martha's later life with such minuteness. Stevenson would have had a great deal of knowledge of the Booth family if he were affiliated with the theater, if he were in truth a resident of Baltimore, and if he were a member of the Cavalry which pursued Booth and Herold. [History tells us that it was the 16th New York Cavalry.] It also pays to remember that every newspaper in the country featured stories of the Booths before and after the assassination.)

The Stevenson family is constantly on the move, which is true of Martha's earlier life as well. It does not make our quest to determine whether she had an affiliation with John Wilkes Booth an easy one. If she did not, then why was she telling everyone in Baltimore, Burrillville and Canterbury that she did? Stevenson is listed as a detective in 1873 and again in 1880. If he in fact followed that profession, he would have known well the ways of investigation and documentation, not to mention the other more unsavory methods used to track people down. In Boston in March of 1875, John applies for a pension due to service related injuries. A letter from the Adjutant General states that there was no evidence of service related disability as claimed and the pension was denied. Both John and Martha are not opposed to being circumvent in their attempts to obtain the much needed money to support their family of five.

In August of 1875, Martha writes to Alonzo that she finds Boston the meanest city that ever was. She is still caring for the ill and dying and tells him that times are very hard. Young Charlie has been running Express all summer, but wants to work for his Uncle Alonzo and would work for $2 a week and board. Mr. Stevenson would work for board only in order to be out in the country. According to Martha, young Harry is always talking about visiting. Ogarita, who is sixteen, will be married soon. Martha asks Alonzo to fill up her pail with berries and send it to her by Willie's Overland Express. She mentions their father's early death and says not to weep for the happy dead. She closes with "May you ever be as happy and prosperous as I, your sister, am wretched and miserable."

By December of 1875, the Stevensons have moved to 44 Porter Street. Martha has been very ill. She tells Alonzo that any exertion tires her. In August of 1876, we learn Charlie is now working with Alonzo and Caroline on the Brown Farm. Ogarita, who is in poor health, will be sent as soon as she gets enough money together to do so. According to *This One Mad Act,* Ogarita appeared on stage in Providence in 1877 in *Oliver Twist* with Minnie Maddern, who later became a well-known actress. Reading these letters from Martha has shown us an entirely different character and personality than the one portrayed by Miss Forrester. We cannot help but admire this strong lady who struggles to keep her family together and accepts the brunt of fate with a certain amount of magnanimity.

It is also known that Ogarita gave birth to Izola Louise Wallingford (Hills?) in 1878 and married William Wilson in 1879. We suspected they were all living in Burrillville in the late 1870s. This was verified by the 1880 Rhode Island census which lists John H. Stevenson, detective, Martha L., young Charles (19), Harry (9), and a Robert Kennedy (43) all living on Wallum Pond Road in Burrillville between Wilson's and Caroline's farms. Charles is working in a textile mill in Pascoag. Robert Kennedy, who died here in January of 1887, was a member of Co. "E" 4th Rhode Island Infantry according to Alonzo's journal. Could he and Stevenson have met in the service? Robert is listed as a boarder and works as a night watchman on the railroad. A casual glance through time period directories indicate that taking in boarders was not an uncommon practice especially when the textile mills began to flourish throughout the villages of Burrillville. Martha is not listed as Izola. When did she begin to use this name in our area and which future generations continued after her demise? We need to consider the fact that the families from Ross Village and Buck Hill might have taken the name from Ogarita's child, the young Izola, and not from the reputed "Izola" Martha.

John Stevenson disappears from view for a time after the 1880 census. In November of 1891, we find him living in the Soldier's Home in Hampton, Virginia, again seeking a pension from his fall at Aldie, Virginia in 1864. As he is physically disabled from chronic rheumatism, resulting diseases of the heart, and a hernia as a result of injuries in the line of duty, his pension is granted this time. His death in August of 1906 lists him as 66 years old, married (*to

Martha?) and last occupation as a government clerk living in Washington, DC for the past 15 years. After being informed by Mr. Wilkinson that John had been buried in Arlington Cemetery, we contacted the records department there and sent the information about the location of the grave site to him. He in turn took a photo of the simple military grave marker, "17154 J.H. Stevenson Mass."

We wish we could let John Stevenson rest in peace, but think it is necessary to pursue his military career at the State Library in Boston where the information on Company "E" of the 2nd Regiment of Massachusetts Cavalry is said to be found. Amongst the roll call we hope to find familiar names which might give another clue into the unknown gaps in Stevenson's life. Hopefully these might shed light on his relationships with Martha, Bellows, or Booth. But to further our studies of the husbands of our Martha, we proceed to the next chapter/file and a look at her next spouse, Edwin S. Bates, who was also her last.

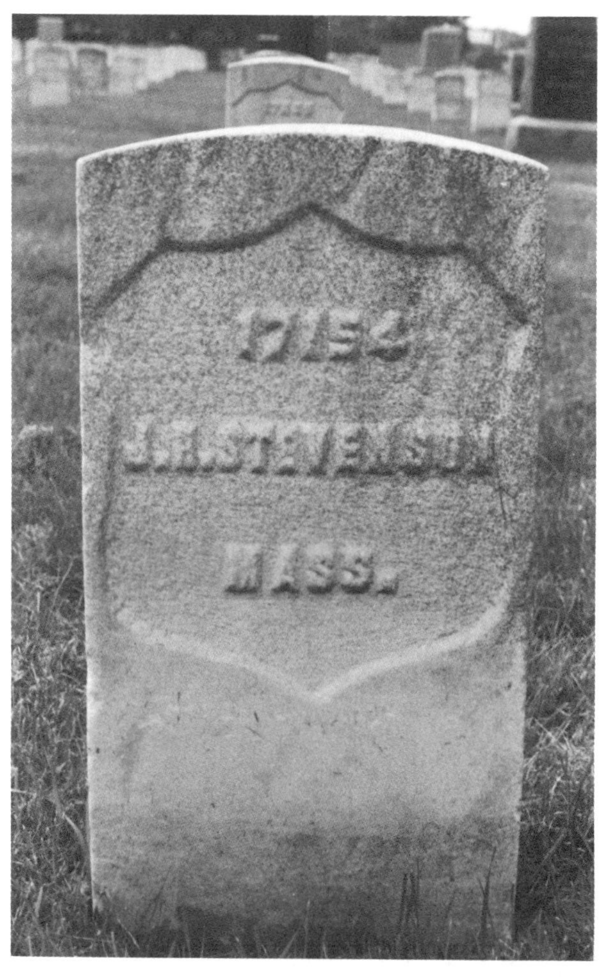

J. H. Stevenson's Tombstone
Arlington National Cemetery
Photo courtesy of Thomas Wilkinson

Chapter/File 14

MORE OF MARTHA'S ADVENTURES

Sources: *Burrillville Town Hall, Burrillville Gazette, and Alonzo's Journals*

We first hear of Martha's next husband from the Burrillville Town Hall records where on September 22, 1881, Edwin Sylvanus Bates, a 28 year old mechanic born in Foster, Rhode Island, and living in Burrillville is married to Martha L. Mills, a 34 year old born in Stanford, Connecticut, and also living in Burrillville. His parents are listed as Sheldon and Phebe Bates and hers as Abraham and Caroline Mills. They are married by the Reverend Lovejoy who is affiliated with the local Baptist Church. Martha is listed here as 34 years of age with no mention of her previous marriage to Detective Stevenson. There were several Bates' families in Burrillville at this time. One, a Francis Bates, who was a respected partner in the Eddy & Bates store, died in 1883 at the age of 31 and was a deacon of this particular church. We suspect he is also either Edwin's brother or a very close relative. Alonzo also notes several Bates in Burrillville and Pawtucket in his recordings. He lists Samuel Millard Salisbury and Mary E. Bates, both of Burrillville, married in 1877 by the Reverend Hopkins Brown Cady. This is a fine example of the use of last names for first and middle names, all too familiar in Burrillville and Rhode Island. There was a family by the name of Millard who were neighbors to the Wilsons and Caroline on the Brown Farm. After reading this, you can understand our difficulty in making definite relationships amongst our complicated Martha and Alonzo families.

Source: *Letters from Martha to Alonzo.*

In January of 1882, we find Mrs. Edwin S. Bates living at Chestnut Hill in East Killingly, Connecticut. Martha writes she has not heard from her family since leaving Pascoag and worries they do not care enough to write to her. Ogarita's chiding in this letter, they didn't write because they lacked a stamp, indicates that Ogarita has left William Wilson and is living with her mother and new stepfather, Edwin, in Connecticut. Letters from Martha dated 1885 and 1886 suggest that they were still displeased with her. We can only speculate on the reason. Was it Martha's marriage to Bates or Ogarita's divorce from Wilson which caused this displeasure? Martha indicates toward the end of her first letter that she still has contacts in Burrillville. She has heard that Bob Kennedy says she took a lounge which belonged to him when she moved from his rented house. She is indignant with the accusation because William's sister, Almira Wilson, gave it to her.

Martha writes that Edwin and she are sorry they gave up the Kennedy place, and would like to either get it back or be somewhere near there in Pascoag. There are two churches where she lives in East Killingly, Connecticut, but no ministers. According to Martha, the children of Pascoag are "angels" compared to the wild "Arabs" here. (*It is difficult for us to believe there is a wilder place than Pascoag, notorious for its lawlessness and "tolerant" ways during this time period.) Martha wants Alonzo and the Reverend Patterson of the local Methodist Episcopal Church to visit on one or two Sundays to help her start a much-needed temperance movement. She continues that the people here bury their dead without as much as a prayer. Furthermore, she writes, people iron, sew, and do anything they please on Sundays. Martha wants to remedy their heathen ways in East Killingly.

(*There is a strange dichotomy found in our Martha, who has married two men without an apparent divorce, claims an affiliation with the then notorious John Wilkes Booth, is not always honest on her vital statistics, and quite probably has distorted the truth about her own actions with many people including her own family. We can sympathize with her need to do all of this considering what the fates have dealt her. On the other side of the coin, she is constantly involved with good works, has a strong sense of family and parental responsibility, is active in the church, and, apparently, has participated in revival and temperance meetings. So did Alonzo and Caroline in later years, which was reported tongue in cheek in the *Burrillville Gazette*.)

We were aware of her affiliation with the Methodist Episcopal Church on Canterbury Plains as it was mentioned in Miss

Forrester's book as well as by Mr. Linwood Tracy, caretaker of the churchyard where she is buried. Inquiries to the United Methodist Church in Providence were answered by Reverend T. C. Whitehouse, who in turn referred us to Mr. Irving W. Lovell, historian of the Southern New England Conference of the Church. Mr. Lovell was most interested in the Douglas Meeting Campgrounds across the border from Burrillville. He sent us information on the Laurel Hill Methodist Church in Pascoag with a listing of the now familiar pastors: Revs. Gifford, Allen, Pack, Cady, and Patterson, who was pastor from 1881-83 and 1887-88. (*Martha quite probably became acquainted with Reverend Patterson when she lived on Wallum Pond Road with Mr. Stevenson and on South Main Street with Mr. Bates, both in the Pascoag area.)

(*It was standard practice for ministers to visit and preach in our tri-corner area holding revivals, rallies, love feasts, and temperance meetings. Caroline and Alonzo held one of their own . . . with a parade, prayers, food, fellowship and a good social time. This type of activity requires a person willing to stand up in front of a crowd and hold forth. There are several indications that Martha had these abilities and the willingness to use them . . . perhaps her acting career was in this form. The revivals were not that far from being good theater and grand productions. This is not suggesting that she and others were not sincere. But, these were an outlet for those who liked to be at the center of attention. After reading in the *Pascoag Herald* and the *Burrillville Gazette* about the excess of drinking, gambling, cockfights and all around rowdiness in Burrillville, it is understandable that a counter action was much needed.)

Mr. Lovell referred our inquiries to Stephen P. Pentk, Interim Library Director of the Boston University School of Theology. According to him, there were no records listing Mrs. Stevenson or Mrs. Bates under memberships or marriages, and none of her children were listed in the baptismal records of the Methodist Episcopal Church in Pascoag. There is no indication that Martha as Mrs. Edwin Bates preached there with the Reverend Patterson. The Methodist Episcopal Church in Canterbury was burned, and all records after 1870 were destroyed by the fire. A second church built there also burned, and the present Calvary Baptist Church was built on the same spot.

Source: *Additional Letters from Martha to Alonzo.*

We do know that in June of 1885, Martha was asked to accept the pastorship of the M. E. Church in Canterbury. She writes to Alonzo that she will give her first sermon at three o'clock the next Sunday. She has already started a Sunday school in a vacant schoolhouse that was "packed" every Sunday and she was the "Supertindent." In 1886 she writes she has added on a room to her house which will be used to hold meetings and carry on Sunday school. It appears they did not retain her services as a preacher, or the possibility is that a qualified minister was found. Martha notes that young Harry is very interested in religious matters, but it takes nearly to the end of her life to convert Edwin S. Bates. We do not doubt her sincerity. She has finally found her niche. When Alonzo and Caroline are having their troubles, she suggests he send "mother" to spend a week with her and Edwin. Martha knows she could straighten out matters at the Brown Farm, "if she could just walk in there."

Source: *Burrillville Gazette January 19, 1883.*

In the *Gazette* Mrs. Edwin B. Bates has published a sermon entitled, *"Let me go! My soul is weary of the changes that bind it here."* She is living in Canterbury at this time but presumably sent it to the *Gazette*. The following is excerpted from this sermon.

"Yes, weary of life. How many there are who are weary of life, weary of its joys, its sorrows, its cares, its pains, toils, hopes, and its laurel crowns, weary of life. How hopeless, how despairing these words sound. We utter them when we have been deceived, when we have trusted and been betrayed, when we have given friendship and received injury and insult in return, when one has shown kindness and bestowed sympathy and have been repaid with ingratitude and slander . . . The clouds have linings of silver, the pathway before us contains roses as well as thorns, yet under the first heavy stroke of sorrow we are apt to deem life valueless or containing naught but sorrow and gloom. . . When called upon to endure crosses and sorrows, let us gather in new strength, gird faith's armor on, and take our places in the ranks with renewed energy to fight the great battle of life. We will find some good in everything and every person on earth if we only go to work the right way to find it. So let us never grow weary of life or in well doing."

We suspect this was meant as a response to some verbal injury Martha received from someone in the Burrillville vicinity and was written before her ministry in Canterbury. Yes, it is filled with the platitudes found in the sermons of the day. She perhaps does not really know the symbolism behind them, but she has certainly felt the

Methodist Episcopal Church on Laurel Hill Avenue in Bridgeton
Dedicated in 1892. No longer standing.
Photo courtesy of the Burrillville Historical & Preservation Society.

pain. From the content of her letters and other writings, we can assume that Martha, and Alonzo as well, have a little more than the average education of the day as they both have the inclination to write and are fairly well read. Martha mentioned writing for the *Danielson Transcript* . Editions of this paper are as hard to come by as the *Norwich Courier*. Both had vital copies destroyed by floods. Fire and water do tend to block our investigations, particularly in Connecticut. Fortunately, the newspaper collection from the State Library in Hartford, Connecticut, came up with a microfilm of the *Windham County Danielson Transcript* from 1860-1890. After spending a few hours scanning the film with anxious eyes, we spotted these little items under briefs from Canterbury.

Source: *Windham County Danielson Transcript from 1860-1890.*

January 18, 1887 - On the 28th of December Barstows and Bates had a family Christmas party. Dwight Barstow gave an oyster dinner and entertainment was provided. But the best of the evening was when little Izola Henderson (*Miss Forrester) ran into the parlor with a hat on one side of her head and sang, *"I have just been down to the doctor's."* Included in this section was the notice that on the first of the year, Mrs. E. S. Bates was presented with a grandson, Charles, by her daughter Mrs. A. Henderson of Chicago.

(*We strongly suspect that Mrs. Bates is the Canterbury correspondent for the *Windham County Danielson Transcript* as the family is prominent on the pages during the years noted. Martha had written to Alonzo that she was writing for this newspaper, "as it was the only paper around here." She is correct, as we also scanned the *Norwich Courier* for the 1880s and found not a mention of Canterbury anywhere.)

February 16, 1887 - Edwin S. Bates was cut by falling on an axe, but improving.

April 4, 1887 - Mr. and Mrs. Henderson arrived on the fourth after eight weeks of being in the West, and they will start out again in May. (*No mention of their being in the theatrical profession, however.)

July 15, 1887 - We read that the beautiful Hilbert House at Fort Ned burned down . . . and in the same paragraph that the Bates have a guest in their home—chicken pox. (*This information causes us to do a double take. Martha and the rest of her family supposedly lived in the Hilbert House calling it Terrace Hall. She reputedly died here after which the household goods were auctioned. No wonder Mr. Linwood Tracy never saw it as the fire predated his birth. This suggests they did not reside there, although for a brief time in 1886 Martha writes to Alonzo from West Canterbury near Hanover where Hilbert's home was located. Martha also describes her home near Hanover as an eight-room, white colonial, the prettiest home in town. Not a description of a Victorian mansion.)

October 12, 1887 - Mrs. A. Henderson is home from the West visiting her mother.

October 19, 1887 - Mrs. Zola Bates was called upon last Sunday to the pulpit to replace Mr. Purdy. We read that she did a credibly good job as little notice was given for preparation. (*This is the first time we have seen her using the name, "Zola" in print.) Miss Forrester was in the congregation and records this in her book. Fact and fiction do tend to meet now and then.

The contributions from the Canterbury correspondent slack off after November of 1887, but the issues which would have listed her death were missing from the files. We read further that Reverend Purdy is now located in East Thompson, Connecticut, which borders the Burrillville area. According to Miss Forrester, Harry Stevenson was tutored by him and boarded with the Reverend after Martha's death. There is also mention made of a Miss Jessie Jencks spending a week with her Uncle J. M. Hyde in Canterbury. Any relation to Caroline and the abundant Jencks family?

(*The reader can imagine our delight while reading these tidbits about our elusive Booths. These do support Miss Forrester's contention that her grandmother wrote for newspapers, if not magazines. A writing talent is obviously there. It continues with Martha's first grandchild and on down through the family into the present generation.)

There was an earlier item of interest which strengthened our belief that Martha was indeed this correspondent. A certain businessman in the village was chastised for operating his store on Sunday and for allowing young men to gamble in his back room. Quickly a letter to the editor appears from the businessman, who is indignant, and says he keeps his store open to allow a family who can only pick up their mail on Sundays—at that time post offices were quite frequently located in stores—and that no gambling occurred there either. And, he knows who put that piece in, a certain member of the M. E. Church . . . and implied with a holier than thou attitude. Another letter appears from "One Who Knows," saying that it was most certainly not a member of the M. E. Church, etc. That is certainly Martha—feisty, tenacious, and pugnacious as the proverbial bulldog.

It is relatively easy to document and fill out Mrs. Zola Bates' life in Canterbury. She is still on the move and changing her address from time to time. In **1885**, she writes to Alonzo that she is two and one half miles from Scotland and two miles from Hanover. The nearest railroad station is in Baltic and the stage passes her house every day. Ogarita has a good husband, Mr. Henderson. Charlie and his wife are in Boston. Harry is in school and will help Edwin farm this summer. She still has contact with Mr. Stevenson in Boston who, she writes, is very ill.

In a letter to Alonzo written in **April of 1886** and addressed from Terrace Hall, West Canterbury, Connecticut, Martha writes that she and Edwin have two homes now and they may rent the first. She has just begun to live, but her health is poor. (*A fact she keeps from her children.) She expects to die here in the state where she was born, and then writes the cryptic sentence,"I suppose you saw by the papers a few months ago that I was left a little money." On reading this, we searched the papers Alonzo would have seen, but found nothing. Our search of local wills and probate records of that time frame also drew a blank. It did cross our minds that the mother of the Booths died late in 1885. Miss Forrester lists Mrs. Booth, as well as Rosalie, sending money and gifts to them in Canterbury. It is a tantalizing thought, but one which probably cannot be either proven or disproven. Nothing has yet been published in any of the discovered material from the Booth family about Martha receiving money from Rosalie Booth. Neither have we actually seen any of Rosalie's letters to Martha of which Miss Forrester writes in her book.

March 18, 1887 - Martha is now living in Canterbury Plains according to her latest letter to Alonzo. What ever happened to Terrace Hall, which she told Alonzo she bought, and which Miss Forrester also confirms? In the Canterbury Town Hall, we found no evidence of her owning this property in their records. She herself never writes of living at the "beautiful Hilbert House."

In an undated letter, probably **1886 or 1887**, Martha writes that Edwin will most likely be elected constable. Edwin also has his problems besides being cut by an axe, he has a liver condition and will probably die young. He is also run over by a wagon, but getting better. We read of his working the farm. She keeps him busy and normally refers to herself as Mrs. Edwin S. Bates.

(*We have not discovered any more about Mr. Tracy's "maternity hospital" in Canterbury nor of Martha's colored assistant, who is buried with her in the unmarked grave in the plains cemetery. This assistant is mentioned in Chapter/file 4. Mr. Tracy is quite positive of these facts and cannot understand why the family members have not mentioned this to us because, "They know this!" The Bellows and Stevenson sides of the family have a sizable number of descendants as well as the next generations in their turn. We do not know which family members have this knowledge, but suspect they do not always work together. Miss Forrester did relate of an Aunt Sarah, who came with Martha from the South. There were also two colored ladies who prepared Martha for burial, a Miss Frances and a Miss Martha.

Still searching for data on the maternity site, we exhausted the collection of local history at the tiny Canterbury Library across from the Prudence Crandall House in Canterbury. We decided this was a good time to actually visit the museum for a tour. Kaz Kozlowski gave us a delightful and informative swing through the individual rooms of the lovely restored house. One thing lead to another and we asked if she had heard of "Izola" Martha and her stay in Canterbury. No, but she did recall hearing of a black midwife, who was related to a servant who worked for Ms. Crandall. She kindly put us in touch with Mrs. Charles Fairbrother, curator for the Canterbury Historic Society. From her we learned that the woman's name was Miss Frederica Olney, who was still practicing midwifery into the 1920s. She was either the niece or grand niece of the aforementioned servant. She might be too young for our "assistant." This lady attended the Westminster Congregational Church and not the Methodist Episcopal on the plains. We are attempting to check this further.

Source: *Norwich Courier article written by Maria Crider in 1975.*

From Mrs. Fairbrother also came the 1975 *Norwich Courier* article, which we had been seeking. This gave us a wealth of material. The Olson family built a home on the site of the Hilbert place and while shifting through the ashes of the burned home found an old perfume bottle made of gold Bohemian glass estimated to be of 1875 vintage. The Olsons believe this bottle belonged to Martha/Izola Bates. (*We are still not convinced she lived there and quite sure she did not own the Victorian Mansion.) The article by Maria Crider continues, stating that Mrs. Booth lived in Canterbury between 1865 and 1887 (*actually 1882-1887) seeking "the loneliest spot in the world." This is curiously the same as the story told in the Burrillville/Bridgeton area in Rhode Island. But of more interest to us was a sign found in the Barstow home on Barstow Road in Canterbury in 1942. At that writing in 1975, the sign still belonged to the Barstow family. It read, "Mrs. Izola Bates, Midwife." The article notes that Miss Forrester failed to mention this occupation of her grandmother or the fact that she was also a housekeeper for George Barstow. Curiously, in a letter to Alonzo from Canterbury, Martha writes she had always wanted to be a doctor and not a minister when she was asked to be one at the little church on the plains.

A member of the Barstow family recalls both Izola and her granddaughter, according to this newspaper article. Young Zola was full of stories and used to come visit them wearing stage costumes. At the age of nine, Zola was insisting she was related to John Wilkes Booth. Some people never doubted the story as "where would a youngster get such a background on the Booths?" A local historian, Charles R. Underhill (*unfortunately since deceased) gathered an incredible amount of data on the Booth legend. He states he can point out gaps even in the parts which took place strictly in Canterbury, but ends the article with "but somehow, in spite of all the flaws, you want to believe it. You just really want to believe." We certainly know that feeling. This information all supports Mr. Tracy's account.

Our lady is full of surprises, and her life history, especially via her letters, reveals a woman of strength and intelligence, who survives and overcomes a great deal of adversity. She is pragmatic when need be, but she certainly inspired her children and grandchildren to reach for higher goals. It is pleasant to read that Martha is living a fairly comfortable life and has become the country wife with chickens, cows, orchards, fields and the like. She is even giving Caroline advice on preserving butter and eggs. She is a busy lady, quite respectable and a somebody in the community. A far cry from her "miserable" and "wretched" situations in Baltimore and Boston. Like any true life story, it will not last long.

The sad letter from Ogarita to Caroline dated November 8, 1887, written at four o'clock in the morning, says, "My dear grandmother. Mother died last night from shock. She went to bed apparently as well as ever." Ogarita is weighed down with grief and she has telegrammed her brother Charlie, who is in Michigan. She continues, "If you could come to the funeral, it would sustain me very much. Lovingly, your granddaughter, Rita."

Martha, as far as we can determine, had nine children. The first chronological chart did not include all of them. We include them here:

1852 - An illegitimate male child by George Shephard who died in 1856. Source: Miss Merrifield's letter to Author Kimmel.

1855 - Harry Bellows who also died in childhood.
Source: James O. Hall to Gail Merrifield.
1859 - Ogarita Elizabeth Bellows (Booth?) died in 1892.
Source: City of Providence and RI State Archives.
1861 - Charles E. Bellows (Booth?)
Source: Mass. State Archives and Alonzo A. S. Mills.
1869 - Stillborn child born in Baltimore, Maryland.
Source: James O. Hall to Mrs. Colony.
1871 - Martha writes that she had five children by Bellows. Two of whom survived—Ogarita and Charles. Source: National Archives/Seaman Bellows Pension Records.
1871 - Harry Jerome Dresbach Stevenson.
Source: Mass. State Archives and Alonzo A. S. Mills.
1873 - Irene Caroline Stevenson.
Source: Mass. State Archives and Alonzo A. S. Mills.

More will be said about these children associated with Booth when we attempt to find definitive proof of their relationship. A continuation of the previous chronological and geographical chart is at the end of this chapter/file. Our trip to Keene, New Hampshire and its aftermath follows in the upcoming chapter/file.

Chronological and Geographical History according to Official Records
*exception - taken from family records
Part Two

1871 - MA/Boston - Birth of Harry Jerome Dresbach Stevenson- Feb. 27.
1871 - MA/Boston - Marriage of John and Martha Stevenson - March 23.
1871 - MA/Boston -8 Lafayette St. Martha applies for children's pension - March 23.
1873 - MA/Boston - Birth of Irene Caroline Stevenson - November.
1874 - MA/Boston - Death of baby Irene - April.
*1875 - MA/Boston - Ogarita on Boston stage as Miss Wilkes.
*1875 - MA/Boston - 26 Mott St.- Martha writes to Alonzo.
*1876 - RI/Burrillville - Charles E. Bellows on farm with Alonzo.
*1876 - RI/Burrillville - Ogarita being sent to the Brown farm.
*1877 - MA/Boston - 804 E. Fifth St. - Martha writes to Alonzo.
*1877 - RI/Providence - Ogarita on stage with Minnie Maddern in *Oliver Twist*.

*1877 - MA/Boston - Martha requests information on her parents from Caroline.
1877 - RI/Burrillville - Death of Edward M. Brown.
1878 - RI/Burrillville - Death of Betsey B. Benchley.
1878 - RI/Burrillville - Birth of Izola Louise Wallingford to Ogarita.
1879 - RI/Burrillville - Ogarita marries William Wilson.
1880 - RI/Burrillville - John H. Stevenson, Martha, young Charles Bellows, Harry, and Robert Kennedy living on Wallum Pond Road between the Wilson and Brown residences.
1881 - RI/Burrillville - Martha marries Edwin Bates.
1882 - RI/Providence - William Wilson divorces Ogarita.
*1882 - CT/East Killingly - Martha and Edwin Bates living at Chestnut Hill.
1883 - RI/Burrillville - Martha's Sermon appears in the *Burrillville Gazette.*
*1883 - ??/?? - Ogarita marries Alexander Henderson.
*1885 - CT/Canterbury - Martha living in her "own" white cottage.
*1885 - ??/?? - Beatrice Rosalie Henderson born.
*1886 - CT/ Canterbury - Martha writes of receiving money.
*1886 - CT/Canterbury - Martha living in "Terrace Hall."
*1887 - CT/Canterbury - Martha living on the plains in Canterbury.
*1887 - IL/Chicago - Charles Henderson born - January.
1887 - CT/Canterbury - Martha's death listed as Izola Bates November.
1890 - VA/Hampton - Stevenson applies for his pension.
1892 - NY/Binghamton - Ogarita dies on tour and is buried there.
1906 - Washington, D. C. - Stevenson's death in August.
*1911 - RI/Burrillville - Mrs. Merrifield contacts Alonzo.
1916 - CT/Canterbury - Alonzo visits his niece.
1917 - RI/Burrillville - Alonzo buried in the Joseph Brown Cemetery.
1937 - MA/Boston - *This One Mad Act* published.

Chapter/file 15

TRIP TO KEENE AND ITS AFTERMATH

Our scheduled trip to visit the two ladies in Keene, New Hampshire, was delayed by unforeseen circumstances until the first of November. Since we usually take the back roads whenever possible, it was a delightful ride from Pascoag to Keene through the Massachusetts countryside. While passing the New Hampshire border, the change is apparent. The older farm houses have their outbuildings, including the barns, cozily attached to the living quarters. (*At one time the snows "layered in" to stay for the winter months in northern New England. With the buildings connected, the farmers could take care of all their chores without going outside in the winter weather.) Mrs. Colony is waiting for us on the porch of her sister's charming Queen Anne Victorian home. Mrs. Putnam has coffee and tidbits ready after our long journey. This comfortable house is filled with a strong sense of family. We are shown photos of those whom we have researched scattered throughout the house. Miss Forrester's pictures show a dynamic and lovely woman. These counter the less than flattering ones of her in *This One Mad Act*.

After refreshments and small talk, all four of us climb the two flights of stairs to the room where the family archives are kept. Clustered around the orderly indexed boxes lugged from a cupboard stuffed with more of the same, we recall that this family has been gathering their history for nearly a century. According to the sisters, every Monday they work on these files and are in the process of transcribing their great grandmother's diaries and family letters. These materials will eventually be stored in the archives at Harvard University. Another sister, "Zola," is coming from California in January. We hope to arrange a meeting in Burrillville with all three sisters and Miss Hazel Hopkins to discuss the name "Izola," and how it got to be so popular a name in our town.

We are like the proverbial children in a candy shop. One of us tackles the files with headings that are of interest, and the other searches through the material from Miss Merrifield's contributions. Peggy (Mrs.Colony) is working on the diary and Ros (Mrs. Putnam) on letters from Ogarita to Martha and Harry, her mother and brother. Bypassing the material that is all too familiar to us, we try to pull out the areas which have served as roadblocks in our research. The family is still working on the Fairfield connection for records of the births of Martha and Abraham. It pleased us to be able to fill them in on materials which they did not have, specifically Abraham's middle name of Amherst and the Canterbury Town Hall record of Martha's death. They were as surprised as we with the Long Island, New York, listing as her place of birth.

Just recently, we received a letter from David A. Overton, historian from the town of Brookhaven, New York, to whom we had written inquiring about the Mills and Millers of Long Island. He wrote of a Martha Mills, who was a member of the First Presbyterian Church prior to 1779 (*this cannot be our Martha because of the age difference) and of a Martha Olive Mills Miller. Mr. Overton was unable to locate a Martha L. Mills or Abraham A. Mills. According to the local genealogists, the Mills and Miller names were abundant in Suffolk County, Long Island, as well as across the Sound in Connecticut.

We were shown the divorce record of Ogarita from William Wilson dated 9/17/1882 and numbered #6473. According to this information, Ogarita was accused by William of risque behavior and of being involved with a company of "playing actors" from the Theatre Comique. These early legal records of Rhode Island are kept at Providence College, but we had not yet been able to find the time to follow through on this particular item. Our next step will be to trace the origins of the acting company mentioned to see whether it has local roots. For one reason or another, theater has always been successful and thriving in Burrillville from early times to the present. We see little evidence of early Burrillville being influenced by the Puritan concepts flourishing in the nearby colony of Massachusetts.

In a letter from Gail Merrifield Papp to her Aunt Ros, she informs her that plans are going forward to erect a monument to Martha in the Canterbury cemetery . . . where many people visit every year looking for her gravesite. According to Gail, Mr. James O. Hall, who has worked with the family for decades to help establish some verified date of the Martha and John Wilkes Booth affiliation, believes that it would not be historically accurate to have the family place the name Booth on this monument. He does suggest that the phrase "Martha Lizola was reported to have associated with John Wilkes Booth in theatrical enterprises" would not stretch the historian's conscience overly far. Does this suggest they have found an association, or does the word "reported" say it all? The family members still insist on Martha's middle name as being Lizola because, "she signed her letters this way."

Miss Forrester's writing career has been extensive. Besides publishing *This One Mad Act* in 1937 (*a research project of 44 years) she also wrote several adventure books for children beginning in 1900 through 1936 with such names as *Polly Page Motor Club*, *The Girls of Bonnie Castle*, and *The Secret of the Blue Macaw*. She wrote for several magazines and was a journalist for leading newspapers as well. The sisters have reason to be justly proud of their mother's accomplishments. We should point out that the ladies have never denied us an answer to any of our questions and inquiries. They have been open with us and have encouraged our quest in every way. Looking at the clock, we cannot believe time has passed so quickly and that it is way past noon. After a glass of Dubonnet, we are led to a delightful corner of windows on the first floor where a table has been set. We chatter all through lunch about the subject at hand.

After our repast, we all return to the archives and there discover correspondence from Mr. Hall regarding a letter written in August of 1869 by Martha D'Arcy. Apparently, Martha is living with or married to a Walter/Arthur/Harry D'Arcy, who according to this letter either died or deserted her. She also writes of the recent death of her baby. Probably this is the sorrow to which she refers in her letter to Alonzo in September the same year. It appears D'Arcy has turned the responsibility of the family over to John H. Stevenson, who married Martha in March of 1869. The suggestion was later made that Arthur M. D'Arcy served in Company "I" of the Massachusetts Cavalry . . . and became a friend of Stevenson at that time. There is no proof to back up this assumption.

Martha mentions she has brought back seeds from California. A trip which we still question, as Martha was in poor financial circumstances most of the time. She refers to her dear mother (*Caroline?) and her grandmother (*Betsey Benchley?) and an Aunt Amy, who we know is Betsey's sister. She states she would like Alonzo to take them in, but would settle for her "mother's house in Providence." (*Does this mean Caroline owns a house there or is another "Mother" living in Providence?) This information does not simplify our determination to validate the local lore. It only serves to confuse the issue more than ever . . . though we ought to expect the unexpected from Martha by now.

No mention is made of any Darcy or D'Arcy in Alonzo's records in our possession, nor in the Burrillville or New England records we have seen to date. Is there the possibility that Martha met D'Arcy and/or Stevenson in the Boston area? Stevenson's Co. “E” mustered out in Virginia but returned in a body to Readville, Massachusetts, for final dispersement. Mr. Hall states the letter suggested that John, Martha, et al, were returning to Boston to Stevenson's parents. This information supports Mr. Wilkinson's and our belief that Stevenson was somehow familiar with our tri-state corner.

In Miss Forrester's book, she introduces Arthur, also known as Harry D'Arcy, as Martha's adopted brother. Since he is the son of Henry and Fanny [Mills] D'Arcy, this would make him her first cousin. According to her story, Harry was a friend and associate of Booth, both of whom served the South with secret missions while Martha and baby Ogarita were living in the Shenandoah Valley. Mr. D'Arcy also signed as their witness in Cos Cob when Martha and Booth supposedly married in January of 1859. Miss Forrester eliminates Harry by having him shot by the Union Army as a spy in Virginia. Fanny returns to Boston after the death of her husband, Henry. The story within the story of Martha Violetta Mills tells of her adopted brother, Henry, whom she was expected to marry. Instead, she eloped with Booth. Halfway through this narrative, she switches the name Henry to Harry. We suspect there are elements of truth in these stories, but how does one separate the wheat from the chaff?

Returning to *This One Mad Act*, we read that Martha wrote her biographical sketch in 1870. The name Harry follows Martha throughout her life and seems to have had a profound effect upon her. The 1860 census records from Boston, unearthed by Mr. Hall, finds Martha with baby Ogarita and a five year old by the name of Harry Bellows. She also names her son born in 1871 Harry. There doesn't seem to be any more information on Arthur M. Darcy other than his death noted by Peggy in her chronology. "Arthur Darcy also known as Harry died January 19th, 1888." Sounds like an Alonzo entry. Mr. Hall adds that according to the pension records, Harry was wounded and left the Union Army. He was back in Boston for a time in 1865 and reenlisted in Co. 1 of the Second Massachusetts Cavalry, which served in the Washington area around the upper Potomac River.

Is D'Arcy the man who tempted Martha or was it Booth? Could Harry have been associated with the theatrical world in any way? There were definitely some facts about the family history that Alonzo was not privy to . . . neither are we. The gray zone in Martha's life includes the years 1862 through 1868. If we could only unearth bits and pieces from these missing years, we might be able to get closer to material which would either validate or invalidate her relationship with Booth. It does seem strange that so much material is available on Martha after 1869 and so little before that date. The only exceptions are the vital statistics which do not by themselves support the possibility of a Booth connection. Martha is becoming more and more like Winston Churchill's description of mother Russia, "A mystery wrapped in an enigma," or was it, "an enigma wrapped in a mystery." Either way, this quote fits Martha's story rather well.

While sorting through this information, Peggy is reading aloud from her mother's diary of an incident when Edwin S. Bates skipped away from Martha in Canterbury. Martha pursues him via train, trolley, and stage through all three states of Rhode Island, Massachusetts, and Connecticut. She finally finds him and bodily brings him back, where we assume he stayed. The other sister, Ros, is reading from Ogarita's letters to Harry in which she writes that Mr. Stevenson is not being a nice man. In another letter, Ogarita writes to her mother, Martha, suggesting that she join the Hendersons in Chicago. They are thinking of starting a theatrical company of their own. Martha would only have to learn a few lines or words to appear with them. This does not sound as though "Izola" was a veteran actress, although the sisters interpret this differently than we. One of the interesting and annoying aspects of research is the fact that everyone reads the same data through different eyes and gives different meaning to the same information.

One of the sisters gives us a chart she is working on of the family of Izola Forrester Page and her ancestors. Glancing at the list, we smile at the many similarities between this one and our own chronological charts listed at the end of Chapter/files 12 and 14. There is no time to study these in detail in New Hampshire. On the way back to Rhode Island, reading them leads to much discussion between us.

Source: *Family Chronology showing excerpts which are either dissimilar to or missing from our own charts.*

1834 - London, England. Oct. 12th, Birth of George Forrester, stepfather of Izola. Educated for legal profession, practiced law. Came to the United States in 1874. Engaged in journalism.

Librarian of School of Commerce from 1908 til death. (*Date not recorded nor place of death. We still do not know what his relationship was with Ogarita and the reason for his adopting young Zola, other than Miss Forrester's account which does not satisfy our inquisitive minds. We read in *This One Mad Act* that Mrs. Forrester (Harriet Newell) is a strict disciplinarian of Mayflower stock.

1847 - Abram Standish Mills dies in Albany, New York, and is buried with his mother, Betsey Bucklin Benchley in a Pawtucket Cemetery. (*We and everyone else agree that this is true even though no one can find the gravesite nor any record of it. Betsey is still listed as the mother of Abram/Abraham. Wonder why? This fact alone justifies the time spent by us and also by Mr. Roger Joslyn on the history of Betsey and the Benchleys. Bucklin is the middle name of Edward M. Brown's mother. This probably means that Edward and Caroline are cousins. In our minds we still have a shadow over Martha Louise/Izola's relationship with Betsey.)

1853 - Newton, Mass. November 9th, Birth of George Wallingford Hills, father of Izola Forrester. He died February 22, 1924 in Washington, DC. His parents were Joel Hawes and Edwina Francesca [Bugbee]. (*Incidentally, Edwina is also the name of Edwin Booth's only child by his first wife, Mary Devlin.) Later, Mr. Hall writes with the information that George was a student at Harvard College from 1873/1874 through 1877/1878 but never received his degree. The family suggests that Ogarita had a romance with student Wallingford while she was on stage in Boston. From local statistics, we read that Ogarita is listed as the widow of George H. Wallingford. We thought she might have been living in Burrillville after 1876 as Martha writes that as soon as she can scrape up the money, she is sending Ogarita to the Brown farm. There is the strong suspicion that all of the Bellows and Stevensons are living on one of the Wilson Brothers' farms, where Alonzo tells us young Zola was born in 1879. The whole family is listed there in the 1880 Burrillville census report, including John Stevenson, Martha, young Harry, and young Charles Bellows.)

1859 - Martha Mills writes in her 1885 diary that "in 1859 Peleg Weaver married me to J.W.B. at his house. His wife and daughter being witness's, also Harry Arthur D'Arcy, my adopted brother. Mr. Weaver was kind to me after the death of my husband." (*Please note the entry was made in her "1885 diary." Many of her informational dates are included long after they occurred.) Authors Bryan, Hanchett, and Kimmel have all put many holes in this information about her Cos Cob marriage. Her marriage in Baltimore to Stevenson as the "Widow Booth" was not registered until nearly two years after the fact. It is the only official record with the exception of family material where the Booth name is used. This leads to two possibilities. Either Martha did have a romance with JWB and kept it quiet until after the assassination. Or, the idea of this romance with a national figure came either before or after her marriage to Stevenson for whatever purpose. Author Bryan more than suggested that "Izola" may have been one of those women claiming to be Booth's wife in order to receive material gains from the Booth family. Even to this date, the popular, rich and famous have problems with paternity suits filed against them.

1859 - Ogarita Booth is born on October 23, "at the residence of my Aunt Amy Benchley, my grandmother's sister in Abbott's Lane, Providence, RI." from a letter from Alonzo to Izola Forrester dated 1911. A letter from Gail to her father undated, "Mr. Hall reports that the muster rolls show it was 'absolutely impossible' for Mr. Bellows to have been Ogarita's father, as Bellows was far out to sea and checking into South American ports all during the critical time." (*They agree that Ogarita's name is Ogarita Elizabeth and not Rosalie. Middle names quite frequently have a strange way of being changed in this family.)

(*This information stating the impossibility of Bellows being her father was startling news to us. Ogarita's birth in Abbott's Lane was on record, and we assumed that Martha returned "home" from Boston to have this child. The Bellows pension files show that Ogarita was not the first child born to Martha. In her *Saturday Evening Post* article, Miss Forrester mentioned her Aunt Amy coming to the Brown Farm and bringing so many good things for all of them. We know that Amy was Betsey's sister, although her history was not included in that particular chapter/file.)

Source: *The New England Historical and Genealogical Register, Volume CXII: April 1988. Whole Number 566 - pps. 184-185. The Benchley-Bensley Family by Roger D. Joslyn.*

Amy is another of those feminist Benchley girls. She was single according to this report, and lived in Providence on Nash's Lane in a house purchased from Joseph Weaver for $250 in 1846. In 1855, she sold this house to Patrick and Owen Raid of North Providence. Amy is living in the First Ward in Providence with William A. Smith from 1850 until they both moved to North Providence in 1865. She was born in 1784 in Smithfield where the Benchleys originated. At the age of 94 years, she died unmarried at the Dexter Asylum in Providence on November 7, 1878. It is curious that her younger sister, Betsey, died the same year in Burrillville, age 86. Both deaths occured before Miss Forrester was born. We suspect her story in the *Post* contains her mother's memories and not those of her own.

It is important to realize that Amy—as things stand at the moment—could not have been a blood relative to Martha L. Mills Bellows. Why is she at Amy's house for the birthing? There is the possibility that Martha is related in some other way to the Benchley family, in addition to being Caroline's stepdaughter. The 1860 Census in Providence lists baby Ogarita, under six months of age, living with a McNamara family a few houses down from Amy. What does all of this mean? The plot thickens but never jells. It is obvious the Benchley gals did not follow the traditional lifestyle of their peers. If Abbott's Lane is today's Abbott Street, then Amy's home was in the downtown area not far from the wharfs and docks of the Providence Harbor. This location is also not too distant from the various theaters which rose and fell quite rapidly in the same time period.

The unequivocal statement by Gail that, according to James O. Hall, Bellows could not possibly have fathered Ogarita is of much concern to us. We had been hesitant to write to this leading authority on John Wilkes Booth, but this entry overcomes our shyness. Mr. Hall not only was kind enough to answer our questions, but sent his micro copy of the log from the US "Preble" upon which Charles S. Bellows, Master at Arms, served a three year tour of duty. A trip to the North Providence Library is in order so we may read and copy this film which contains selections from January 1859 through the 1860 log, courtesy of the National Archives.

Charles S. Bellows enlisted in Baltimore in December 18, 1857 for a three year tour of duty ending December 17, 1860. We recall that he signed up for another tour a month after his marriage to Martha in 1855. She wrote in the request for his pension that "he joined the Navy when a boy and served in the service until his death, never remaining at home over three months at a time." This information is worth restating. In the early part of January, 1859, the "Preble" is located off Lobos, Argentina.

On January 12th, the "Preble" goes into port in Montevideo, the capital city of Uruguay, to take on Marines, equipment and guns. They leave port on January 20th and see the Point India Light. Apparently they are part of a flotilla of US Navy ships prowling about searching for our "Manifest Destiny" in Central and South America. The official title of the Preble assignment is the Norfolk to Paraguay Expedition. The selections from the ship's log end at this point and do not start again until March of 1859 with the ship back in Montevideo.

From our reading of this log, the statement that Charles S. Bellows did not father Ogarita is not proven. Biological counting is tricky business, but using the old medical practice of counting 266 days back from the date of birth, October 23, 1859, the conception could have occurred the last day in January give or take a few days to account for mother nature's vagaries. If the "Preble" went stateside and the crew were given shore leave, there is the possibility that Martha could have been with Charles. There was enough time for the ship to make home port. This all needs to be examined further.

On the muster/enrollment charts, recruits sign on throughout the three year's tour. It is obvious that the "Preble" goes stateside as men sign on at various United States cities including Norfolk. We discover a name familiar to us, a James Wilson, who enlisted in Norfolk. There is a James Wilson buried in the Douglas Cemetery just across the Burrillville border in Massachusetts, who served in the US Navy in that time period. These Wilsons are related to our local families, but it does not prove this is the same man. It is time to return to the family historical chronological chart.

1860 - Martha Bellows is in Boston Third Ward, House 896. Mr. Hall writes that she is in a millinery shop working for a woman named Geneva Webster. Martha L. Bellows is listed as a dressmaker, 22 years old, and born in Connecticut. Her two children are Ogarita E. eight months old and Harry Bellows five years old, born in Massachusetts. He later died at a young age. (*Apparently, Martha has collected Ogarita from the McNamara's house in Providence. Here is the Harry of whom we wrote earlier, who was born the year Martha and Charles were married in 1855. Charles was not listed as he was aboard the "Preble" during this census taking.)

1861 - Charles Alonzo Bellows is born on May 16th. (*In Cambridge, and his birth certificate reads Charles E. Bellows. Possibly the "E" is for Elijah Bellows, seaman Charles' father.) In the same letter as quoted previously, Gail writes, "The case is almost as strong for him not being Charles Alonso's father either. The ships logs show that Bellows was far out at sea again." (*Back to our notes on the log, we read that the "Preble" is anchored near the Mississippi River. On March 25th it proceeds up the Mississippi, back down to New Orleans the end of March and beginning of April, and over to Florida on April 10th. The log skips from April 12th to June 4th where it is at the Warrington, Florida Navy Yard, and again from the June date until August 19th where it is again in upper

Florida Bay. The log between August 22 and September 17th is missing. On September 18th the "Preble" leaves the area and goes out to sea. The ship is listed as standing up Boston Bay on September 20th. On September 29th it is put out of commission.

Using the same method of the 266 days, we estimate Charles's conception as being around the 26th of August. There is no firm date on the "Preble" or Charles at that time. Since the ship is located in the Florida Gulf area for a lengthy time, the crew may have been given shore leave. Again we cannot state with certainty that seaman Charles is not the father of Charles E. We will take Martha's advice given to Alonzo and look more before we leap into any unequivocal statements concerning paternity.

***Source:** Continuation of Family Chronology by Izola Forrester*

1869 - Martha Mills goes to California. (*No source or further information. Our thoughts on this are known by now although anything is possible with the persistent and feisty Martha.)

1869 - John H. Stevenson marries Martha L. Bellows, March 2 in Baltimore. (*Not Martha Booth?)

1875 - Martha writes to Alonzo, "Do not be surprised to hear at any time of her (*Ogarita's) marriage, letter dated August 26th.

1878 - Ogarita Booth gives birth to Izola Louise Hills on November 15th at the Mills home in Pascoag, Rhode Island. The child of a romance, her father, George Wallingford Hills, when he was at Harvard and her mother acting in Boston at the time. (*We now believe that young Izola was born in a Wilson Brother's house as written by Alonzo. The Stevenson's are probably renting from the Wilsons.)

1882 - William Wilson and Ogarita married in 1879, divorced in 1882.

1883 - Ogarita marries Al Henderson, a director of Light Opera. (*Miss Forrester wrote of this happening when she was six years old.)

1885 - Ogarita Booth gives birth to Beatrice Henderson. (*Beatrice Booth Henderson Clutts Colony who started the summer theater in Keene, New Hampshire.)

1885 - Martha moves to Terrace Hall, Canterbury, Connecticut. "I suppose you see by the papers that I had been left a little money." Martha writes to Alonzo in a letter dated April 2, 1885. (*Actually, the correct date was 1886 according to the handwritten letter we have seen from Martha to Alonzo. There is still the doubt of Terrace Hall being the Hilbert's Victorian Mansion due to the *Danielson Transcript* article.)

1888 - January 29, Arthur M. Darcy also known as Harry Darcy died. (*No source or location given.)

1893 - Ogarita Booth Henderson, aged 32, died of pneumonia while on the road in a theatrical company in Binghamton, New York. She is buried there.

1893 - Izola is living with the Forresters in Chicago, and is adopted by them the following January. (*No source given. This ends the chronology as given to us. Before this chapter is completed, however, a few more words concerning John H. Stevenson should be said, as we were rather rough on him previously.)

The three year account of the 2nd Massachusetts Volunteer Cavalry in which John Horatio Stevenson served is in our possession thanks to the Chief of Special Collections, Brenda Howitson, of the George Fingold Library at the State House in Boston. This information was compiled from the Massachusetts Adjutant General's report, *Massachusetts Soldiers, Sailors and Marines in the Civil War.* The first company "A" was raised in California and known as the "California Hundred." Later in California, four more companies were mustered in and Co. "E" was amongst them. The Californian Battalion “rendezvoused” at Camp Meigs in Readville, Massachusetts, which is south of Boston.

The main body of the regiment left for the seat of war May 11th, proceeded to Washington, DC, and camped near there until July 19th. During that time, it was engaged in raids and scouting expeditions in the region between Washington and the Blue Ridge. Joined by the rest of the regiment on August 6th, the Californians fought Mosby's Battalion near Fairfax Court House and then proceeded to Muddy Brook, Maryland, where they did picket and patrol duty during the fall and winter. This regiment fought many battles during the following two years, and they were in the thick of it a good deal of the time. We read that they suffered heavy losses at Dinwiddie Court House and Five Forks. These engagements broke the Confederate right, uncovered the Southside Railroad, and insured the fall of Petersburg. In April of 1865, they assisted in the capture of Lee's supply trains at Appomattox Station and on the following morning were with the troops who stopped the further progress of the Army of Northern Virginia at the Appomattox Court House. Stevenson certainly earned his pension.

The Battalion was in the Grand Review in Washington, DC on May 23, 1865, and was mustered out at the Fairfax Court House

July 20th. They returned as a body two days later to Camp Meigs, Readville, Massachusetts, where the men were paid off and the regiment disbanded on August 3rd. This places John H. Stevenson in the Boston area during the same time we assume Martha is located there. From the muster enrollment, we were surprised to read that Stevenson gave his residence as St. Joseph, Michigan. Was that his last stop before heading for California? He is listed as 22 years old and a laborer. This destroys our faint hope that he was a musical conductor and associated with the theater. This account also states the fact that his "name was also borne as John H. Stephenson." This strengthens our belief he was related in some way to our Stephensons/Stevensons in Burrillville. There were no other familiar names listed in Company "E", which was disappointing. Stevenson was in Winchester near the supposed site of Izola Martha's home in the Shenandoah. We found no other familiar names on this roster.

As you can see, the trip to Keene and its aftermath brought us much needed data on our Burrillville Booths. Much of Martha's history is still a mystery, and we have not yet resolved the question of her association with Booth. In the next chapter/file, a comparison will be made of time and place to consider the plausibility of Martha's meeting JWB.

Chapter/File 16

PLAUSIBILITIES AND EXPLANATIONS

At this point, one may well question the reason for our continued and relentless pursuit of the Burrillville Booths without any substantial evidence they are affiliated in any way with the Booths of Maryland. Verifiable vital statistics along with chronological and geographical charts appear to favor the unlikeliness of Martha meeting John Wilkes Booth. There are periods of Martha's life, particularly in her younger years and during the 1860s, which allow room for speculation. Please remember that it has never been our prime interest to "prove" that Martha and John were married. We are investigating the local lore concerning this "romantic" pair by presenting a history of Martha and her extended family. If in the process the evidence leads to Ogarita, Charles or Harry being a child of JWB, it would be the frosting on our cake. We have tried to keep an open mind and to weigh the facts and information carefully as it came into our hands. Admittedly, the information has caused us to sway back and forth with our opinion between the possibility of a romance between Miss Mills and JWB or the plausibility of a complex and continued fabrication of this romance by Martha and her descendants . . . knowingly or unknowingly.

Modern critics do not take Miss Forrester's claim overly seriously, although one or two admit to the chance of a romance, but not to any marriage. Miss Forrester is herself at fault for much of this skepticism and disbelief with her discrepancies, contradictions and obvious omissions of any family facts which stood in the way of her romanticized history. As a journalist, she must have been aware of the gapping holes in her account, and that critics would check the reliability of her sources. The scarcity of information before 1869 and the abundance of letters, diaries and news articles after that time is also questionable. Miss Forrester's explanation is that Martha destroyed anything that would associate her with Booth after the assassination. From several sources including Asia Booth Clark and Eleanor Ruggles, we read that the Booth family destroyed materials pertaining to JWB. Yet, when Martha marries Stevenson in 1869, she lists herself as the "Widow Booth." And, according to our investigations, she freely informed those living in our area and in nearby Connecticut that she had been Booth's wife.

There is still no hard core proof that Martha arrived with Ogarita and Charles either in Burrillville or Canterbury in 1865, although local lore in both towns claim this is so. We are inclined to agree that Martha and her family were in Burrillville in the mid 1800s if only for short stays or prolonged visits. In her letters to Alonzo, she writes that the children want to see him and want to be on the farm with him. Martha sends her best to "mother" Caroline and Mr. Brown. It is obvious they have been in contact before her 1869 letter from Baltimore. The birth of Ogarita in Providence at Aunt Amy Benchley's and her writing of "mother's" house in Providence indicate that she is also familiar with the complex Benchley family. There is no evidence so far that Martha was brought up in the South as Miss Forrester claims. The mysterious Aunt Fanny [Mills] D'Arcy has eluded everyone. We believe Martha is more familiar with this tri-state corner than with the South. Alonzo's recording Martha as "of Pawtucket, Providence and Boston," only strengthens our case. We also suspect that she was living in Boston in 1865 where she probably met either John H. Stevenson or Arthur D'Arcy. There is an embarrassing lack of factual data on Martha's whereabouts between the years 1861 and 1867. This period of time is one of those vast gaps mentioned in the beginning paragraph.

Speaking of John H. Stevenson, the history of Co. "E" 2nd Mass. Cavalry tempered our judgment, and we omitted some of his less than flattering personal history. After reading his service record from the National Archives, we decided this information might add a clue or two to the unresolved mystery of the Burrillville and the Maryland Booth relationships. We add the following reluctantly, but with the belief that if Booth were not Ogarita's and Charles's father, then this fabrication began in Baltimore with Stevenson's advice and consent. There is little to support the claim that Harry Stevenson was also Booth's son.

Source: *Information from Mr. Wilkinson (grandson of Harry Stevenson) and Virginia and Washington Street Directories.*

1891 - John Stevenson is at Hampton Home in Virginia.

He is listed in Washington, DC in 1892 under various addresses and occupations. In 1900 he is living at 507 13th Street "enumerated with Amelia Whitman as a boarder." Mr. Stevenson died August 7, 1906, with cerebral syphilis listed as the primary cause of death and exhaustion as the immediate reason.

Source: *National Archives, Washington, DC.*

Stevenson's service record is confusing and suggestive. He is accused of desertion at Muddy Brook on July 10, 1864, from Capt. Eigenbrodgt's Co. "E" 2nd Mass. Cavalry. He was confined at Washington, DC. on August 1, 1864, and released to duty on September 25, 1864. Stevenson was present on the Muster Rolls until April 10, 1865, when he was listed as absent on duty with Company Commander in Washington, DC. On June 17, 1865, he is listed as deserted at Clouds Mills, Virginia, and placed on the descriptive list of deserters. After returning to duty on the 9th of July, he was mustered out at the Fairfax Courthouse, Virginia, on July 20, 1865. The charge of desertion was removed on July 17, 1865, per Special Order 127 from the War Department in Washington. (*It appears that either Stevenson had a big "in" with someone or he was engaged in undercover work with his commanding officer's acknowledgment. His later occupations as detective, government clerk, and watchman would have been of help in the preparation of an elaborate fabrication.)

A distress signal was sent out to James O. Hall for his interpretation of the log of the USS "Preble" in his possession. This is in regard to the time after January 20th when we left mariner Bellows in Montevideo Bay. Mr. Hall explained that it would have taken the ship at least two months to get back to Norfolk or Boston. Still we were not satisfied with that explanation. We requested the information on the "Preble's" February 1859 log from the National Archives. These verified that the "Preble" with Bellows aboard is cruising up and down the Parana River before returning to Montevideo. Unless Martha were also on board, Ogarita has an unidentified father. This does not prove that Booth fathered her, but it certainly eliminates Bellows.

This brings us to the question of Martha's relationship with Charles S. Bellows. It might sound strange to modern ears that Bellows signed up for a tour of duty less than a month after he married Martha in Boston, but one has to think in terms of the realities of the time period whenever possible. Choices of occupation were limited, especially for the working class. The sea, the land, a few businesses, and a handful of professions were the main stay of livelihood. Sea captains and crews were gone for months, even years, at a time. It was a fact of life and no insult to their wives. We have been unable to locate his birth record in Roxbury or Boston, but the surname Bellows is prevalent in Pawtucket, Burrillville and Boston. We contacted William M. Bellows, a family genealogist, who told us that the Bellows of Pawtucket came from New London, Connecticut, in 1892. He cannot find a listing for our Bellows in his records.

It is difficult to say when Martha and Charles parted. He is listed as a mariner, boarding in Cambridge in an 1861 directory but not there the years before or after. Martha is not included, but the archivist who gave us the information said that women were not often listed unless they were widows, owned a home, or had an occupation. We assume Martha is in Cambridge with him as Charles Alonzo Bellows was born there. According to the testimony of Dr. Putnam and Mr. and Mrs. Averill on her pension request in 1871, Martha is Mrs. Bellows and the children are those of the deceased Charles S. Bellows. By that time, she is also married to John Stevenson. There are so many shady items involving Martha and her choice of mates. We wish we could find Booth among them.

We do accept that mariner Charles Still Bellows could not have fathered Ogarita, but we continue to hedge in favor of his being the father of Charles A. Bellows. (*Massachusetts State Archives list his middle initial as "E" but Boston records indicate "A". We first thought the "E" stood for Elijah, the name of the senior Charles's father. We now accept the "A" for Alonzo as found in his journals.)

Mr. Hall was also asked his opinion on the letters from Mrs. Elijah Rogers to Dr. William Stump Forwood in reference to their influence upon Stanley Kimmel's acceptance of the common law family of John Wilkes Booth. He wrote back that he had known author Kimmel, who had lived at Tudor Hall while researching the material on the Booths for *The Mad Booths of Maryland*. This former home of the Booth's was owned by Mrs. Mahoney. (*She conducted Miss Forrester on a tour of this house.) Mr. Hall thought that perhaps Mr. Kimmel had changed his mind about the common law family of Booth after his first edition in 1940 and included them in the 1969 Dover edition along with the information from the Merrifields. According to Mr. Hall, he was never consulted about the change.

We are more than pleased to read that Mr. Hall allows for the suggestion we made in Chapter/files 6 and 11 in regards to Mrs. Rogers' knowledge of Martha, Ogarita and Alonzo (*probably young Charles). "Izola" visited Elizabeth Rogers at Tudor Hall and told her these were John Wilkes Booth's children. We surmised that Martha made this trip to Bel Air while she and Stevenson were living in Baltimore somewhere between 1868-1870. Ogarita would have been about ten and Charles, eight.

Source: *Sketches of Tudor Hall and the Booth Family by Mrs. Ella V. Mahoney, privately published in 1925. From the U.S.Army Military History Research Collection.*

It is all rather curious that Mrs. Ella V. Mahoney, who knew Mrs. Rogers, wrote that a woman did indeed visit Mrs. Rogers with two children in tow and declared JWB to be the father. This woman asked for advice about promoting the girl (*Ogarita?) on stage as the daughter of Booth and was advised against it. Then, Mrs. Mahoney writes, they disappeared and were heard of no more. We are not convinced the above statement is one hundred percent accurate. Copies of the letters sent to Dr. Forwood by Mrs. Rogers are now in our possession. It was a struggle to locate them at the Library of Congress as they were listed under "Family Papers of Junius Brutus Booth, Senior." One has to know "where" to look.

Bits and pieces are excerpted from these letters. We felt a complete set would help set the record straight regarding our elusive Booths. We are grateful for those at this Library who were willing to seek and find. This would be a proper moment to exonerate those who work in the various museums and record departments of Maryland and Washington, DC. They have interest, knowledge and willingness to share information in an efficient and gracious manner. It is true that our first request for Martha's marriage was either lost or misplaced, the one fault of these guardians and dispensers of historical facts. The encountering of terse, seemingly uninformed or disinterested, not to mention tardy, counterparts in our own New England States does embarrass us. There have been exceptions, of course, and that is the reason we have mentioned them.

Source: *"Biography of Junius Brutus Booth" by William Stump Forwood, M.D. Unpublished manuscript from the Maryland Historical Society.*

While searching for those letters, we requested and received two reels of microfilm entitled "Stump on Booth #1039" via the Interrelated Library System which we had been told Mrs. Roger's much-quoted letters were found. Unfortunately, the selections in which she referred to our elusive Booths of Burrillville were not included. (*Yes, we are now convinced that it was our Martha who visited Mrs. Rogers with the belated news that JWB was the father of her children. The above information is supportive data for this conviction. What are the probabilities of another family having the names Izola, Ogarita and Alonzo in that exact time period. This does not confirm that Booth was father and husband, but that Martha did relay this information to someone else outside our tri-state corner of New England.)

Although the excepts for which we were searching in "Stump on Booth" were missing, we did discover answers to the questions posed in Chapter/file 6 regarding the exchange between Forwood and Rogers. Dr. Forwood was president of the Harford Historical Society and was collecting the history of noted residents of Harford County including the Booths. With his eldest daughter, who was an admirer of Edwin Booth's acting, he visited Tudor Hall in 1885 while Mrs. Rogers was there. This sparked the flow of information from the friend and former neighbor of the Booth family. The good doctor felt it necessary to apologize to his reader for including John Wilkes Booth in his accounts even as late as 1887. (*But Martha in 1869 is brave enough to declare herself Widow Booth in Baltimore when she married Stevenson! This correspondence predates Miss Forrester's research by several decades.)

We learned that Mrs. Mary Ann(a) Booth died October 22, 1885 in New York at the home of her youngest son, Joseph. Maggie Mitchell (1832-1918), an actress renown for her role as Fanchon, was first cousin to John Wilkes Booth. This might explain the fact that during his budding career, Booth often had walk-on parts where Maggie Mitchell was engaged on stages in various cities. (*The Mitchells were the children of Junius Booth's sister, who lived on the farm with the Booth family much to everyone's dismay. Her husband was a no-account, who, not unlike Arnold Benchley in Pawtucket, enrolled his children in factories in Baltimore . . . disdaining work himself.)

The Booths lived on Exeter Street in Baltimore during school and during the winter months, and also attended the Rock Spring Church in the same city. Mrs. Rogers, herself, was living on Hanover Street by 1887, the same year the Mahoney family purchased Tudor Hall. From Mrs. Rogers' letters and other readings, we know that this friend and former neighbor of the Booths kept in touch with the family, in particular with the elder Mrs. Booth and Rosalie. In fact, it was Mrs. Elizabeth Rogers who directed undertaker Joseph Weaver to the gravesite of the departed Booths on the Harford County farm. She wrote that she clipped a lock of John's hair for his mother while he lay in his "elegant" coffin before his final burial in Greenmount Cemetery in 1869. This lady also offered to accompany Rosalie or any family member to collect the money John had deposited in a Canadian bank prior to the assassination. Edwin forbade it, and the money was lost to the family. This is not difficult to understand, and we recall that the government finally released JWB's body after many pleas from Edwin on the condition that the family not attempt to perpetuate John's name or fame in any way.

It is difficult to believe that anyone accepts the escape theory after reading the many accounts of the identifications of JWB's body by friend and foe. The subsequent descriptions of the deterioration of his leg during and after the twelve days on the escape route, and the actions and reactions until he was finally laid to rest in Greenmount Cemetery in 1869, tend to confirm his death.

Source: *Mrs. Rogers' letters to Dr. Forwood. Courtesy Library of Congress.*

Mrs. Rogers' recollections of the Booth family members dart in and out as she writes of "Marrien" (*Marion was the daughter of Junius Booth, Jr.) at the funeral of her grandmother. Out of a clear blue sky she writes, "None of the family takes any account of John Wilkes' children but Rosalie; she is very kind to them; does not visit them; but sends them money every spring and fall. Calls them her children." This certainly suggests to us that Mrs. Rogers talked to Rosalie concerning her visitors and that Rosalie accepted them as John's family. We recall Edwin writing to a friend that one of those "widows" got hold of poor Rose and robbed her of all the money she had. Apparently, Edwin was not convinced of these "children" and their bloodline.

Elizabeth [Brown] Rogers continues about a beautiful girl "Ogretia" and a son "Alonso." "Izalia" was not married to John and she did not know what her maiden name was. Rose is given two oil wells by JWB and told to take care of his children. (*From the book written by Ernest C. Miller, *John Wilkes Booth in the Pennsylvania Oil Region*, published by the Crawford County Historical Society of Meadville, Pennsylvania, we read that Rosalie did receive stock certificates in the Pithole well from her brother, John Wilkes Booth, around 1865. Mr. Miller further suggests that she received a portion of the $1,400 for damages awarded in a suit against Valley Railroad around 1868. According to Edwin Booth, a self-styled widow of his late brother, John, robbed poor Rosalie of the little money she had. The money Rosalie received from this suit might be the money in question.) Mrs. Rogers writes in 1886 that both the children mentioned are married. (*In 1886 both Ogarita and Charles are indeed married. All of this leads us to believe that Miss Forrester's account of a relationship between Rosalie and her grandmother has some basis in fact. It suggests as well that Martha kept in touch with Mrs. Rogers, or that Rosalie confided in her and kept her abreast of the news of John's children.)

In addition to this we have a letter dated July 16, 1888, from Ogarita in Minneapolis to her younger half-brother Harry Stevenson at Hotel Superior in Chicago. Ogarita writes that she had a "beautiful letter" from Mrs. Rogers in Baltimore, who is going to find out Aunt Rosalie's address. Apparently Rosalie is living somewhere in New York with "Uncle Joseph." (*Rosalie Booth died on January 15, 1889 and was buried at Greenmount. We do not know whether Ogarita ever received that "address".) We also learn that Ogarita and Henderson are separated. She writes of a "Maggie" with whom she frequently corresponds. (*Could this be Maggie Mitchell?)

Our thoughts fly back to the description of a visit to Aunt Rosalie in New York from Ogarita and young Zola from *This One Mad Act*. It is one of those paragraphs that makes us wonder if Miss Forrester were unconsciously questioning the validity of the whole Booth affair. She writes that twice a year they visit Aunt Rose whenever they are in New York. According to the letters, these visits would have had to been either before the 1888 letter or between July 1888 and January 1889. The visit was not like a "family one" but under some sort of strain, "something of a ceremony." Ogarita and Aunt Rose are talking when "someone came down the staircase into the front room and stopped to greet my mother. Rose shielding her eyes while this person was in the room." Later, Ogarita tells young Zola it was her uncle. (*Joseph Booth, we assume, certainly not Edwin!)

Another time Miss Forrester relates the discovery of a package of letters from Aunt Rose to her grandmother with dates from 1866-1887 with a gap between 1867 and 1871. (*We have not seen nor did Miss Forrester reproduce any of these in *This One Mad Act*.) She explains that Harry thought these were destroyed quite purposely by Martha so as not to endanger JWB with whom she was united during that time period in California. Booth as Harry's father and the California episode tend to destroy the credibility of Miss Forrester's account. This inclusion might be explained by the fact that she is fond of Uncle Harry and wanted to include him as a blood relative of her own grandfather. (*Incidentally, the sisters informed us that much of what their mother wrote came from Harry, who was about seven years older than Miss Forrester and would have been more aware of the family history.)

At one time, Miss Forrester writes that Rosalie tells Martha not to write directly to her address but to forward her mail to Marion Booth (*Junius Brutus Booth, Jr.'s daughter) or Joseph Dabney (*affiliated with the theater?) both of New York. Could this be because Rosalie is then living with Edwin, who does not approve? She also adds later that Rosalie died at her younger brother Joseph Booth's home in Long Branch, New Jersey. Rosalie actually died at his home in New York City according to the State of New York Death Certificate.

Apparently, Martha asked Rosalie for help in getting Ogarita's stage career off the ground. It was said that Rosalie wrote back that this might cause Ogarita much unhappiness. Aunt Rose also writes with a "fluttering anxiety" about her brother, Edwin, as though she were "afraid of his displeasure." It is suggested that someone in the Booth family helped Ogarita gain her first minor role in 1875 as one of the sons of Malcolm in *Macbeth* at the Globe Theatre in Boston. Charlotte Cushman, who played Lady Macbeth, was a famous actress who starred in both male and female roles. Although she does not look like Martha, she shares the rather strong and unfeminine facial structure. It is not difficult for us to envision either one of them as Lady Macbeth or Medea. The above farewell performance of Miss Cushman in Boston is listed in an unidentified newspaper given to us by Martha's family. The role of Donalbain is played by a Miss Wilkes, a surname that both Ogarita and John Wilkes Booth used in their early stage appearances. She later was known as Rita Henderson and Rita Booth on stage.

(*From our point of view, there was correspondence as well as an association amongst Rosalie, Martha and Ogarita, to what extent is uncertain. Miss Forrester said she never saw Edwin perform because her grandmother and he had had some kind of a feud between them. Strangely enough, this animosity toward Edwin Booth has carried through to the present generation of Martha's descendants. According to Bryan's account in *The Great American Myth* (*see Chapter/file 6), Edwin Booth received intimations from a Boston lawyer that he would be hearing from one of those "widows" again. Edwin was reacting to a newspaper article in the *New York Tribune* which appeared in 1885 concerning an unnamed "widow" of Booth with two children, all of whom had lived in secrecy for over twenty years.

In the middle of the 1800s, Martha is living in Canterbury, Connecticut, as Mrs. Edwin S. Bates. Stevenson is at the Tremont House in Boston. Young Zola accompanies her grandmother on a visit to him. She notes her grandmother becomes visibly upset during the conversation with her former husband. (*Does this have anything to do with the letter in the newspaper about the widow and children?)

Why Mrs. Mahoney was not aware of Mrs. Rogers' letters when publishing her book in 1925 is puzzling. Perhaps the letters had not been discovered at that time, but she certainly should have known about them from Mr. Kimmel's research at Tudor Hall. The legitimacy of Mrs. Rogers' letters are crucial to our summation of the tie between Rosalie and Martha. To be fair, we must mention that Mr. Kimmel's scholarship has also recently come under question. This is not all that unusual. It is part of the process of writing history where the last kid on the block discredits the previous one who held his standing amongst his peers.

The main criticism is not so much Kimmel's acceptance of the common-law family of John Wilkes Booth. But, it is critical of his theory that Booth turned to oil and land speculation along with participation in the conspiracy to kidnap President Lincoln because he was losing his stage voice and knew his stage career was ending. There has been much published pro and con whether this has any basis in fact. We read of theater critics who noted Booth's ignorance of voice control on stage and his occasional hoarseness. We also read of his missing many engagements between 1864 and 1865 because Booth was busy with other concerns. These bouts with throat problems did not appear progressive, but not all the past was recorded. There is only so much information available for study and interpretation.

The actual meeting of Martha and Booth has not been proven, but the stage has been set for the possibility, if not the plausibility. Neither we nor Martha's descendants have been able to place her on stage at any time. Our search for firm data has continued with the gathering of much information concerning the theater in this time period. The stage names used by Martha, according to Miss Forrester's book, as well as her splicing of names, must be considered. Orianna and Violetta—reputedly used as stage names by Martha—are names of people in our locale who were peers of "Izola." (We did find a Violetta Angell, daughter of Darius and Nancy Angell, in Alonzo's journals.) We sense participation in the theater by the Brown, Benchley, Wilson and Jenkes families, but every time an attempt is made to nail this down, it alludes us. Amy,

Betsey, Caroline and Edward all lived in the cities of Rhode Island a good part of their lives, and their surnames appear in association with the various theaters, museums, halls, and opera houses in Providence.

It should be noted that Providence was a lively center for the stage performances pre- and post- Civil War, mainly because it was a rail, ship, and stagecoach stop between New York and Boston. The brightest stars of the time would shine on the boards of Providence. Theater had its ups and downs in the early history of Providence with its many friends and foes. The upper crust saw the stage as culture, and the lower as entertainment and escape. We read that the audiences of Providence were an active and rowdy lot similar to the ones in Shakespeare's time. Actors and actresses who gave poor performances were pelted with day-old vegetables and hustled out of town in fear of their lives. The youths of the city, both the townies and the ivy leaguers of Brown University, were much involved in the theatrical scene. In between the appearances of stars and touring companies from out of town, the local acting groups kept the theaters going. Leading townsmen and businessmen alike invested money in the various halls, museums, and opera houses. It is not impossible that Martha L. Mills might have ventured upon one of these stages, although it is apparent that she did not blaze across the theater scene. Even the likes of Miss Charlotte Cushman made her first appearance in Boston in 1830 listed on the playbill as merely, "a young lady," with many a minor role played by "a young woman or a young man." Martha just might have been one of these, but we believe Miss Forrester's account of her playing leading roles at the Boston Museum is just another romanticized exaggeration.

A small dent has been made researching the available material on the theatrical world found in the mid-eighteen hundreds. The Boston and Providence stages are fairly well documented, but the special interests of the recorders must be considered. Our early efforts were concentrated more on the Providence scene as we believed that Martha was in Rhode Island when the romantic interlude with Booth occurred—if it did. Ogarita was born at Aunt Amy's house here in 1859. The Providence Directory in 1860 lists Martha L. Bellows living at 13 Abbott's Lane there in her own house. According to the 1860 census, Martha is earning a living as a dressmaker in Boston with eight month old Ogarita and five year old, Harry. On the 1860 Providence census, six month old Ogarita is living with a family by the name of McNamara. It is possible that Martha was living in Providence, later moved to Boston, and then to Cambridge, a suburb of Boston, where Charles A. Bellows was born in 1861. She could have returned to Providence after her husband Bellows signed up for a tour of duty in August of 1855.

Martha's great granddaughters were unable to locate any evidence in their archives of her ever having been on stage, which was discouraging to us. We begin our search for Izola's elusive stage appearances with a collection of "just about everybody who was anybody on the stage," according to the author. We offer a few tidbits of interest from this publication. The copy received was leather bound and secured with red thread ties. It was delightful to turn the old pages and read the print . . . far more satisfying than reading microfilm. These selections should also convey our frustration in the attempt to make an affiliation between Martha's extended family and the legitimate theater. We know there are connections to be made, but are unable to do so.

Source: *History of the American Stage. Biographical sketches of nearly every member of the profession that has appeared on the American Stage from 1722 to 1870 by Allston T. Brown. Dick & Fitzgerald, Publishers (New York, 1870). (*Quite an undertaking, and we suspect that Brown missed a few minor personages, but not many. The dates studied would eliminate Ogarita's appearance, but not Martha's. Many of the surnames and information were of interest, but were unable to locate Martha in any of this material.)*

John Brown Mills who came from England in 1818. On stage in Boston and Philadelphia in 1838. Retired to a farm in New York in 1870. (*Brown is a common name among theatrical people in this time period. Families do tend to follow in their father's footsteps. There is a link between our extended family with those living in Boston, Philadelphia and New York.)

George F. Brown, born in New Hampshire in 1833, was on the Tremont stage in Boston. Settled in New York and ran an English Alehouse there.

Fanny Brown born in Cincinnati in 1837. (*Fanny became a rather well known actress and appeared with John Wilkes Booth. She was one of the five pretty faces found duplicated in John Wilkes Booth's diary after his death.)

Frank M. Bates made his debut in 1858 at the Howard Athenaeum in Boston and was manager of the Metropolitan Theatre in San Francisco in 1868.

Asa Cushman was born in Providence, Rhode Island, May 10, 1833. Appeared at Cleveland Hall in Providence. (*Whether this is Charlotte Cushman's relative, we do not know. Alonzo mentions a

Hulda Cushman who died in 1879 age 92 and a Rebecca Cushman died in 1876, age 88, widow of Samuel Clarke of North Smithfield.)

Charlotte Cushman was born in Boston in 1814. (*With whom Ogarita made her first stage appearance as Donalbain in Miss Cushman's final dramatic stage appearance in 1875. We have also read the year 1874 for her final appearance. She made several of them. Alonzo records her death in 1876 in his journal.)

Mr. and Mrs. Alexander Wilson. He was a sea captain, merchant and speculator in land and goods as well as an actor and stage manager. He retired to a farm in New York State and first appeared on stage in 1817 and died in 1854. (*Many Wilsons were found on stage or in theatrical enterprises in Providence and Boston during this time. Among them were Francis Wilson, author of a book on John Wilkes Booth, and George W. Wilson, who appeared on stage in Providence and Boston and also with Edwin Booth.)

***Source**: An Historical Account of the Providence Stage: Being a Paper Read Before the Rhode Island Historical Society, October 25, 1860 (with additions) by Charles Blake. Published by George H. Whitney. (Providence, RI 1868). (*We obtained the loan of this book from the Pawtucket Library. We understand it is the first published book about theater in and on Rhode island. The date of the lecture series pleases us as it predates the assassination year, 1865.)*

Much is learned about the various theaters, halls, museums, and opera houses that rise and fall in Providence between 1846 and 1860. Maggie Mitchell was immensely popular in this city and was onstage as early as the 1855-1856 season, returning many times through 1860. All the greats of the day played to crowded houses. Some of those in Providence were: Charlotte Cushman, E. L. Davenport, Fanny Davenport, Fanny Vinning, Kate and Ellen Bateman, Mr. and Mrs. J. W. Wallack, Edwin Forrest, Lola Montez and Junius Brutus Booth, Sr.

It more than interested us that Booth, Sr.., was a familiar figure in our city. Mr. Blake has him here in 1829 arriving in Providence on foot and nearly unclad. He walked from Boston, having missed the stagecoach, after one of his famous mental aberrations on the Boston stage in December. Booth goes to the familiar Deming's sailors boarding house at the junction of South Main and Wickenden Streets in Providence. He had many friends in Providence, one of whom, Colonel Josiah Jones, takes Booth to his home on Aborn Street where Junius remains until he has recovered.

John Wilkes Booth
Looking more like a conspirator than an actor.
Photo by Silsbee, Case & Co.
From the Richard & Kellie Gutman Collection

Flocks of visitors arrive at the Colonel's home and Junius Sr. entertains the guests by readings from the Bible. We find the older Booth on stage in Providence from 1836 through 1850. This would suggest that Edwin Booth would also have been a familiar face around the haunts of Providence as he attends to his father as keeper and dresser at the age of fourteen in 1847.

We have not seen any of Martha's reputed stage names. The closest we can come is a Sallie St. Claire appearing at Forbes' Theatre during the 1857-58 season. We read that The Pine Street Theatre at the corner of Pine and Dorrance Street in downtown Providence opened on September 5, 1858 under the management of E. Varrey and W. A. Arnold habitues of the Providence Museum and Forbes' Theatres. In the winter and summer of 1858 and 1859 when it was known as Swarts' Hall, a small company played here under the management of Mr. George Wyatt. Playing starring engagements upon this stage according to Mr. Blake were: Maggie Mitchell, Fanny Herring, Cordelia Howard, J. W. Wallack, C. W. Couldock, and J. W. Booth. (*Mitchell and Booth together once again and on a Providence stage. Unfortunately, the author does not give the exact dates of the individual appearances The Pine Street Theatre closed in the winter months of 1859 as receipts became too small to pay for the necessary heating fuel. This would indicate one of JWB's earliest engagements in Providence, and the first time we have seen it mentioned.)

Martha is living at 13 Abbott's Lane during this period. This Lane is located near the North Burial Grounds off North Main Street. It is not that far from the city of Providence where the churches, businesses, theaters, and wharfs were located and is in walking distance to the Pine Street Theater. We write immediately to those who might be able to either verify or disclaim the above information, but do not allow our hopes to get too high because those with more extensive knowledge of Booth's career might deem otherwise. It is interesting that his name is included in the 1860 series of lectures given at the Rhode Island Historical Society. Still we have to consider the "with additions" in the title.

This is perhaps our third strongest hint of the possibility of a Mills/Booth romance. The other two are Martha's relationship with Rosalie and Mrs. Rogers and the fact Mariner Bellows could not have fathered Ogarita. There is the chance that Martha might have met Booth and that Ogarita was the product of that romance. The name Ogarita is from a French adaptation of a melodrama popular in the mid-eighteen hundreds entitled "Ogarita" or "Sea of Ice." Author Gordon Samples has Booth in this play at the Wheatley's

Arch Theatre in Philadelphia on November 26,1857; at the Dudley Hall in Lynchburg, Virginia on November 10-13, 1858, and at the Richmond Theatre October 18, 19, 20, and 28 in 1858. We read that this little melodrama is still playing to Providence audiences in the 1870s . . . without Booth, of course. As noted earlier, theater and the brighter lights of the stage were all the rage. News of the stars' stage appearances and personal lives were as anxiously read and transmitted as the rather wearisome accounts of their modern counterparts are today. It would be unlikely that Martha L. Mills Bellows was immune to all the Booths' stage appearances both in Providence and Boston. There is a sense of the dramatic about Martha as revealed through her letters and certainly in the documentated milestones of her life. She was not the model New England seawife who walked the widow's walk atop her house waiting for the return of her sailor.

During the crucial 1859 period, Martha is probably between twenty-two and twenty-four years old, married to Bellows—if only by name—and has had two or three children. Her son, Harry Bellows, would have been around four years of age. She is living at 13 Abbotts Lane in 1860 but not listed in 1861. Booth would have been 21 and well into making a stage name for himself under the name of J. Wilkes. His reputation as a ladies man had already been firmly established. Later he was reputed to have a lady in every city: Ella Turner (Starr) in Washington, Etta in New York, and Jennie Candsomeone (Hoppin) in Boston. No particular lady's name is listed for Providence from what we have read.

According to undated photographs in Miss Forrester's book, Martha appears to be short of stature and more than well endowed. Her strong facial features are a square flat forehead, a protruding, determined jaw and a not-pleasing nose. Her eyes appear to be her best feature. Martha is shown once as a Spanish lady wrapped in a shawl, her dark hair pulled severely back with a Spanish comb, but her facial structure belies the pose. Her strong, assertive and feisty features are also noticeable amongst some older families in our area We call them the determined ladies with their strong bull-dogged British chins. Their opposites are the tall, sparse, high cheek-boned Yankee ladies. Searching for a word to describe Martha, it would be dramatic-looking, as Miss Forrester writes herself. Glancing through *A Pictorial History of the American Theater: One Hundred Years 1860-1960* by Daniel Blum and viewing the ladies of the stage during Booths and Martha's time period, it is easy to see that excess weight was not considered unattractive. The voluptuousness of Lillian Russell is *de rigueur*.

Another thought has crossed our minds after reading *The Divine Eccentric* by Doris Faley printed by Westernlore Press in 1969, which gives the history of Lola Montez. We began to think that perhaps Martha, who claimed her mother was Spanish, took the letters from Lola Montez's name and created the name Lizola or Izola. Maybe far fetched, but we read in Blake's account that Lola was at Forbes' Theatre during the 1856-1857 season for two weeks. She endeared herself to the Providence audience when she chastised the boys in the gallery for making fun of an elderly actor by name Poor Duffy as "second old man." She also helped the wife of a light comedian, David Palmer, who was dying of consumption at his home on Fulton Street. Blake wrote of Lola that when she left Providence, "hearts remembered her and blessings followed her . . . Sick, and ye visited me." This same type of concern for others comes forth in Martha's letters when she writes of tending to the sick and dying.

This chapter/file closes with an overall chronological and geographical chart of John Wilkes Booth and Martha Louise Mills. This suggests that they were not near one another that often, but as we have seen all too often vital statistic milestones do not always reveal the truth of a human situation. The exact whereabouts of Booth at specific times and specific places are hotly debated by those who study this actor/assassin. We have relied on the more sophisticated pursuers of John Wilkes Booth to tell us where he was and when. This research is far beyond our scope of activity and reliability. We have been fortunate to stumble upon the so-called Booth Mafia (those who are currently tracking Maryland Booths for whatever purposes). This information came from a "Boothie" in England, Arthur Kincaid (dramatist/actor/author), who passed on the names and addresses of those thus engaged. Mr. Kincaid wrote that, "Booth scholarship is the most remarkable process of cooperation we've ever encountered." This is true, otherwise we would not have been able to place John Wilkes in Providence and in Boston as well as we have.

It is with some amazement we have finally begun to see the possibility, if not the plausibility, of the Burrillville and Maryland Booths meeting. There was little hope for this when our investigations started. Our findings are a long way from being confirmed or denied, but there is just the slim possibility that this meeting did occur. The gaps in Martha's life during the 1857-1869 time period need to be filled before we, or anyone else, could wager on the hint of this romance. It does bother us that Alonzo is the only member in the family to breath the words actress or theater until

Miss Forrester begins to write of her mother, Ogarita. A.A.S.M scatters throughout his journals such tidbits as the first theater in London, and mentions famous actors' and actresses' births and deaths. He also adds other standard squibs from the newspapers of the day, although they may have no special significance to him.

The comparison chart on the next pages is a composite from the following authors with the emphasis on Booth's stage appearances. The times and places of interest pertaining to our elusive Booths of Burrillville have been highlighted. Our next chapter/file shall continue with more of the Booths' appearances in both Providence and Boston.

Source of chronological and geographical comparison chart:

Charles Blake. *History of the Providence Stage. An Historical Account of the Providence Stage: Being a Paper Read Before the Rhode Island Historical Society* October 25, 1860. Providence: Published by George H. Whitney, 1868.

Stanley Kimmel. *The Mad Booths of Maryland,* New York: Dover Pub., 1969.

Clara E. Laughlin. *The Story of Booth's Plot, His Deed and the Penalty.* New York: W. W. Norton & Company, Inc., 1953.

Eleanor Ruggles. *Prince of Players, Edwin Booth.* New York: W. W. Norton & Company, Inc., 1953.

Gordon Samples. *Lust for Fame: The Stage Career of John Wilkes Booth.* North Carolina and London: McFarland & Company, 1982. (*Author Samples has been most generous sharing his research material with us. His listings of Booth's stage appearances have been most helpful.)

George O. Willard. *History of the Providence Stage 1762-1891.* Providence: The Rhode Island News Company Publisher's Agent, 1891.

Francis Wilson. *John Wilkes Booth Fact and Fiction of Lincoln's Assassination.* Boston and New York: Houghton Mifflin Company, 1929.

Arthur F. Loux. *John Wilkes Booth - Day by Day.* Unpublished

Chronological and Geographical Comparison of John Wilkes Booth and Martha L. Mills

Bold Print indicates when JWB was in this general area.

1838 - MD/Harford County John Wilkes Booth Born May 10.

1840 - 1855 - MD/Harford Cty. & Baltimore. Raised on the farm and attends Episcopalian Military School.

1855 - MD/Baltimore - John W. Booth makes his stage debut.

1857 - PA/Philadelphia - JWB begins his stage career with small parts at Wheatley's Arch Theatre. **Appears in "Sea of Ice."**

1858 - VA/Richmond - Appears in **"Sea of Ice"** at the Richmond Theatre.

1858 - PA/Philadelphia - Again at Wheatley's Arch Theatre in **"Sea of Ice."**

1859 - VA/Richmond - Member of the Richmond Theatre stock company on a steady basis.

1859 - **MA/Boston** Appears with Edwin Booth at Howard Anthenaeum Oct. 26-28. Returns to Richmond and the Stock Company.

1832-1837 - NY/MA/RI/CT - Martha born September 11th.

1846 - RI/Providence - Abraham Mills marries Caroline Jenks.

1847 - NY/Albany - Abraham Mills dies in October.

1847 - RI/Pawtucket - Alonzo A. S. Mills born April 13th.

1850 - RI/North Providence - Caroline and Alonzo living with Betsey Benchley.

1855 - MA/Boston - Martha marries Charles S. Bellows.

1857 - RI/Pawtucket - Caroline marries Edward M. Brown.

1857-1858 - MA/Boston - Charles S. Bellows listed in city directory at 2 Sigourney Street. We assume Martha is also there.

1859 - Ogarita conceived in second half of January. Bellows at sea.

1859 - RI/Providence - Ogarita born in October at 13 Abbott's Lane. (*Martha appears there in Providence City Directory of 1860.)

1860 - VA/Richmond
1860 - GA/Columbus
at Columbus Theatre.
1860 - AL/Montgomery

1860 - MA/Boston - Martha here with Harry Bellows age 5 and Ogarita age 8 months.

1861 - NY/Rochester & Albany
April 26th in Albany, actress Henrietta Irving slashed Booth in the face with a knife. Little record of stage appearances until October.

1861 - MA/Cambridge - Charles A. Bellows born in May.

1861 - MD/Baltimore &
RI/Providence - Pine St. Theater October 21-25 as John Wilkes Booth.
NY/Buffalo
MI/Detroit
OH/Cincinnati
KY/Louisville

1861 - MA/Cambridge - Charles S. Bellows, mariner, appears on city directory as a boarder at 3 Washington Street.

1863 - MA/Boston - Boston Museum Jan. 19 - Feb. 13. Edwin & Mary, living in Dorchester, went to see him.
1863 - PA/Philadelphia
DC/Washington
MO/St. Louis
OH/Cleveland
MA/Boston - At the Howard Athenaeum Sept. 28 - Oct. 10. Enamored of a well-known courtesan, Jenny Hoppin.
1863 - MA/Worcester & Springfield
RI/Providence - Rave reviews at Academy of Music Oct. 16-19.
1863 - CT/ Brooklyn & New Haven. Fanny Brown involved romantically with Booth on tour.

1863 - Martha's whereabouts unknown. Caroline, Alonzo, Betsey Benchley, and Edward Brown move to Joseph Brown Farm in Burrillville.

1863 - 1864 - MA/Cambridge - Charles S. Bellows not indexed in street directory but is listed under Naval Service.

1863 - DC/Washington
OH/Cleveland

1864 - Booth in Louisville, St. Louis, Nashville, Cincinnati & New Orleans.

1864 - MA/Boston - Boston Museum April 25-27. Parker House July 26 - ? Some historians believe he met with conspirators at this time.

1864 - CT/New London - July 30 - Travels from Boston to visit relatives Junius Jr., Edwin, Asia and her husband, John Sleeper Clarke.

1864 - NY/New York City Aug. 2 - John and Edwin return to the city.

1864 - Canada/Montreal - October 24 - Corby's Hall with solo dramatic reading.

1864 - MD/Baltimore - Nov. - In Baltimore during election.

1864 - NY/New York City - Nov. 25 - Junius, Edwin and John star together in *Julius Caesar* at Winter Gardens.

1864 - 1866 - MA/Cambridge - No listing for Bellows in directories.

1864 - Martha's whereabouts unknown.

1865 - DC/Washington - Jan. 29 - One performance at Grover's Theatre.

1865 - NY/New York City - Feb. 11- visits Edwin and Junius.

1865 - DC/Washington - March 18 - One performance at Ford's Theatre.

1865 - **MA/Boston & RI/Newport** - April 5-6.

1865 - DC/Washington - April 14 - Assassinated Lincoln.

1865 - Martha's whereabouts unknown.

manuscript. (*Mr. Loux of Stilwell, Kansas, is gathering an account of the daily activities of JWB. Nearly as difficult a pursuit as our own. He shared with us some of his data on Booth's appearances on the stages of New England. Once his accounting is completed, it will be an invaluable source for students of Booth and the assassination.)

Surratt Courier. A publication of the Surratt Society. Clinton, Maryland. (*We have gleaned bits and pieces from their various featured articles. The Surratt Society offers a broad appeal to both modern day Confederates and Yankees in search of information on the many aspects of the time period during the Civil War.)

Chapter/File 17

BOOTHS AND THEATRE IN PROVIDENCE & BOSTON

Charles Blake, author of the first history of the Providence stage, Clerk of the Rhode Island Supreme Court and a local thespian, aroused our hopes to the possibility of J. Wilkes Booth being on stage at the Pine Street Theatre in Providence during the winter months of 1858-1859. The Manuscripts Department at the Rhode Island Historical Society Library was contacted in an attempt to locate the original lecture given there by Mr. Blake in 1860 . This was the basis for his book, *History of the Providence Stage,* published in 1868. If Mr. Blake had mentioned J. Wilkes Booth at the Pine Street Theatre in his 1860 lecture, it would prove Booth was in Providence at an earlier date than previously recorded. Unfortunately, Mr. Blake did not leave his lecture notes to the Historical Society.

J. Wilkes, the name used by Booth in his early appearances, was busy as a stock member at the Richmond Theatre during this time frame. Supportive data to strengthen our hope that JWB was in the Providence area at this early date is lacking. Most authorities on Booth are inclined to discount the possibility. Gordon Samples does have him "disappearing" from Richmond on October 25th and "hopping" a train to Boston to join his brother, Edwin, for the last three nights of a two weeks' run. This occurred shortly after Ogarita's birth in Providence in October of 1859. It does not prove he dashed up north to see her, nor does it prove his paternity. It is generally accepted that Booth had an impetuous nature and was inclined to disappear and reappear seemingly at will. Mr. Samples has him taking a week off from the Richmond Theatre from January 10th to the 17th in 1859, but there is no indication of where Booth went during that time.

(*We have yet to find a shred of evidence that Martha and Booth were in the same spot at the same time in any given city during the time of Ogarita's conception. As the investigation has progressed, we are more convinced than ever that solid evidence and actual truth are not easy items to package, especially since vital statistics are not always to be trusted. It is this set of circumstances which makes it necessary to give a sense of the social structure and general ambience of this time period in order to understand Martha and her extended family. We are not attempting to create a scenario to sway the reader this way or that, but are attempting to bring more insight into the entire process of documentation as a method of discovering secrets from the past. The following information is offered on the transportation system of that time period which allowed for the restless movements of both Martha and John Wilkes Booth.)

Source: *American Economic History by Harold Underwood Faulkner. Fifth Edition. Harper & Brothers Publishers. (New York and London, 1943).*

The Erie Canal was opened as early as 1825 for hauling passengers and goods between New York City and Buffalo, and thereby to all points west. A charting of railroad systems of the 1860s shows that the east coast and the near west were blanketed with iron rails and wooden ties. It explains how Booth can appear in Portland one week, in Detroit the next, continue on to Cincinnati then to Louisville and finally down to New Orleans. The New England states are crisscrossed with railroad lines. Fares are reasonable enough to enable Martha to go from Boston to Providence and later on to Baltimore. Even Alonzo and Caroline in Pascoag can visit Martha in Boston or Canterbury if they are willing to make several changes. Steam and packet ships run regular routes between New York, Providence, New Bedford and Boston. Public transportation, as well as horse and buggy, probably provided the public with better connections than we have today.

We were pleased to discover a book written by fellow actor and friend of Charles Blake, George O. Willard. He continues the history of the Providence theatrical stage where Blake left off in 1860. It is fascinating reading for natives of Rhode Island. It is also a rich mine of detailed information on actors and actresses, stock and touring companies, production and stage managers, board of trustee members and the various stars and plays on the stages in Providence between 1862 and 1891. Martha or Ogarita have not been found listed under any of their known stage names. There are countless familiar surnames involved with every aspect of the stage in our state, names which Alonzo also lists in his journals. We can smell the grease paint in the Benchley/Brown/Wilson family, but cannot find an individual face to put it on.

Source: *History of the Providence Stage 1762-1891 by George O. Willard. The Rhode Island News Company Publisher's Agent. (Providence, 1891). (*The Rhode Island Historical Society Library on Hope Street has a good collection on local theater as does the Providence Public Library on Empire Street.)*

Pine Street Theatre closed in the early part of 1860 and was rechristened as the Providence Theatre on October 7, 1861. Here J. Wilkes Booth, Joseph Proctor and Lucille Western acted under the management of J. C. Myers. Arthur F. Loux also has Booth in Providence from October 21st through October 25th with rave reviews from the *Journal* and *Post.* (*Martha is living in Cambridge having given birth to Charles Alonzo Bellows in May of that year.)

Booth reappears in Providence in 1863 at the Academy of Music located in a "capacious hall, provided with a stage and some of the appliances of a theater" in the recently completed Phenix Building built upon the ruins of Forbes' Theatre. In October of 1863, Booth starred with Mrs. Barrow on the 15th, 16th and 17th. Willard writes of our actor as being twenty-five years of age and "as handsome a man as ever graced the stage. He retired from the profession soon after this 1863 Providence appearance to speculate in oil." The author adds that, "This terrible deed—the assassination of President Lincoln—is the more remarkable for the rarity of criminals among the dramatic profession."

We read that Miss Maggie Mitchell is still the ever-popular star in Providence and Boston with regular scheduled engagements year after year. Willard's sketch of Maggie has her born in New York in 1832. Mrs. Rogers writes of her being a first cousin to the Booths of Maryland and growing up barefooted on the farm in Harford County. The venerable lady writes, rather saucily, that this is the reason Miss Mitchell can play so well the role of the winsome, barefooted innocent. A leading authority on Booth states unequivocally that Maggie is in no way related to the Booths. This is another one of those contradictions which serves to confound our investigation into the local lore of Burrillville. We do know that Booth had small roles in Miss Mitchell's engagements during his early career, and there was chatter of a romance between them. (*We still question whether the "Maggie" that Ogarita refers to in her letter to her brother, Harry, is the actress, Miss Mitchell.)

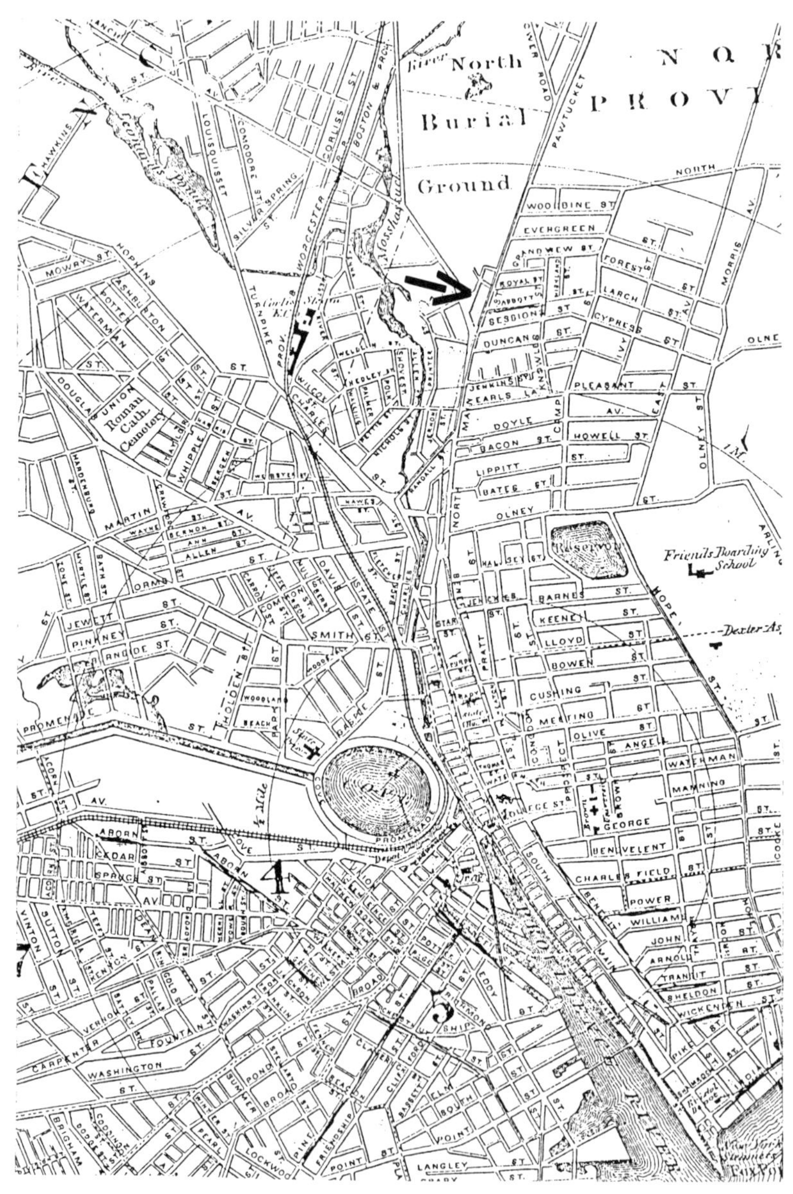

Providence from Beers Atlas - 1870
Arrow shows Abbott Street at end of North Burial Ground
between Royal and Session Streets.
Notice proximity to downtown Providence.

Willard writes of visiting Maggie Mitchell in 1871 at her home in Long Branch, New Jersey. (*Where the youngest Booth brother, Joseph, later lives and in whose home Rosalie dies.) The author meets a neighbor by the name of William Henderson, whose wife Ettie is also a stage actress. One thing leads to another, and Henderson becomes the first manager of the Providence Opera House located on the corners of Dorrance, Pine and Eddy Streets. His first production number was on December 4, 1871. Mr. Henderson began as an actor and made a fortune in Pittsburgh where he managed two theaters before coming to Providence. In 1877 he left this city to manage the Standard Theatre in New York where he was also successful. He died in 1890 managing the Academy of Music in New Jersey. (*There is no mention of a son by the name of Alexander Henderson, director of light opera and last husband of Ogarita.)

Charlotte Cushman is another favorite and frequent performer in Providence. Her last farewell appearance was at Edwin Booth's Theatre in New York in 1875 when William Cullen Bryant "presented her the laurel" for her long and fine acting career. (*Miss Wilkes appeared in Miss Cushman's farewell appearance at the Globe Theatre in 1875.) The famed actress died in Boston at the Parker House in 1876 and was buried at Mount Auburn. She died a wealthy woman . . . due to her Yankee thrift, notes the author.

The appearance in Providence of a solo dancer from Cadiz, Spain, next attracts our attention (*According to Miss Forrester, Abraham Mills first wife, Maria, came from Cadiz.) Isabel Cubas was born in 1831. She died in New York in 1864 leaving behind a beautiful daughter about six years of age. (*We are still clutching at straws in an attempt to discover the why, when and where of Martha's adopting the name Izola/Lizola. Performers during this time period had a fondness for Italian and Spanish names. We still believe that "Izola" was an attempt by Martha to romanticize herself just as her granddaughter did several years later. There is no solid evidence that Martha used that name officially. It does appear on her death records in Canterbury.)

We did find "Little Minnie Maddern" in Providence in the 1874-75 season appearing in *The Nights in a Barroom*. Willard does not record the child actress as being the "Artful Dodger" in *Oliver Twist* in 1877 along with Miss Ogarita Wilkes. He does mention a stock company in this city staging *Oliver* but not in 1877. There is always the possibility that he missed a few here and there.

Sources: *The History of the Boston Theatre 1854-1901 by Eugene*

Tompkins. Boston and New York: Houghton Mifflin Company The Riverside Press. (Cambridge, 1908) and The Prince of Players by Eleanor Ruggles. W. W. Norton & Company, Inc. (New York, 1953).

In 1867 Edwin Booth appears as Hamlet at the Academy of Music in Providence. Willard mentions Booth's first appearance at the Boston Museum in a minor part in *Richard III* on September 10, 1849. We surmised that Edwin would have been with his father in our two cities before he "bursts upon the town at Burton's Theatre in New York on May 4, 1857 as *Richard III*. He has ever since been recognized as one of the foremost American tragedians." Edwin had previously wooed and won audiences—among them Dr. Samuel and Julia Ward Howe as well as Louisa May Alcott—at the Boston Theatre in April of the same year. Boston was recognized as having the most critical and exacting audience possible. Edwin Booth went on to conquer the stage in New York with confidence after this. He continued to "play" Providence and Boston throughout his long stage career.

We tend to think of the Booths as being from Maryland, which they were, but the adult lives of Edwin, Junius Jr., John and Joseph were spent in the cities of the north and west. At one time, we entertained the idea that perhaps it was not John who fathered Ogarita but one of his brothers. Junius Jr. is eliminated as he was in California for ten years prior to coming east in May, 1864. He returned once during that time to get a divorce from his first wife. Joseph is too young, and also spent most of his time studying to become a medical doctor in Charleston and New York. In his early stage career, Edwin was every bit as much a dandy, womanizer and imbiber as his younger brother, John Wilkes Booth. Because Edwin was in both Boston and Providence earlier than John, we zeroed in on him. He was also the target of hostility in Miss Forrester's book, an animosity that continues down to the present generation. As early as 1857, Edwin was smitten with a tiny actress, Mary Devlin, whom he later married.

It is worthwhile to note that three of the Booth brothers spent a good deal of time in the Boston area, although not always at the same time. We have mentioned Edwin's earlier appearances in 1847 and 1857. He returns to Boston for two weeks in September of 1857 and again in March and October of 1858 at the Boston Theatre. On November 12th, in the same city and theater, he plays "Romeo" to Miss Devlin's "Juliet." Edwin marries Miss Devlin in New York on July 17, 1860. Brother John comes up from Richmond to be in attendance. (*We believe Martha Bellows is living in Boston during this time period. The evidence points that way as the city directories find Charles S. Bellows, mariner, house at Two Sigourney, Boston in 1857-1858, in Cambridge in 1861, and boarding at Three Washington. According to vital statistics, Charles A. Bellows was born there in 1861.)

On the chart in the previous chapter/file, we noted John Wilkes Booth's long run at the Boston Museum during the month of May in 1862. Toward the end of this year, Edwin, Mary and baby Edwina have a home in Dorchester where John occasionally visits. We have read that JWB may have owned property in Boston as well, quite probably in his mother's name. Mr. and Mrs. Edwin Booth are in the audience of the Boston Museum when John struts his stuff on stage in *Pescara* in January of 1863. His performance is acclaimed "extraordinary" by the *Boston Transcript.* (*Photographs of Booth were secured from Richard and Kellie Gutman, authors of *John Wilkes Booth Himself*. By telephone, we learned they have also published an article in the "Surratt Courier" about JWB buying land in Boston. They forwarded it to us along with an article from the *Boston Sunday Herald* dated April 11, 1915.)

From the Gutmans' article, we learned that in 1863 Booth requested his business manager, Joseph H. Simonds, to bid on lots on the north side of Commonwealth Avenue and the south side of Marlborough Street along with a corner lot on Commonwealth Avenue. JWB purchased the lot at 115 Commonwealth Avenue in Boston but listed it in his mother's name, Mary Ann Booth. Rosalie sent the first payment, and John the second. This indicates Rosalie was involved in John's business affairs to some extent, which confirms what other sources have said. Joseph H. Simonds was a teller in the Mechanics Bank. This friend, advisor and business manager of Booth was approximately the same age though he was born in Fitchburg, Massachusetts, and Booth in Maryland. We read that Simonds faded into obscurity after the assassination. He died in Buffalo, New York in 1888.

Orlando Tompkins, father to Eugene Tompkins, was also a friend of the Booths. Tompkins, born in 1818, was from Adamsville, Rhode Island, which is in southeastern RI in the Little Compton area. This friend had an apothecary shop in Boston and was part owner of the Boston Theatre. (*Edwin was playing in Boston when Booth assassinated the President.)

From both the Boston paper and the Gutmans' articles, we read that John Wilkes Booth gave Orlando a ring engraved "J.W.B. to O.T." on his last visit to Boston on April 6, 1865. These memento rings were often given between men as a token of friendship from the 1600s through the 1800s. (*According to Miss Forrester, Martha is said to have a similar one on her finger engraved "J.W.B. to I.M.M. see chapter/file 4.) This information supports our contention that Booth spent a great deal of time in Boston along with his appearances on stage. We now return to the previous source.

While Edwin is on stage in New York, his wife Mary stays in Dorchester. She is probably consumptive and is being cared for by a Dr. Erasmus Miller and his wife, who says, "It's a pleasure," caring for this young wife and mother. (*Strangely these are the very words Martha uses in her letter to her brother when she describes herself caring for the ill and the dying.) Shortly after John stopped at Dorchester on his way to New York in February of 1863, Mary passes away. The funeral service is held at Mount Auburn Cemetery in Cambridge with John and his brother-in-law, John Sleeper Clarke, coming up from Philadelphia. Edwin and Mary had a select coterie of friends in Boston, among them Julia Ward Howe (*author of the Battle Hymn of the Republic), Professor Agassiz (*he famous naturalist), Mrs. Cornelius Felton and a "spinster" lady from Cambridge, Emma Cary, (*both sisters to Richard Cary, a friend of Edwin's who is killed in the Civil War), and Wilson Barstow who is a relative of Mr. and Mrs. Richard Henry Stoddard. The Stoddards, poet and author published in *Atlantic Monthly* and *Harpers* magazines, were friends of Edwin and Mary when they lived in New York.

In the fall of that year John is back at the Athenaeum in Boston for a September and October run, where he has to fight off the ladies getting to and from the theater. The magnetism of the Booths for the ladies on and off stage makes us smile. The male authors, with great seriousness, tell us that neither Edwin nor John ever debauched the young innocent ladies as they were busy enough with actresses, ladies of the night—from the higher class brothels—and married ladies who had nothing better to do. It is not known whether our Martha was one of these married ladies who pursued the Booth brothers in the late 1850s or early 1860s.

John's last appearance on stage in Boston was during the months of April and May in 1864. Arthur F. Loux in his day-by-day account of JWB has him at the Parker House in Boston in late July. Others registered there, some with fictitious names, were from Toronto, Montreal and Baltimore. Several authorities in the field view this meeting as John's serious commitment in the plan to kidnap President Lincoln. (*It is interesting that Charles S. Bellows is no longer recorded in the city directories from 1864-1865 although he is listed as being in the Naval Service in that index. We believe he and Martha have more or less parted by this time.)

On the fifth of April, 1865, John Wilkes Booth is in Newport, Rhode Island, at the Aquidneck Hotel with a "lady". This lady is thought to be none other than the daughter of Senator Hale from New Hampshire to whom JWB is secretly engaged. He is back in Washington, DC, on the 11th, three days before the assassination. There are so many unanswered and unexplored intriguing situations in the Booth/Assassination story. They should keep both the professional and amateur historical detectives busy for years to come.

(*Unless some startling new facts appear, we have two final commentaries on the Booth/Martha association in this chapter/file. On the surface of things, it would appear unlikely that John became infatuated with Martha in 1859, 1860 and 1869 and fathered Ogarita, Charles and Harry Jerome Dresbach. Booth is wrapped up in a world of theater, oil/land speculation and intrigue. His attentions are devoted to actresses, ladies of the evening and the "other" ladies from high society who have political connections. As early as 1859, Martha has had at least two children before Ogarita's birth. In 1860 she is living in a boarding house with six months old Ogarita and Harry Bellows age five, and working in a millinery shop. As far as we can determine, Martha's life was a struggle to provide for her family. She is not a part of the glittering social and theatrical world of the time . . .though we are aware that all was not "glitter" in either one of these worlds. Still and all, what has plausibility or possibility got to do with that mysterious and erratic little fellow, Cupid?)

The feasibility of Martha "Lizola's" affiliation with the theatrical world as a dressmaker is a good one. If the clothes on Martha, Ogarita and young Zola in Miss Forrester's pictures are examples of her handiwork, then Martha was a fine seamstress. We still feel that there is a strong possibility our Burrillville Booths rubbed shoulders with those of the stage personalities in this manner. Especially since there doesn't seem to be any kind of evidence that Martha by any name was actually on stage, with the exception of Miss Forrester's undocumented assertions. This scenario of Martha being a seamstress for the theatre was proposed to Martha's present day descendants, but was met with a cool and no comment attitude.

(*It is difficult to believe this lady would have destroyed any playbills or news clippings proclaiming her as a fine actress in the role of Lady Macbeth or Medea. She reputedly saved those of all the other Booths. In the earliest pictures from *This One Mad Act*, Martha is a handsome and engaging looking woman, and obviously attracted the menfolk. We are not downgrading her attractiveness to the opposite sex in any way. She is both assertive and formidable, and when she wants something, she goes after it. For example, Martha's great granddaughter read us a story of her tracking down and bringing Edwin S. Bates back to their Canterbury home.)

Edwin was on stage in Boston when President Lincoln was assassinated. For a time it appeared America's most notable tragedian would forsake the stage forever due to his own and the public's reaction to his younger brother's crime. He appears as Hamlet in New York on January 32, 1866, and receives a standing ovation before the performance begins. Edwin has a six-week run in Boston the same year and continues regular engagements for some time, as does the durable Maggie Mitchell. In the early 1880s, Edwin and his daughter Edwina are living in his gray mansion at 23 Chestnut Street in the Beacon Hill area of Boston. The actor is a familiar figure in the streets of Boston. His natural melancholy has by now become "solid" as his offstage life becomes more tragic than those of his onstage characters. These tragedies involved his brother's assassination of the President, the death of his much loved first wife, Mary Devlin, and then the insanity and death of his second wife, also called Mary. He was America's living and breathing Hamlet. Curiously enough, not too many miles from Newport, Edwin and Edwina spend their summers at the cottage, Boothden, overlooking the "Seaconnet River and the glittering Atlantic." We have heard that a direct descendant of Edwin is still living in Rhode Island to this present day, but have not been able to verify it.)

Junius, Jr., has been slighted, but we add that he, too, was no stranger to Boston and its environs. The eldest Booth brother was acting manager for the Boston Theatre from 1865-1871. Junius, along with his actress wife, Agnes Perry, occasionally starred in Providence and Boston. This couple later established a grand Victorian summer hotel in Manchester, Massachusetts. June, as he was called by his family, was a well known and well liked figure in this city-by-the-sea. Junius and Edwin were both buried in Massachusetts soil. Junius in Roseland, and Edwin at Mount Auburn with his first wife, Mary.

(*The Booths were very much on the Boston scene. Martha et al would have had ample opportunity to see them on or off the stage. The possibility is suggested of Martha approaching Edwin regarding the father of her children and requesting aid. We can envision the cold fury of rejection by Edwin and a furious or stunned Martha. This could account for her family's hostility to his name. It is evident Ogarita received little help in promoting her career as an actress from any of the Booth family. This leads to one remaining item concerning the theater. We have been combing the indexes of various libraries looking for material which might lead us to more information on the stage careers and appearances of both the Maryland and the Burrillville Booths, when we came across another history of the Providence Stage. It is written by a fellow after our own hearts, who declares that apostrophes are a mystery to him, and then proceeds to write a most delightful accounting of the inside and outside theater scenes in Providence during the gay nineties.)

***Source**: Temples of Illusion by Roger Brett. Published in the USA by Brett, Theatrical. Printed by E. A. Johnson Co. (East Providence, RI, 1976).*

We learned a good deal about the varied entertainment and diversion to be found in Providence in the late eighteen hundreds and the early nineteen hundreds. The excitement and competitive show time fairly leaps at the reader from the pages of Mr. Brett's *Temples of Illusion*. He shows us for the first time the inside and the outside of theaters, museums, and academies where Edwin and John Wilkes Booth held forth to packed houses and entranced audiences. Now we know that "ballet girls" are not dancers but bit part actresses who could make from eight to fifteen dollars per week in Providence. Those who kept the illusion intact earned more. If Martha were a wardrobe mistress, she would have earned thirty dollars per week. Stage carpenters were valued at fifty dollars and scenic artists did best of all earning from sixty to one hundred per week. Some "stars" did not fetch more than a hundred dollars. Ogarita and Martha are kept in mind while reading about the "temples" in our own city. Miss Forrester has Ogarita Wilkes Booth on stage in Providence as early as 1877 with Minnie Maddern. (*An educated guess would have Miss Wilkes [Wallingford/Wilson] acting in Providence between 1878 and 1882. An promised accounting of Ogarita's trouping taken from her family's records has not yet been received.)

Local business people were often involved with theaters. A local stove manufacturer, Amos Barstow, built Music Hall on Westminster Street in 1871. The opening of the Theatre Comique in 1870 introduced the world of burlesque to the city of Providence. This "theatre" was housed in a wooden building on the northwest corner of Weybosset and Orange Streets. It was originally known as Lafayette Billiard Hall where the dashing young blades of Providence made frequent visits. Archer Stalker and John D. Hopkins introduced our city to this form of entertainment which had its American beginnings in New York at Niblo's Garden in 1866. Burlesque was a parody of a well known production with an ample supply of girls wearing scanty costumes. Needless to say polite society did not attend, but Stalker and Hopkins earned a goodly sum of take home pay each year.

(*The Theatre Comique has appeared before in William Wilson's divorce papers from Ogarita. The play actors he mentioned were not a local Burrillville troupe as previously suspected. Ogarita was well known here in our community as an actress, as was her mother, Martha. Providence is located about twenty-two miles from the Wilson Place, but by the 1880s trains were running on a regular basis between Pascoag and Providence.)

By 1876, the Theatre Comique had cleaned up its act, and the full length burlesque metamorphosed into minstrel and variety shows. A well known burlesque comedian, Don Mason, produced shows more appealing to the general public. We read that some of the best variety shows were held in the city of Providence with Friday nights as amateur night. (*We can envision Ogarita starting here and progressing to a stock company that played *Olivette, The Pirates of Penzance,* and even *Oliver Twist*. William Wilson on his farm/mill complex in Bridgeton must have been scandalized by his wife's behavior.) We read that under Mason and his partner Morrow, many a star of caliber began their stage careers here. Ogarita's name is not mentioned in *Temples of Illusion*, but the author did not mention many of the "ballet girls." The end man and the burlesque comedian were far more important. We would be remiss if we did not give a patriotic cheer to Providence's Yankee Doodle Dandy, George Michael Cohan, who was born in a tenement house in Wickenden Street in 1878.

Our investigations into the theatrical aspect of our case are just about complete. A few newspapers of the time will be scanned to see if Ogarita is listed anywhere. Even if she acted upon the stages in Providence, her small role as one of the "ballet girls" would not be mentioned. This in no way detracts from her ability as an actress, and we have read one favorable account of her stage presence. Her subsequent tours with various companies attest to her career as an actress.

We have come a long way from the bits and pieces related by residents in our northwestern corner of Rhode Island in regard to Martha and Ogarita, wife and daughter of John Wilkes Booth. Like Miss Forrester, we have sizable gaps in our pursuit of the "truth". It is time to reorganize and enlist some willing hands to make one more sweep of the available material. After this is accomplished, a

Theatre Comique - 1888
Photo courtesy of the Providence Public Library
Providence, Rhode Island

summation of the major and minor personalities discovered in our investigations will be given. Our most important goal is to find Martha's whereabouts during those hazy days between her birth and her marriage to seaman Bellows, along with the confused years shortly before, during, and after the Civil War. This is no small task we historical detectives have taken upon ourselves.

Chapter/file 18

ARTHUR "HARRY" D'ARCY - MARTHA'S OLD FLAME

We promised a summation of the major and minor characters in the last chapter/file, but an avalanche of information on "Harry" came to light within the last two weeks. As suspected, Arthur M. D'Arcy plays a significant role in Martha's life. This made it necessary to devote an entire chapter/file to him. Martha's elusiveness is not wanting when we begin to document both their lives.

Arthur "Harry" D'Arcy was not a fellow Confederate activist of John Wilkes Booth nor was he shot as a spy in West Virginia by Union soldiers, as written by Miss Forrester. He and Stevenson both wore Union blue and not Confederate gray. D'Arcy's death is recorded in the family chronology as January 28, 1888. It is curious the way both Miss Forrester and Martha eliminate this "gentleman" from their family history. Martha has him vanquished by two methods. In her "autobiography", she writes that she has "escaped" the charms of her adopted brother (Henry/Harry/Arthur), who was attentive to her only when "the other girls were not about."(*Miss Forrester reproduces her grandmother's dedication page in this "autobiography" by M. I. V. B. The handwriting compares favorably with that of Martha's on her pension application as well as in her letters to Alonzo and the insert in his journal. There is little doubt in our minds that this "story" was indeed written by Martha.) Her own words might shed some light on their relationship. "We were too much alike to be happy (wild, headstrong and self-willed) . . . he was after every handsome face he saw . . . I know there is many a one who has cause to remember him, to her dying day . . .but I did not love him. . . and I escaped." Martha also has Walter (*Arthur) dying in Baltimore in 1868 or 1869. This relates in some way to Miss Forrester's finding the death notice of Martha D'Arcy in a Baltimore newspaper in September of 1868. In order to look into this further, we need to return to Martha's letter written to Alonzo in 1869.

Source: *Letter from Martha L. D'Arcy from Baltimore to Alonzo dated August 18, 1869. Information gleaned from James O. Hall's commentaries to the sisters regarding this letter. Copy of his letter in our possession. (*Unfortunately, our request to the sisters for a copy of the original was not forthcoming. Apparently, they decided it would not be in their best interests to give it to us. There has been no reason given, but we respect their decision. Since they had given us a copy of Mr. Hall's reply when we visited Keene, it seems odd to hold back on the original letter.)*

According to this letter, Martha signed her letter "Martha L. D'Arcy." The "L" being for Lizola, a name she signed to other documents. (*We have yet to see this name on documents or anything else, but that does not mean it was not so.) She is living or married to a man she identified as "dearly beloved Walter" who is probably Arthur D'Arcy. He has either died or deserted her leaving her impoverished in Baltimore. (*We did check with the Enoch Pratt Free Library in Baltimore. Wesley L. Wilson, Department Head, promptly sent back the following: The surname of D'Arcy/Darcy does not appear in Baltimore City Directories from 1866 through 1869.) D'Arcy has his three children living with them in Baltimore. His parents took these children, leaving Martha with her two, Ogarita and Alonzo (*Charles A. Bellows). (*We have our doubts of the D'Arcys living in Baltimore with all five children.) Walter must have been the father of the baby born dead recently in 1869. (*If this is the case, John H. Stevenson married Martha when she was pregnant with D'Arcy's child. Could this have been related to the September 1868 death notice of a Martha D'Arcy about whom Miss Forrester writes? It seems more plausible that the child who died was named Martha D'Arcy.)

"Walter" turned Martha over to a friend, John H. Stevenson, whom she plans to marry and move to Boston, where his parents reside. (*At this writing she had been married to John since March. The fact that his parents live in Boston strengthens our case that John was known in that area.) She refers to "dear mother and grandmother" and "Aunt Amy." (*Of course we know these are Caroline, Betsey Benchley and Betsey's sister, Amy, who also appears to play a large roll in Martha's life.)

Martha states she has been to California and brought back

some seeds for Caroline from her favorite kind of plant. (*Miss Forrester's book and this letter both mention the seeds. Perhaps Stevenson or D'Arcy visited there after the war. We have our doubts about Martha with all those children trekking out to California with either one of them.) Martha wants Alonzo to take her in but would settle for her "mother's house in Providence." (*This is probably either Amy's or Caroline's house. Martha's appeals for help are more often directed to Alonzo rather than Caroline. Understandably, Martha appears to have some reservations regarding her stepmother.)

Mr. Hall suspects that Martha is not being entirely candid with her brother. The Baltimore address is a puzzler. Miss Forrester has her grandmother living in Pleasant Valley, Maryland, in 1865 after the assassination. (*This location is close to Westminster and about thirty-five miles or so from Bel Air, not that distant from Booth's Tudor Hall. Pleasant Valley was a mustering out point for the Union Army. Could Martha have been there to meet either D'Arcy or Stevenson? We have not read of either of them being discharged there. It may be one of Miss Forrester's ploys. She also writes of a friendship between Booth (D'Arcy?) and Stevenson, who comes to Martha's rescue at various times. Mr. Hall suggested that "Harry" and John may have met in the service where they served in the 2nd Regiment of the Mass. Cavalry, but in different companies. There is the possibility Miss Forrester might have taken this friendship and spun it into the Order of the Golden Circle story regarding Booth's and Stevenson's roles in the assassination and its aftermath.)

Source: *National Archives Military Records: D'Arcy's service records, declaration for pension for his widow, Sarah, marriage and death certificates, and several depositions from various family members. (*These records are of enormous help in doing this type of research. The Military National Archives do have an efficient and effective process. The following material prompted our separate chapter/file on D'Arcy. After reading this information, our thinking has shifted somewhat concerning Martha Louise Mills' activities and relationships. The Burrillville Town Hall records of Ogarita's marriage to William Wilson lists her mother's name as Martha Louise Mills.)*

Widow's Pension File: Sarah J. D'Arcy aged 62, widow of Arthur D'Arcy, living at 193 Warren Avenue in Boston. She applies for pension on October 10, 1890. Her husband was a private in the 8th Battery Mass. Light Artillery for six months from May 2 to

November 19, 1862. He died on the January 19, 1888 in Brooklyn, New York. Witnesses to this statement were Ella P. Gordon and Charles E. D'Arcy.

Marriage Certificate from the city of Boston: Sarah J. Smith age 21 and Arthur D'Arcy age 23 married on the 28th of November 1850 by Reverend Edward T. Taylor. First marriage of both parties who are both residents of Boston. From the Commonwealth of Massachusetts records of this marriage, we learn a bit more. He is listed as a carpenter born in Nova Scotia and her birthplace as Boston. City of Boston Registry Division could not find a birth for Sarah J. Smith between 1800 and 1849.

General Affidavit in pension claim of Sarah J. D'Arcy: Charles W. D'Arcy aged 49 who lives in the City of Boston in Suffolk County writes that Arthur M. D'Arcy is my brother . . . He left his family in East Boston in 1864 or 1865 or soon after the war. (*This is probably one of the times he was living with Martha and her family.) The person buried in Brooklyn under the name of Henry D'Arcy was my brother, Arthur D'Arcy. (*Was it Arthur/Harry/Henry/Walter who began the subterfuge of fictitious names?) He lived in New York City and Brooklyn for many years. After receiving word of his brother's death, Charles W. made burial arrangements in their father's lot. The telegram to Brooklyn arrived too late, and Arthur was already buried there. Charles states that Mrs. M. F. Walker (*his niece and Arthur's daughter) received a letter explaining why this was done.

Affidavit of Charles D'Arcy: Aged 35 living in the City of Boston. He states he knows Arthur M. is the husband of Sarah J. Charles, visited him in Brooklyn the last time in December of 1887, and lived with him there at one time. Arthur was living with a woman named Charlotte Byington who called herself Lottie D'Arcy and "he called her so." "He was also called Harry and Henry D'Arcy and he was my father." Charles notified his Uncle Charles of East Boston about making arrangements for burial. He has seen the letter from the woman called Lottie, who explains that she had not received the telegram in time to ship the body to Boston. Lottie also states that Henry D'Arcy was actually Arthur D'Arcy. (*Arthur/Henry apparently had an eye for the ladies as Martha stated in her story of her life. He shares some of the not so endearing traits of John Wilkes Booth.)

General Affidavit of June 27, 1890 from Warren C. Morse: (*Could he be from the family of Morses mentioned earlier in Chapter/file 7?) We learn that Sarah is an incurable invalid requiring constant care. An appeal is made for the government to support her claim as she is now supported by charity. Witnesses are L. W. Howes and Wm. M. McLean.

Affidavit of Ella P. Gordon, aged 42, of the City of Boston: Witnesses by C. Smith and S. C. Durfee. (*Alonzo writes of a Cyrus E. Smith of Burrillville born 1843, son of Samuel and Merenda Smith.) She also knows that Arthur D'Arcy is husband of Sarah J. as she visited him in Brooklyn before his death. He was called both Henry and Harry. Lottie D'Arcy's real name is Charlotte Byington, who has been living with Arthur in Brooklyn. (*Is Ella the daughter of Arthur? She does not state so.)

Affidavit from Charlotte C. Byington: Aged 45 living in Brooklyn, County of Kings, dated April 30, 1891. She was acquainted with Arthur D'Arcy, who died in her house and was buried as Henry D'Arcy. She knows he is the same person who was the reputed husband of Sarah J. D'Arcy. She has known him from about 1883 until his death. (*Looks as though she changed the 1883 after writing 1873. . .might be a slip of the pen.) She notified his daughter, Mrs. Walker, that her father was dead. But, she did not receive the telegram asking that he be buried in Boston until the afternoon after the funeral. In a day or so she wrote to Mrs. Walker acknowledging the receipt of the telegram and the circumstances encountered. Signed Mrs. Charlotte C. Byington. Witnesses were Emily J. Cameron and Maria E. Walker. (*Signature was written over. Mrs. Byington wrote D'Arcy and then corrected it. Looks as though Mrs. Walker went to Brooklyn to get this deposition for her mother.)

Transcript from the records of Deaths in the City of Brooklyn: Henry D'Arci aged 62 died in January 29, 1888, in the city of Brooklyn at 63 South Fourth Street of valvular disease of the heart. He resided in the city for ten years. Nova Scotia was the birthplace of "Henry" as well as that of his mother and father (*though not named). He was buried at Linden Hill by William H. Bryan, undertaker, and George St. Lindsey served as the coroner. (*It is curious that Ogarita did not wear the brooch with John Wilkes Booth's picture in it until both Martha and Arthur D'Arcy died.)

Deposition in case of Sarah J. D'Arcy No. 471575 on the 18th of June, 1891 at Boston. Maria E. Walker appears before J. A. Williamson, a special examiner of the pension office. Marie is 32 years old and the wife of Charles M. Walker living at 361 Westchester Park. She is the daughter of Sarah J. D'Arcy, who until this time has supported herself but now she is "laid up" and is dependent upon her children. Her father's name was Arthur McNult D'Arcy, but he never liked the name "McNult" and he never signed

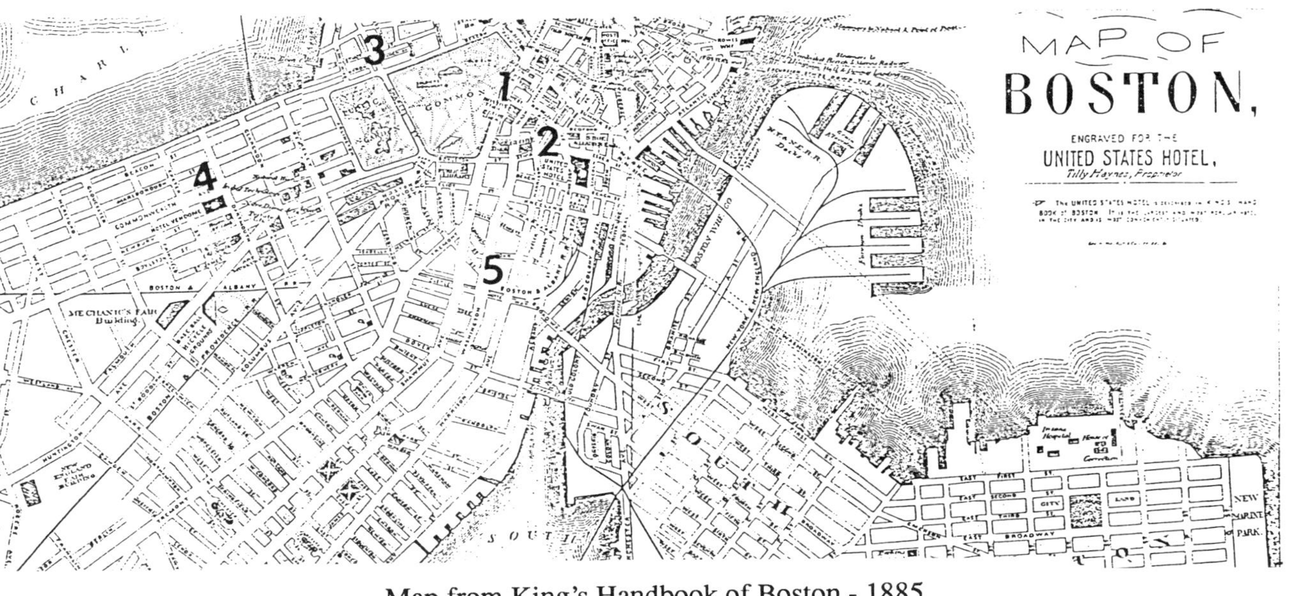

Map from King's Handbook of Boston - 1885
1 - Boston Theatre - Where Edwin Booth starred.
2 - Globe Theatre - Where Charlotte Cushman appeared.
3 - Chestnut Street - Edwin and Edwina live at #23.
4 - Commonwealth Avenue - John W. Booth purchased a lot here.
5 - Washington Street - One of Martha's many street addresses.

Map from King's Handbook of Boston - 1885
1 - East Boston - D'Arcy Family lived here at Lexington Avenue.
2 - Pearl Street - Where Miss Forrester attended school.
3 - Boston Museum - Where John Wilkes Booth appeared.
4 - Howard Athenaeum - Another theatre where JWB appeared.

his name in any other way except Arthur D'Arcy. She states her father, shortly after his discharge, got into the habit of "leaving my mother and going with other women." (*This could be as early as 1862 when he was indeed discharged due to wounds received. He reenlisted in November of 1864 and was recorded as a deserter in May, 1865.) The first was a Mrs. Martha Bellows. (*Not Izola?) After staying awhile with her, he left and went with another woman named Mrs. Mason. (*We have come across several Masons in our quest. A comedian, Dan Mason of the Theatre Comique, came to Providence in 1877 and became one of its proprietors and stock members in 1880. Edward M. Brown had a sister named Mrs. Mary O. Mason, who would have been too old to be the person mentioned. Alonzo mentions several Masons in his journals. Among them are: Ben Mason died 1873 age 95 in Swansea, Massachusetts, Edmund Mason died 1873 age 66 in Pawtucket, and Sarah Mason, widow of George Mason, died 1871 age 68 in Pawtucket.) Maria relates that her father left Boston for New York City, probably with the Mason woman. He returned to Boston and lived with Maria and his brothers at different times. (*Unfortunately, no dates given). During this time, he told her he was living in New York with a woman but did not say what her name was. Maria continues that when she went to Brooklyn last April to see about her mother's pension, she learned the person was Charlotte Byington. (*This appears to be in the late 1880s after her father passed away.) She recognized Charlotte as the woman who caused her father to leave his family when Maria was fifteen years old. Maria was born in 1859 around the same time as Ogarita. D'Arcy apparently returned around 1874 to live with his wife, Sarah, for a short time at his father's request. Arthur would not work or help support his wife and she finally asked him to leave. This is when he took up with "Lottie" Byington.

Arthur returned to Boston about five or six years prior to his death in very poor health. He tried to sell subscriptions to books. Maria assisted him with money, not because she approved of his conduct towards her mother, but because "he was my father and I felt sympathy for him in his condition."

(*We assume he went back to Lottie after this, because that is where he died.) She continues with material similar to the other depositions adding that Mrs. Byington said she always called him "Harry", and that his occupation was renting rooms. (*Rooms to Mrs. Byington's home, we suspect. Our Harry appears to be a roving man with a roving eye and tends to let the women in his life support him. The above depositions do confirm that he lived with

Martha Bellows at least for a while shortly after the war, or perhaps as we have suggested, during the war. We suspect that their relationship began earlier. There is another possibility of a family connection which we will relate later in this chapter/file. It is clear that Mrs. Walker knew Mrs. Martha Bellows though she did not know the first names of Mrs. Mason nor Mrs. Byington until later years. This also suggests that Martha knew of the D'Arcy family and that they knew who she was.)

Pension File results: Apparently Arthur deserted on May 27, 1865 from the 2nd Mass. Cavalry. A letter from the War Department in Washington to the Commissioner of Pensions states this charge was removed on August 18, 1891. Sarah did not live very long to enjoy the eight dollars per month pension. On November 30, 1895, we read that her pension is dropped due to failure to claim. The pension process which began March 4, 1890 takes nearly two years to complete. (*Military and federal red tape was as prevalent then as now.) Witnesses on one of the general affidavits regarding Sarah's pension claim were Ella P. Gordon of 396 Northampton Street and W. C. Morse of 296 Northampton Street in Boston.

Source: *Arthur M. D'Arcy Service Records. National Archives.*

We already know from Sarah's deposition that D'Arcy enlisted in May of 1862 and was honorably discharged on November the same year. This is supported by an undated letter from John N. Coffin late Lieut. 8th Mass. Battery, who writes that Private Arthur D'Arcy while in the line of his duty in service at the battle of South Mountain, Maryland, about September 14, 1862 was struck by a grapeshot in his left side, which broke two of his ribs, and thereby incapacitated him from performing military duty. (*We assume he returned home to Boston a hero.)

Arthur reenlists on November 11, 1864 in the 2nd Regiment of Cavalry Massachusetts Volunteers for three years, "unless sooner discharged by proper authority." We learn he was born in Annapolis, Nova Scotia. He is thirty-one and a carpenter. He received $100 of his bounty at South Hadley in Hampshire County, Massachusetts. (*Apparently a military base similar to Readville where Stevenson's outfit originated.) He is 5 feet 10 1/2 inches high with hazel eyes, dark hair, fair complexion. (*The tallest of Martha's beaux thus far. The dark hair is interesting as Miss Forrester makes a great deal of the black hair in her family . . . particularly of her grandmother's, Ogarita's, Harry's and, of course, Booth's. Don't we wish we had a picture of Private Arthur D'Arcy.)

Desertion charges against Arthur D'Arcy from various records: These do get confusing and an attempt will be made to strip the information down to the bare bones. The first offense was at the permanent camp of the 1st Cav. Div. on January 21, 1865 when "this man D'Arcy" absented himself from camp without permission and returned after the detachment to which he belongs (*2nd Mass.) had left. The Brigade Sergeant had sent for him and notified him of the intended departure of his detachment, which he failed to obey. The major writes that "I do not believe that the man would desert if an opportunity offered, but he disobeyed orders and remained absent a day and night returning after his company had left . . . and alleges as a reason that his wife was sick." The sergeant further states, "D'Arcy came to camp and packed up his clothing, camp and garrison equipage, and then left the line."

(*The sick wife excuse lingers on to our modern times. Which "wife" was it? Sarah or Martha or someone else? If he is in Maryland, he certainly would not have had time to get back to Boston and Sarah. As there are no further statements, we assume he found his detachment and continued to serve. Both he and Stevenson are in the 2nd Mass. Cavalry though in different companies. It is possible they met during the War Between the States.)

The second desertion charge was more serious and had ramifications. D'Arcy deserted May 27, 1865 at Bladensburg, Maryland. (*This is after the war was over.) He is still missing on the muster roles of Co. "I" at Clouds Mills, Virginia, on May 31, 1865 and again when the Company musters out at Fairfax Court House, Virginia, on July 20, 1865. D'Arcy was not paid his ordinance due $63.80 nor is he entitled to the second half of his Massachusetts bounty. (*John H. Stevenson also shows up missing and listed as deserted on the muster out of Company "E" on the same date. Even though both Stevenson and D'Arcy are listed as deserted in Fairfax, they did not necessarily desert there. We are not suggesting they left together, but rather that the 2nd Mass. Cavalry en mass went from the Grand Review in Washington, DC on May 23rd to Clouds Mills and on to Fairfax Court House to be mustered out. According to Stevenson's records, the 2nd Mass. Cavalry went from there to the Fairfax Court House—without Stevenson and D'Arcy—and then dispersed to the individual camps of their home bases, such as Readville and South Hadley, Massachusetts. Apparently, they both decided to miss the fanfare after the end of the war. We are not sure where Stevenson stayed after he left the service, though we know Arthur made his way back to Boston.)

A letter from Headquarters East in New York City by command of General Hooker to Colonel Clark in Boston dated July 2, 1865, states that Private Arthur D'Arcy be held prisoner along with the witnesses subject to Lt. Corbin's recognition. (*How D'arcy made out is unknown, but we would be very interested to see who the witnesses were in this case.) The charges of desertion were not removed until August 18, 1891. A discharge certificate was then given stating he left the service as of May 27, 1865. The Adjutant General's report of the 2nd Regiment of the Mass. Vol. Cavalry does not record Arthur D'Arcy as deserted. A great many names on the same page have this disgrace posted for posterity. Another source, however, lists him as being a deserter.

Source: *Record of Massachusetts Volunteers, 1861-1865 Published by the Adjutant General of Massachusetts. Volume 1, Wright & Potter. (Boston, 1868).*

DeArcey, Arthur. 2nd Regiment, Cavalry Massachusetts Volunteers, Co. "I" Age 31. Bounty 4325. Residence or place credited to enlistment: So. Hadley, MA on November 11, 1864 and listed as deserted May 27, 1865.

Source: *Arthur M. D'Arcy Service Records. National Archives.*

An undated and unaddressed letter from Lt. Col. Fitzsimmons of the 2nd Mass. Cavalry puts in a good word for D'Arcy. He says, "It appears he was left behind his detachment owing to the illness of his ribs. He bears an excellent reputation as a soldier. Please release him unless you know of some flagrant violation of camp rules on his part other than those stated." D'Arcy was "held" on the second charge of desertion, so this is probably referring to the May 27th incident. There is another note dated August 2, 1865 from Readville (*also the mustering out place for Stevenson's company). "Respectfully returned to Col. Clark with the remark that D'Arcy deserted from the Guard July 29th, 1865." Signed by a captain, but we are unable to decipher his name.

(*There were no more papers or commentaries regarding D'Arcy's desertion. Since his wife, Sarah, had to have the charges removed before she could collect her pension, we assume his final status was as a deserter. Could this interesting bit of information have anything to do with Martha's so-called flight in 1865, not from the Shenandoah Valley but from Massachusetts to Burrillville and/or Baltimore. And, with Arthur D'Arcy and not John Wilkes Booth?

This is the proper time frame for her appearance in Burrillville, approximately three months after the assassination.)

It is difficult to say how Martha actually fits into the above scenario except that she lived with both Stevenson and D'Arcy and married John in Baltimore. Certainly their service records indicate they both would have known the Virginia, Maryland and Washington areas rather well. None of this tells us where, when or how Martha met either one of them. We have suggested that the naming of two of her sons, Harry (Bellows b. 1855) and Harry Jerome Dresbach (Stevenson b. 1871) may indicate she was enthralled with "Harry" D'Arcy at an early age. He and Sarah J. Smith were married in Boston in 1850.

We have been informed of a love poem written in 1856 by Martha about D'Arcy in the possession of Gail Merrifield Papp. This certainly suggests that Martha had a case on Harry long before the "shortly before or after the end of the war" indicated by Arthur D'Arcy's brother in his deposition. This was a romantic age, and Martha was very much a part of it. The writing of poetry was prevalent in America during this time period. Both men and women labored over poetic lines devoted to the love of a person, place or thing. There are a few examples of Martha's poetry in *This One Mad Act*.

A few remarks on desertion may be in order. In nearly every Civil War muster or roll call we have seen, desertion is prevalent. It was not always intentional, but mainly the failure of a soldier to appear at the roll call of his company, detachment, or regiment. In other circumstances, the man was missing, lost, wounded or hastily recruited by another company or commanding officer. We are not defending D'Arcy or Stevenson, but giving more of the whole picture so the "truth" may be found. The desertion dates of both Arthur and John H. have not matched. Stevenson's blots on his record were removed on July 16, 1865 and again on September 8, 1874. This means he actively sought to have them erased. D'Arcy's were not changed until after he died. There is no firm evidence in our possession that D'Arcy and Stevenson were service buddies, but the possibility is there.

It has been suggested that the D'Arcy family of Boston, not Baltimore, brought up Martha, as Miss Forrester relates in her story, but with differences. Mr. and Mrs. D'Arcy were friends of Abraham A. Mills and took in Martha after her mother's death, or possibly after her father's death in 1847. (*Mrs. D'Arcy [the elusive Fanny?] could be Abraham's sister. If she were, Martha would have been infatuated with her first cousin, Arthur. Though this is possible, we still contend that Martha lived and was brought up by the Benchley family of Providence for part of her childhood. Granted, we have not been able to locate her in any census even as "a female child between such and such age.")

(*Our main concern with the D'Arcy relationship is the fact that Martha never really discovered the names of her maternal grandparents or even where her parents were married. If indeed the Mills and the D'Arcys had been life-long friends and/or Fanny related to Abraham, why wouldn't they supply Martha with the knowledge she so desperately wants in the latter years of her life? We agree that Martha was in some way acquainted with the D'Arcy family . . . other than just her romance with Arthur. Could she have worked for the family as a young girl and became infatuated with the engaging Arthur McNult D'Arcy? Young women were often employed in this manner just as were young men "hired out" to relatives and neighbors. There has been no evidence found that puts Abraham in Boston where the D'Arcys reside. His associations seem to be with Providence, Pawtucket, Albany and various places in Connecticut.)

The Bellows family, who were native to the Boston area, could well be affiliated with the D'Arcys. There were two named Charles in the D'Arcy family as well as two in the Bellows family. Charles Still Bellows' mother, Sarah, is living as a widow in Cambridge in 1860 and 1880. Stevenson could also have been a Boston boy at one time, as Martha mentions in her letters to Alonzo that they are going back to Boston where John's parents are living. Being in the same area during the same time period does not a relationship make, but the possibility is there. We are disappointed in the lack of positive evidence of the Mill/Bellows/D'Arcys/Stevensons sharing more than just Martha.

We along with other researchers have recently unearthed some facts about the D'Arcy family of Massachusetts. Many discoveries appear to be made in this manner—independently and simultaneously. David Putnam, son of Mrs. Rosamond Putnam and a genealogist in his own right, gathered this information by the various means of his trade. In our research, similar information has been discovered at the Fingold Library at City Hall in Boston and from the Archives of the New England Genealogical Society on Newbury Street in the same city. The following is a composite of these unearthings.

The D'Arcy family came from Nova Scotia when Francis and Eleanor D'Arcy came to Boston about 1830-1840. They are listed in the 1850 Boston Census. Francis died in 1857 and was buried in Woodlawn Cemetery in Everett, Massachusetts. Eleanor is living as a widow at 18 Lexington Street in East Boston from 1863-1865. It has been suggested that Eleanor might be Aunt Fanny, although we find the name, Fanny, to be a full name and not a nickname during this time period. According to Miss Forrester, she and her grandmother, Martha, visit Aunt Fanny in the Back Bay area in the late 1880s on their expeditions to Boston from Canterbury.

Source: *Vital Records of Rhode Island (Providence). Birth, Death and Marriages Volumes I and II 1851-1870 as compiled by Edwin M. Snow, M.D., City Registrar. Published by Sidney S. Rider (Providence, Rhode Island, 1880).*

(*This might be a good time to add a few D'Arcys located in the Rhode Island Directories. A Francis E. D'Arcy, son of John, died in Providence in 1863. A Mary D'Arcy married Patrick Sullivan in 1865, and a William D'Arcy married Lucy Keith in 1858. There is a Charles A. Bellows who married a Clara Carpenter in 1867. Our Charles Bellows was born in 1861 in Cambridge, so this is not he. There are many D'Arcys in both Pawtucket and Providence using a variety of spellings of the surname. The Nova Scotia D'Arcys tend to use the European spelling. A Michael D'Arcy, marble polisher, is living at 109 South Main Street in 1852-53. A Thomas D'Arcy in 1854-55 is at 44 Broad Street, occupation laborer. In 1859 Thomas is at 301 Broad Street where he has a market, then he disappears from the city records. The 1859 date is interesting as this is the conception and birth year of Ogarita.)

Source: David Putnam, Fingold Library at City Hall in Boston, Archives of the New England Genealogical Society.

We find James and Jerusha D'Arcy appearing in Boston living next to Francis in 1850. They also may have been in Boston area previously to this appearance. Several children were born to them in Nova Scotia and in Boston. Among them are: Edwin B., Charles W., John S., Stephen J., and our own Arthur McNult. Martha claims in her autobiography to have been adopted by a family of several sons, and here is one tailored to our investigations. We also learn that the D'Arcy's have a daughter named Maria and possibly an Ella as well. with the girls much younger than the sons. Martha wrote to Alonzo in the beginning of 1886 that she received money from "someone". It could not have been Jerusha D'Arcy because she died in September of that year.

Abraham Mills' middle name was Amherst, and Mr. Putnam notes that there is an Amherst in Nova Scotia . . . as well as in New Hampshire and Massachusetts, we might add. Is it possible that the Mills and D'Arcy families both originated in Amherst, Nova Scotia? Consider the fact that the D'Arcy family has two people named Charles amongst them, and in the 1860 census, Eleanor D'Arcy has three of her boys listed as seamen. Charles Still Bellows would have been closer to their age group than Abraham Mills. It can be seen just how far one has to stretch the imagination to connect two seemingly unrelated points. The surprising thing is that fifty percent of the time there is a connection.

Boston City Directories record the D'Arcy family living in East Boston during 1861-1865. (*Wives names are not listed.) There are two Arthurs and two Johns. The men in the family tend to lean toward the building trades. James, the father, is listed as a carpenter living at 77 Princeton with Charles W., a clerk . An Arthur D'Arcy and a John Arthur D'Arcy are plasterers living on Lexington Street along with Eleanor, widow of Francis. We nail down our Arthur in 1865 where he is listed as a houseright, at Harmony Place, East Boston, Mass. Cavalry. We can safely conclude that Martha, the Bellows, and the D'Arcy family from Nova Scotia are all in Boston during the 1850s and 1860s. For the most part, this is supported by various vital statistics from Boston.

Source: *This One Mad Act by Izola Forrester.*

It is time to review what Miss Forrester tells us about Arthur/Harry D'Arcy and his role in her grandmother's life. She writes that Harry is the only member of this family to remain loyal to Martha after her elopement with John Wilkes Booth in 1859. The D'Arcy boys are growing up in Maryland not too far from the Booths farm near Bel Air. It is not quite clear whether they are acquainted with the Booths. (*If they had been, then JWB would certainly have known Martha.) Arthur is in love with his cousin. Nevertheless, he is witness to Izola and John's marriage in Cos Cob, Connecticut. (*Could we substitute Charles Bellows for Booth and Boston for Bel Air and Cos Cob? We need to remember it is a young Zola who is recording her grandmother's past.) According to her, several people saw the marriage certificate from the Connecticut marriage. Among them were Mr. Forrester, Harry and Harry's wife, who destroyed much of the family papers when she divorced him. It is our belief that no one takes much stock in the marriage of Booth and Martha. But, the marriage certificate which appeared is interesting. Mrs. Gayle Merrifield Papp wrote of it in her accounts to her aunts in New Hampshire. It was in the possession of James O. Hall, who later declared it a forgery. He wrote us that this JWB used the name John Byron Wilkes Booth on this paper. The spurious marriage record was dated January 9, 1859, and shows D'Arcy as a witness to the wedding of Martha Mills D'Arcy and Booth at Dingletown, Connecticut, Rev. Peleg Weaver officiating.

There are so many curious items here. Where is Dingletown? Why didn't Martha use the name Izola? Why the inclusion of Byron in Booth's name? The elder Booths did have a son who died named Byron. The wife of Eugene Allen of Pawtucket, Adir or Ader B. Homer, claimed to be a relative of Lord Byron. She and Eugene (*cousin to Alonzo A. S. Mills) were married in 1876 at Central Falls, Rhode Island. This information was received from the same lady, Mrs. Collins, who knew the location of Caroline's gravesite. Mrs. Collins is also a descendant of the Benchley/Allen families.

We are not sure the above means anything at all, and question if Dingletown is in jest Dingle Bay in Ireland. Mrs. Papp had written to her aunts that it was a forgery—a joke. And so it would seem. (*We suspect Arthur McNult D'Arcy has something to do with this story about his being a witness to Booth's and Martha's wedding, though we have our doubts about his being involved with the forged certificate.)

Miss Forrester tells us of the friendship that develops between Harry and John Wilkes Booth. They join the Richmond Grays when John Brown raids Harpers Ferry and stand guard after he is captured. (*Wilkes did stand guard over John Brown, though he was not actually a member of the Richmond Grays. He was not at Harper's Ferry during the raid.) As the war continues, they both devote themselves to the Southern cause serving as spies. The most interesting point here is the notation that D'Arcy is stagestruck and a follower of Booth. There is the veiled hint it was Arthur D'Arcy who attempted a stage career. This would fit neatly into naming Ogarita after the character in the melodrama "Sea of Ice."

D'Arcy shares a great deal of the looks and personality of JWB . . . dark hair, fair skin and a ladies' man. Young Zola describes him from a picture in Aunt Fanny's house. He is handsome with an engaging and frank face with a black moustache carefully curled, as Ogarita adds at one point in the story. (*The friendship between Booth and Stevenson might reflect the same between Arthur M. D'Arcy and John H. Stevenson. This is exactly the way Miss Forrester and Martha blend reality with fiction. Including D'Arcy in this complicated story tends to negate a romance between Martha and John Wilkes Booth. Was Arthur D'Arcy the real love of our Burrillville Booth and possibly Ogarita's father? Our main problem with this suggestion is that we have no firm dates to verify when D'Arcy and Martha were romantically active. The early love poem of 1856 and the deposition of Arthur's uncle suggesting he left Sarah before or after the war (*1862-1865) suggests a decade of an on-again off-again romance between them. Sarah's children certainly know about this woman, Mrs. Martha Bellows, and are not very pleased.)

How the long-suffering seaman Bellows fits into this picture is another question. Could it have been Arthur who was witness to the marriage between our mariner and our Burrillville Booth? Was it Arthur, who resembles Booth, and not Stevenson, who encouraged Martha to become a Mrs. Booth in Baltimore in 1869? Did he also encourage her to visit Mrs. Rogers during that time frame? Again we are stymied by the lack of definite times and definite places. We are not convinced that D'Arcy was ever in Baltimore living with Martha. We do know Stevenson was there as early as 1867 and Martha in 1869. There is a veil thrown over Martha's activities during this particular time in the 1860s. The destruction of family materials for whatever reason for this period is questionable. Miss Forrester writes that Martha did it out of fear for her life after the assassination and to protect Booth after she learned of his "escape." She also has Ella Stevenson destroying the same materials in order to erase her "Harry" out of her life. Once again it is Miss Forrester, who in her endeavor to prove her mother's Boothness, tends to destroy the possibility of it. Still, there is a nagging doubt in our minds, probably because we cannot actually prove that it did not happen. (*As the historian of Canterbury, Mr. Underhill, said in the *Norwich Bulletin*, "You want to believe it.") None of this discounts the slim possibility that Martha met Booth in 1859 in Providence or Boston, with Ogarita being the love child, as a result of this meeting. Maria D'Arcy was born in the same year, if our addition and subtraction of dates are correct.

One final attempt is made to resolve some of the contradictory and/or missing data from our files. A sweep of the available data will be made to see if some of the empty spaces can be filled in our investigation of the Burrillville Booths. As promised at the end of the previous chapter/file, we begin with a summation of the major and minor personalities involved.

Chapter/File 19

SUMMATION OF MAJOR & MINOR PERSONALITIES

While the exploits of Arthur McNult D'Arcy are still fresh, we would like to extend a possibility which has little verifiable data to back it except for the time frame coincidence and a few other facts already noted. Although the local lore concerning the elusive Booths of Burrillville does not always offer us the same picture, there is one segment which remains constant. It is the belief that John Wilkes Booth was here in Burrillville and "hid out" for some time. Lore has it that his gravesite is located in the Bridgeton area. It is, supposedly, not too distant from the Brown Farm at the top of Whipple Hill and Warner Lane near an old granite quarry site. We have been unable to locate it even after being given directions. Those who have never heard of Martha and her family still insist that Booth was here "after the assassination of President Lincoln on the Wilson and Brown farms." (*This area is considered to be as close to the end of the world as it is possible to get. Even those who surveyed for Roger Williams in 1660 declared it uninhabitable.)

Our belief that Booth did not escape from the Garrett Tobacco barn has been presented previously. To eliminate any doubts in our mind, we needed to find someone who would be hiding in this area in 1865 who resembled JWB. Seaman Bellows' likeness has already been noted with the exception of his dark complexion. Booth was famous for the marble-like quality of his complexion along with his glossy black hair. Another candidate for the mysterious stranger in the northwest corner of Rhode Island is Arthur M. D'Arcy. His description fits that of the actor/assassin as well, if not better, although he was a shade taller. Arthur's moustache in particular and his fondness for the ladies make the resemblance even stronger. If D'Arcy were on the run from the military officials after May 27, 1865 and again on July 29th, it would fit in rather well with the appearance of a stranger in our midst. He may well be our mysterious Burrillville Booth. Martha seems to have known Arthur at least since 1856 and was still associated with him as late as 1869 in Baltimore. It is still our belief that Martha and her family were on the Brown farm now and again during this same time. The closeness between Martha and Alonzo, and her familiarity with the Brown farm and those who lived in this area, seem to make this plausible. Of course, this is all sheer conjecture on our part.

All our suspects have not been chased down and put into neat little catagories. But, we are not writing fiction, and life is not always as obliging or as controllable as it is in a good detective story. Real life cases are seldom sewn up to everyone's satisfaction. At this point, we should like to round up the last of our findings and fill in as many of the missing pieces as possible.

Case One Abraham/Abram Amherst Mills (1820-1847).

Research done by others did turn up an Abram Mills marrying a Mary A. Whitney August 14, 1836, in the Baptist Church in Stamford, Connecticut. Both are listed as of Stamford. Some researchers think this is indeed the mother and father of our Martha L. Mills. They are in the correct time frame, and Martha often lists herself as being born in Stanford/Stamford. Further investigation lists a Mary Anne Whitney born March 19, 1801 in Stamford. If this were indeed the correct Mary, then Abram was only sixteen when he married the thirty-five year old Mary A. Whitney, daughter of Josiah Whitney and Mary Smith. This Mary also married George Mather at Darien, Connecticut, on October 22, 1826. They lived in Darien as late as 1874. Of course, there could have been another Mary A. Whitney who was younger and living in Stamford, though she has not been found in the Connecticut records. Neither has Abraham A. Mills., though there was an infant named Abraham Mills who died in Stamford on May 7, 1841. He may or may not fit into our Mills family portrait. We learned from the Rhode Island Seaman's Protection Registry that Abraham Mills was certified as a mariner on December 28, 1844. His name here is Abraham A. Mills, age 25, from Southport, CT, and of light complexion. These facts convinced us he was indeed from Southport. The names Mary A. Mills and Abraham/Abram Mills, are common in our southern New England States. According to the Pawtucket Records, an Abraham Mills from England died in 1898 at 66 years of age. His mother's name was Sarah.

Thanks to the enduring research of Miss Shinsel, we know

that Abraham Mills was a member of the Good Samaritan Lodge #8 of the I.O.O.F. According to the newspapers of that day, he was given a lodge funeral service both in Albany and Providence. The Lodge Order #8, which began in April of 1845, is still active in the city of Pawtucket. We were disappointed in not finding his name amongst their records. It is possible he transferred his membership from somewhere else, as the names listed in the Pawtucket Order only include those who were originally initiated into that particular lodge. Abraham/Abram's middle name of Amherst has been of little help in locating him.

Strangely enough, Miss Forrester continues to insist throughout her writings that Martha's father's people were a combination of Mills, Standish and Benchley. One of Abraham's death notices has his parents as John and Sarah Mills of Southport. Another lists them as Joseph and Sarah Mills. Sarah's maiden name is not indicated. Is it possible Sarah was from the Benchley family? This might account for Miss Forrester's confusion about the Benchley family name. Alonzo has the name Standish as his second middle name, but that, too, has not been of much help. There doesn't seem to be any other affiliation with either the name Amherst or Standish in this extended family. Both of these middle names come from Alonzo's journals.

The Pawtucket City Hall death records note that Abraham died of ship's (typhoid) fever. It does not say he died aboard ship. If he were on board and near Albany, New York, he could possibly have been traveling up the Hudson over the Erie Canal and onto the Great Lakes. New York was the waterway to the west. There are many New York state affiliations with Martha's family as well as with those who lived in Burrillville.

A letter was received from Arthur R. Raymond, treasurer of the Good Samaritan Lodge #8 I.O.O.F. of Pawtucket, Rhode Island, just as we were closing the file on Abraham/Abram Mills. Mr. Raymond resides in Florida during the winter months and did not review our request for information until he returned to Rhode Island for the summer. He was both kind and patient enough to scan the minutes of the Lodge's meetings during the time mariner Mills would have been in Rhode Island, according to the RI Seaman's Records in 1844. Mr. Raymond provided us with six pages of documentation on Martha's father which tended to contradict the information we had previously received.

In September of 1846, Abraham A. Mills was placed on the ballot for membership into the Pawtucket Lodge #8. He was initiated into the order in October of the same year along with Alexander

Young. Many familiar surnames are listed throughout the minutes of these meetings: I.T. Jenks, Nathan M. Brown, Charles Allen, etc. As we suspected all along, this indicates that Abrahm was in close association with the extended families of the Benchleys, Browns, Allens and Millers in the Providence/Pawtucket areas. Seaman Mills moved quickly through the ranks and was appointed Guardian in January of 1847. Brother Barton Miller was the secretary at that time. Another Miller/Mills association is found.

We followed Barton Miller's participation in the I.O.O.F. with interest. The death of Caroline's husband and Alonzo Mills' father in Albany in 1847 was duly noted. It was Brother Miller who went to Albany to bring back Abram Mills' body. The Lodge also paid the expenses for his funeral, $35.90. It was Barton Miller and John Perry who headed the committee to take care of Brother Mills' funeral arrangements. Joseph Smith requested and received payment for wood and coal delivered to Widow Mills (*Caroline) in October. The title "Brother" is used for lodge members. This probably explains Alonzo's use of that term throughout his journals. We made much ado of Brother Morse in Chapter/file 7 in relation to his capitalistic and evangelistic activities in Putnam, Connecticut, and the Douglas Camp Grounds in Massachusetts. Obviously, Brother Morse was a lodge member known to Alonzo and quite probably to Martha as well. The surname, Morse, was also on one of the D'Arcy affidavits. (*We still wonder why Alonzo did not include the D'Arcy name anywhere in his discovered writings. Martha signed her name as D'Arcy when she wrote him from Baltimore; therefore, he was aware of the name. Was Alonzo being discreet when he failed to mention it? Or was there another reason for his forgetfulness?)

As mentioned previously, Lodge member John Perry helped with Abraham Mills' funeral arrangements. From the New England Historic Genealogical Society's archives, it was discovered that John Augustus Perry's family share not only a plot but a "large upright stone" inscribed with both the D'Arcy and Perry family names in the Woodlawn Cemetery at Everett, Massachusetts. If John Perry were a member of the same family, it would explain his interest in helping the Widow Mills. There are too many coincidences in Martha Mills' history not to take at least some of them as the truth.

From these archive records, we learned that James D'Arcy, father of Arthur (*Harry/Walter/Henry) McNult D'Arcy, is buried here along with Jerusha, his wife. In 1914, Sarah Francis D'Arcy was the last D'Arcy to be interred here. The Perry family members were exhumed from this plot and moved to Forestdale Cemetery in

Malden in 1920. Unfortunately, the death year for John August Perry is not recorded. We could not positively connect the Samaritan, John Perry, with the one whose family shared their final resting place with the D'Arcy family. On looking further, neither a Bellows nor a Mills were discovered buried near the D'Arcy/Perry plot.

Francis D'Arcy, either brother or uncle to James, shared his plot in Woodlawn Cemetery with a Kendric family, John F. Buckley, and Charlotte Babcock. We also learned that Francis came from Ireland and his parents were Bridget and Patrick. James came from Halifax, Nova Scotia, and his parents were Mary and Patrick. It should be recalled that baby Ogarita was left with an Irish family by the name of McNamara in Providence when she was six months old. All of this does not make a positive relationship with either the Mills, D'Arcy, or Bellows families. We still believe the D'Arcys were acquainted with Martha's extended family in some manner other than just the relationship between D'Arcy and Martha.

One final word on the notes from the I.O.O.F. Lodge #8. Among the brothers of this Lodge were George Smith and Edmond C. Tompkins. The Smiths, as we know, were intermingled with the Benchley family members, and John Wilkes Booth was friendly with the Tompkins in Boston. The Tompkins from Boston were originally from Adamsville, Rhode Island. We know this name game is as dangerous as the shadow play found in both Miss Forrester's account of her grandmother and in the lore perpetuated in Burrillville, but we believe this information should be brought out.

The *Commemorative Biographical Record of Fairfield County* in Connecticut was spoken of earlier. The spelling question of Patterson or Batterson might be resolved here. There is a John Mills who marries a Sarah Batterson. Miss Forrester has Sarah [Standish] Mills marrying a Batterson after her husband's death. Previously, we thought the named was spelled "Patterson", which would have made it a local surname. Again, we suspect Miss Forrester, the author, had access to this book and spliced a few names together to fit into her story line. The time frame is slightly askew. The Mills and Miller families are intertwined throughout the histories of southern New England and Long Island, New York. Nothing comes easy in this family. After checking the Mills' names Alonzo listed in his last journal, we were only able to verify one Mills living in Thompson, Connecticut. We regret not catching our elusive Abraham and putting him into a neat time slot. It is still our contention that Abraham A. Mills is buried in Pawtucket with Betsey B. Benchley as Alonzo's records have indicated. Others are still searching for

Abraham's birthplace.

Conclusion: Case of Abraham Amherst Mills - Unresolved.

Case Two Fanny [Mills] D'Arcy.

Aunt Fanny is another shadow figure in our real life drama. Who was she and where does she fit on the family tree? Or, is she just another composite pieced together by Miss Forrester's lively imagination? Aunt Fanny is described by Miss Forrester as being in her sixties with large meditative gray eyes and graying light brown hair. She is decidedly the grande dame of the family who expects ruffles and flourishes from those whom she has honored by her presence while visiting them at Terrace Hall in Canterbury or on the Brown Farm in Pascoag. Even the formidable Martha is subdued. The two ladies are often at odds over the pictures and photographs of certain menfolk. A full length portrait of John Wilkes Booth hanging in Martha's parlor at Terrace Hall sparks a debate and a departure. (*Could we translate the portrait into a photograph, and of D'Arcy and not Booth?) Aunt Fanny refers to "that actor" and the disgrace he has brought on the family name. (*Could this read deserted from the Company "I" of the 2nd Mass. Cavalry?) When young Zola and Martha visit Aunt Fanny in Boston's Back Bay, there is yet another episode over a picture. This time it is Harry D'Arcy's picture—Aunt Fanny's son who was shot as a spy—according to Miss Forrester. It is the last time young Zola sees her great-grand aunt who died in 1887 shortly before or after Martha's death.

As suggested by David Putnam, we have already offered the possibility of Aunt Fanny being Eleanor or Jerusha D'Arcy. Mr. Putnam in a letter to his aunt offers a Fanny Gilman of New Hampshire, whose family were close friends to the Mills, as another possible candidate. This Fanny was sister of Andrew Gilman of Bartlett, NH, who married Dolly Pike. They were the parents of Hanson Pike Gilman mentioned in *This One Mad Act.* We learned the Gilmans traveled from New Hampshire to Boston, and several of Andrew's clan married in Boston. Fanny Gilman supposedly died in 1869, unfortunately for Miss Forrester's time frame. (*Could this be the Fanny who took baby Martha and raised her for a few years? Or, is she just another facet of Miss Forrester's composites.)

The Gilman family was met before in Martha's family history as written by Miss Forrester. Apparently, young Zola Wallingford Henderson boarded for a time with cousin Susan and uncle Gilman in Weston, Massachusetts. (*We found Andrew R.

Gilman, farmer, Central Ave. Weston MA from 1887-1893, but not listed in 1907, in the available Weston directories at the Fingold Library.) Writing of them, Miss Forrester notes that Aunt Fanny has died and that she and Uncle Charles and Aunt Mary (*Charles Bellows and wife?) are all distant relatives of the Mills Branch. Cousin Susan also has gray eyes and auburn hair, and is one of the few relatives who appears not to mind that young Zola and Ogarita are stage people. Zola is left with Mr. and Mrs. Hanson Pike Gilman of Charlestown, Massachusetts, while Ogarita goes on tour. Uncle Pike, we are told, is tall, spare, and from Dover, New Hampshire, who had "gone to sea in his boyhood" even down to the west coast of Africa. (*Could he have been friend of Abraham Mills?) Alonzo does mention two Pikes, both of Providence. A Mrs. Cynthia H., widow aged 87 who died 12/1/1887 and her husband Jonathan who died 1/13/1878 age 85. (*We suspect the Pikes and Gilmans are relatives of the extended Brown/Mills family and quite possibly connected with the Bellows as well.)

While living with the Gilman family, Zola attends Pearl Street School up near Bunker Hill Monument with a close friend named Musetta Brown. Musetta is twelve years of age, and we assume young Zola is around that age as well (*1890?). Zola tells her teacher, Miss Hill, and the Gilmans that she is the granddaughter of the assassin, John Wilkes Booth. The Gilmans and Miss Hill are horrified. Uncle Harry is living close by. He writes to Ogarita, who comes and whisks young Zola away. Miss Forrester writes that she never saw the Gilmans and, we assume, Musetta Brown again.

There was no Fanny D'Arcy listed in the Boston Directories. But there is a widow Fanny Mills, a seamstress, who shows up in the Providence City Directories. She is living at 33 Transit Street in 1854 and 1855. In 1860 this Fanny has moved to 155 Wickenden Street. Could she be the real Aunt Fanny? If she were Abraham's sister, her married name would not have been Mills unless she followed the Benchley women's pattern of retaining their maiden names.

Fanny was a rather popular first name during this time , and we have a candidate of our own for the composite Aunt Fanny. James M. Wilson's second wife was Fanny Z. Bliss, native to Vermont. James Monroe Wilson and Fanny had one child, Myrta Elvira born November 13, 1870. James died in 1890 and was buried in the family lot near his brother, William Wilson, one time husband of Ogarita. Fanny later moved to Worcester, Massachusetts, where she lived with her daughter, Myrta. Alonzo notes her visits to the Wilson homestead in Bridgeton. She died in 1894 in Dudley,

Massachusetts, and was buried in Worcester. Of further interest is the fact that James Wilson's first wife was Elvira M. True, a native of the state of Maine, whose father was James K. True. Mr. True at one time lived and worked in the Laurel Ridge area in Bridgeton before moving out west to Iowa. Elvira True Wilson died in childbirth in 1860.

The combination of the Wilson and True names rang a bell for us. . . and not in association with the Wilsons of Burrillville. We finally found the combination in Miss Forrester's book. A curious tale ensues. The author met Dr. Clarence True Wilson in California in 1932. Dr. Wilson had studied the case of Booth for nearly forty years (*the same number of years as Miss Forrester) and had collected what he believed were proofs of Booth's escape from the Garrett Farm . . . see page 474 in *This One Mad Act*. The Doctor maintains that the man who stood in for Booth was a Confederate soldier named Gerald Boyd, who had reddish hair. He had "proof" that Booth and Boyd had taken an oath of allegiance to the same secret order (*Knights of the Golden Circle?) and were initiated the same night. Dr. True had also personally checked the entire route of escape and was satisfied with the probability of JWB escaping. (*See Hollywood's version in *The Lincoln Conspiracy* by David Balsiger and Charles E. Sellier, Jr. Or, read a more accurate account by Michael W. Kauffman in the *Blue & Gray Magazine*, June 1990.)

Miss Forrester finds some fault with Dr. True's research as he bases his story on the fact that Booth turns up as John St. Helen and/or David E. George known to a Finis L. Bates. When "Booth" dies, Bates has the body mummified which the public could view for 75 cents. Our own Doctor True Wilson was in possession of this mummy for three years and was convinced it was John Wilkes Booth. We have heard many versions of the above., but are interested in the Dr. True Wilson of California who contacted Miss Forrester in 1932. It could be a fluke that the True/Wilson combination surfaces once again in our Burrillville Booth search. We also came across a series of articles starting in March, 1898, written by M. B. C. True who was the son of James K. True. In the *Pascoag Herald,* he reminisces about his boyhood living in the Laurel Hill/Ridge area between 1848 and 1858 and relates of his sister's marriage to James Wilson and her early death in 1860. Mr. True also heads out west, as did most of his family.

Another thread is pulled when we discovered that Herbert M. Wilson, the only surviving male Wilson, was a son of Elvira True and James Monroe Wilson born in 1856 on the homestead farm in Burrillville. In 1881 Herbert married Maria Sayles, daughter of

Aunt Fanny D'Arcy
Hamilton Photographer, Boston
Photo courtesy Mrs. Colony and Mrs. Putnam

another textile entrepreneur Albert and Maria [Ross] Sayles. He later took over and ran the Wilson Mill. He became involved with business complexities—which reliable Uncle William Wilson paid off—and skipped out to California sometime after 1900.

We wrote to the sisters in New Hampshire regarding the Dr. True Wilson of California and the True/Wilsons of Burrillville hoping for some enlightening commentary. The response we received was that "it was downright scary" for them to read of this, but no further comment. It is similar to the reaction of our suggestion of Martha being a dressmaker for the stars. (*This is shaky ground, but we do bet there is a relationship here. It is tantalizing as the Wilson surname is affiliated with Booth, the assassination, and its aftermath on many national levels. The Burrillville lore has Booth hiding out in Burrillville on the Wilson farm. At the same time, there is no mention of the Martha L. Mills/Booth episode.)

The warning should be given that in this time period there were many hoaxes played on a gullible public. Our own locals were not above getting mixed up in one or two themselves. The families affiliated with the Brown/Mills were particularly involved in this form of entertainment. We have a gut feeling that someone in our extended Burrillville family was somehow involved in the real life tragic drama, probably in a minor role, and blew it out of proportion for the sake of amusement. (*Excluding or suspending the belief that Martha was Booth's paramour.) The fact there were—and still are—Booths living in the area would have helped these stories along. It is easy to see how one name "Fanny" can conjure up so many threads to a complex story.

Conclusion: Case of Fanny [Mills] D'Arcy - Unresolved.

Case Three Sarah [Simmons] Mills (1853 - ???)

The elusive Sarah [Simmons] Mills appears for a brief time, only to disappear again just as quickly. In our possession are a series of depositions from an interesting divorce case. They concern the petition for a divorce between one Sarah Mills and Alonzo A. S. Mills in October, 1874. The depositions are from William R. Wilson, James M. Wilson, Caroline Brown, Edward M. Brown and even Betsey Benchley. These people all attest to the fact that Alonzo A. S. Mills was a hard working and frugal man, who provided well for his wife. Great grandmother Benchley testifies the only time Alonzo tussled with his wife was on one occasion when Sarah was saucy to her, personally. Apparently, Sarah does get her divorce as Deputy Oliver A. Inman comes with her to gather her belongings from the Brown farm. It is certainly a small world, and we live in an even smaller state, as it is Charles Blake, author of the first *History of the Providence Stage*, who signs the affidavits as Clerk of the Supreme Court.

Our educated guess in Chapter/file 11 was really on target concerning Sarah. She is indeed the granddaughter of Edward M. Brown. Her late mother, who was Edward's daughter, had married Thomas Simmons. Sarah's little drama is an unhappy one. Her father tosses her out when he remarries, or when one of his wives returns. It is Caroline who goes to rescue Sarah with Edward's blessings. At one time Sarah walks in the mud from Pascoag to get to her grandfather's farm. She lives there from 1869 on and off until she leaves around 1874. Sarah is not a good housekeeper and does little to help Caroline. Even their good neighbor, William Wilson, admits that when she worked for him for a short time, she wasn't much help either. In his deposition, Edward said he told Sarah his home was her home, etc. We believe it is Sarah's actions that precipitated Edward's transferring his property to William Wilson so that his granddaughter would not be able to get her share of the Brown farm. Mr. Wilson returns the property to Caroline shortly after Edward's death. No doubt Sarah is "that girl" Martha warns Alonzo about in her 1869 letter from Baltimore. Obviously, Martha does not know who she is, and she also refers to Edward as Mr. Brown. When we consider that Caroline married Edward two years after Martha and Charles Bellows were married, this is understandable.

Sarah received an inheritance upon coming of age from the property left her by her mother. Shortly after receiving the property, Sarah's former associates began coming around "putting ideas into her head" according to Caroline Brown. It is also the feisty Caroline, who tells Sarah to get $18,000 and not $15,000 for this property, the amount she did receive.

From these depositions, we learn that Caroline has a house in Providence worth $3,000, which she offered to Alonzo and Sarah after their marriage. They preferred to stay on the farm where they planned to build a home. This house in Providence is undoubtedly "her mother's house" of which Martha writes to Alonzo in 1869. We also learn that Alonzo goes to Providence during his marriage to work for the Bumps' delivering milk. This is probably the same Bump family mentioned in Roger Joslyn's report, a member of whom mutinied with the Benchley girls' father for higher muster out pay. They nearly lost their lives in the process. This also points out a circumstances of the times. People generally remained in a close circle of family, associates and friends. When they moved or visited another city, letters of introduction were carried which enlarged the circle geographically but still included the same families.

For this reason, we are inclined to believe the names in Alonzo's journal and those associated with Martha and her friends in other places are all related in some way. The further we investigate, the more this has proven true. Admittedly, sometimes the connection hangs by a thin thread. We really don't know what became of Sarah, but believe she is not an important link in our search. She appears and disappears quickly in this whole scenario.

Conclusion: Case of Sarah [Simmons] Mills - Resolved.

Case Four Brown Farm Residents: Edward M. Brown (1801-1877), Caroline H. [Jenks] Mills Brown (1819-1907), Alonzo Abram Standish Mills (1847-1917)

Study of the deeds of the sale between Andrew Luther and Edward revealed that the full payment of $1,500 for the ninety-two acres was not made at once. Mr. Luther took a quit claim deed for the balance due on the property, which Mr. Brown paid in full in 1874. Reading Edward's deposition on Sarah's petition for divorce revealed a rather simple man who called a spade a spade and was not prone to the observation of detail. It is simply impossible to believe he dashed out to California, married a Hannah Fawcett in January of 1857, and rushed back to Rhode Island to marry Caroline in the fall. Both their names are found in the census and street directories on a fairly steady basis here in Rhode Island. It is possible, but not plausible. Edward M. Brown, a mason by trade, shows up regularly at Green Lane and then North Main Street, both in Providence, prior to his marrying Caroline in Pawtucket.

We were delighted to receive a letter from Mrs. Colony, Izola's daughter, containing correspondence from Clarence E. Barnett of Philadelphia, Pennsylvania, to Mrs. Mann Page in Santa Monica, California, dated June 8, 1927. Peggy was seeking information on Mr. Barnett, who was a former Burrillville resident. The early Barnetts lived in the Wallum Lake/Buck Hill areas from the 1880s and gradually worked their way down to Bridgeton and Pascoag. Clarence writes that he has read articles by Miss Forrester. In particular, he mentions "Green Acres" in which he recognizes his hometown with its Fountain Square and ice cream parlor. He is quite a fan of hers, and notes that a motion picture starring Geraldine Ferrera (?) was based on a script written by Izola Forrester. Mr. Barnett speaks of how proud Alonzo was of his niece, the writer, and that he kept all of her articles stored in his attic library. He is writing to Mrs. Page seeking advice on a writing career, as he has read in another article that she is not a trained writer and writes to please herself more or less. He wants to write about Uncle Lonnie (*Alonzo), who would be an inspiration to any writer. Clarence goes on to describe Alonzo with his little blue eyes and black bushy side whiskers and kindly nature. (*Alonzo has gone from a mustachioed dandy to fashionable whiskers, and finally to the full white beard of which Brandon Patterson spoke so many, many pages back.) He writes that the Mills farm was a summer and winter paradise to the youngsters in the village. They were always welcomed to take a few apples or pears and to pick the seasonal berries. In the winter months, they could cut Christmas trees and skate on nearby Wilson's Pond. Alonzo never turned anyone away in contrast to the neighboring Standfields who would chase everyone off their property.

The attic in the Brown house must have been a busy place. Miss Forrester played up there amongst the trunks of her great grandfather Abraham and her grandmother Martha. Alonzo has his library there and can point to any article he speaks about. There is real antique furniture up there, two spinning wheels, yoke for oxen, and a rocking chair, probably the one in which great-great-Grandma Benchley rocked.

Alonzo recites poem after poem and sings many of his own rhymes to entertain his guest. As Mr. Barnett wrote to Mrs. Mann Page in 1927, "Alonzo Mills was an inspiration for anyone who would care to write . . . he was a suggestive character . . . since I first met and listened to him, I have had the desire within me to write." Whether the former Burrillville resident ever published a story on Alonzo, our unique character from Bridgeton, is unknown.

Conclusion: Case of the Brown Farm residents - Resolved.

Case Five Charles Still Bellows (1827 - 1869)

Source: *Massachusetts in the Army and Navy 1861-1865 Volume II. Wright & Potter. (Boston, 1895.)*

Under the listing of United States Navy Officers from Massachusetts on pages 12 and 13, we find Charles S. Bellows. He was born in and is a citizen of Massachusetts. Appointed January 23, 1863 as Acting Master's Mate. He served on the vessels "Arthur", "Aroostook", "Powhatan" in the West Gulf and the South Pacific. His service was terminated by Honorable Discharge on August 2, 1868, with the rank of Acting Master's Mate. Charles Still Bellows surpassed both Private Stevenson and Private D'Arcy in military accomplishments. (*Bellows tour of duty between 1863 and 1868 in the West Gulf and South Pacific is interesting. This is the grey zone in Martha's life for those trying to locate her. Is it possible she did go to California at some point during this time, not to meet JWB but to see her husband, Charles Bellows? Martha wrote on her pension application that her husband served aboard the "Arthur.". This indicates she knew of his whereabouts at all times even if she were not living with him as his wife. Martha's family had seashells which Miss Forrester wrote could only come from the islands in the South Pacific. She uses them as proof that Martha and Booth were there for a short time during Martha's jaunt to the west coast. It is more likely that Charles Bellows brought these shells back to his family. This might also explain Martha's reputed knowledge of San Diego, San Francisco and Sacramento . . . though the information may have originated with John Stevenson, who was also on the west coast in 1863.)

Both Charles Bellows and Arthur D'Arcy are approximately the same age. They are nearly a decade older than Martha, if her birthdate of 1837 is the true one. At the Federal Archives in Waltham, Massachusetts, we were unable to find Charles, but his mother, Sarah, is listed in the Cambridge 1850 census. She is 56 years old and indeed from Maine as noted on Charles' marriage certificate to Martha. Mrs. Sarah Bellows is living with a Charles and Mary Still, two of their children and two boarders. They are, apparently, her brother and sister-in-law. One of the boarders was Nancy Wheelock, age 52 and married. (*Alonzo married his Sarah at Smith Wheelock's home, located near the Brown farm.) We read that in 1880, Mrs. Sarah Bellows is still living in Cambridge. Charles is listed as a boarder at Three Washington Street in the same section in 1861. We have mentioned his living at Two Sigourney Street in Boston in 1857-1858 and his Naval Service from 1863-1864 as a Cambridge resident. Charles Bellows is not listed anywhere between 1864 and 1866. This, of course, does not say that Martha was living with him at any of these particular times, but there is always the possibility she was.

We have accumulated a mass of material on Bellows' service records, which are confusing and contradictory. Martha's sworn statements when applying for his pension do not jibe with these records. It is impossible to locate Martha at any specific time using them. It is safe to say that Charles Bellows was a seaman from his young manhood until his early death in 1869.

Our confidence in Dr. Dana Putnam has also waned after reading seaman Bellows' medical report. The doctor wrote Martha's husband was in good health when he reenlisted in August 31, 1868. According to the muster roll call of the ship "Guard," he was received on board on July 7, 1869. On October 13, 1869, he was sent to the hospital in New York with "Rheumatism Chronic" which he had had for three or four years. In November, Charles requests transfer to the Chelsea Naval Hospital. He failed steadily and died on December 16th of the same year. The muster list from "A" through "F" lists more than half the crew being sent to the hospital the same time as Charles. We are not doctors, but the description of the illness and his swift decline sounds more like a type of lead poisoning. Dana Putnam, M.D., is in the 1870 -1871 Boston Directory living at 71 Cambridge Street, but not in either the Boston or Cambridge directories for 1865-1869. Since the Doctor said he cared for Bellows and his family for three years before his last enlistment in August of 1868, it would mean he cared for them between 1865 and 1868. The Doctor's statement would place Martha in Boston during that time. We discovered another Doctor Putnam, along with some pertinent maps of the city, in *King's Handbook of Boston* dated 1885. Dr. Charles P. Putnam was in charge of the Dispensary for Diseases of Children at 18 Stanford Street.

Bellows' role in Martha's life is not easy to ascertain. She obviously lived with him as his wife for a good period of time though he constantly "went to sea". Joseph and Jane Averill were sworn witnesses to the fact that Martha was Mrs. Charles S. Bellows with Ogarita and Charles Jr. as his children. They are listed in the Cambridge directories of 1863-1864, 1865-1866, and 1866-1867 with Mr. Averill an officer at the State Prison residing at 109 Cambridge Street. Unless we are willing to admit that both he and his wife as well as Dr. Putnam are lying under oath in order for Martha to claim her widow's pension, then Martha is living in the Cambridge/Boston area during this time. We suspect her stay in Baltimore was a short one between late 1868 and 1869.

Conclusion: Case of Charles Still Bellows - Resolved.

Case Six John H. Stevenson (1839 - 1907)

Source: *Record of Massachusetts Volunteers, 1861-1865. Published by the Adjutant General of Massachusetts Volume I, Wright & Potter. (Boston, 1868).*

Stevenson, John H. 2nd Regiment, Cavalry Massachusetts Volunteers, Co. "E". Age 22. Bounty $50. Residence or place credited to enlistment: St. Joseph, Michigan on February 5, 1863. (*This does not necessarily conflict with his California enlistment notation from other sources.) His service was terminated July 20, 1865, at the expiration of his time. Mr. Thomas Wilkinson, great grandson of John H. Stevenson, has tried to find his birthplace with the same lack of success we have had. He went to Cleveland, searched the city directories and the available census, but could not find any recording of John H. Stevenson. Neither could Mr. Wilkinson find John's parents, Albert and Adelaide Stevenson. Stevenson says they were born in Cleveland, but he later amends this to England. Mr. Wilkinson agrees with us that Stevenson, after living in Burrillville between 1878-1881, moved to and lived in Boston until he appears at Hampton House, Virginia, in 1891. There are several John H. Stephensons and John Stevensons in the Boston City directories between 1857-1890. There is a John Stevenson, clerk, living at 65 Southan St. between 1857-1858. If this is our John, who often worked as a clerk, it would place him in Martha's view at an early date. (*This would be prior to his going to Michigan and/or California where he enlisted in the 2nd Mass. Cavalry.) In 1884-1888, there is a John Stevenson living first at 140 Marginal and later at 37 Cottage in Boston who is a fireman on a tug boat. In 1890, John Stevenson is listed as a waiter rooming at 165 Charles St. in Boston. We believe this is our John H. Miss Forrester has him rooming at the Tremont House in Boston in the late 1880s.

From the Baltimore City Directory 1867-68, a John H. Stevenson, clerk, at 67 S. Eden is, we believe, Martha's one time husband. Both he and Martha are listed there in the 1870 directory, which would probably mean they were there in 1869. They were both in Boston in the 1870s seeking civil war pensions. The 1867-68 directory is filled with Stevensons. There are two other John Stevensons, one a doctor and the other a chairmaker. Could Stevenson be the Southerner in Martha's life? Reviewing the material from Thomas K. Wilkinson, grandson of Harry Jerome Dresbach Stevenson, we note with interest the listing of John H. Stevenson's addresses. On his pension file, Stevenson recorded two addresses: (1) 26 Mott St, Boston, Suffolk, MA 9/17/1875. (2) 507 13th NW Washington, DC 9/20/1875. Later in 1896 through 1906 he is found again at the 13th Street address boarding with Amelia Whitman. This is rather suggestive. Is Amelia Whitman a relative and/or a friend? We recall that Stevenson was affiliated with Martha as early as 1869 in Baltimore, in Boston in the 1870s and finally in Burrillville until 1881. Who is this Stevenson who claims many places as his address but tends to end up in the South?

We will probably never discover his birthplace nor those of his parents. Why did he choose to change his parent's birth and place of residence so many times? Service records indicate that he spelled his name Stevenson and/or Stephenson at various times. Why do all of these people associated with Martha have this tendency? The only exception is Charles Still Bellows. Stevenson allowed Martha to use the name Booth on their marriage certificate in Baltimore. He either knew this was true or was willing to "go along" with her story. His many talents would serve well for one who wanted to fabricate a story and make it believable.

Stevenson's silent disappearance from the house on Wilson's Hill is another puzzler. Where was he when Martha married Edwin Bates, who Miss Forrester claims looked like John Wilkes Booth. We are sure that the Reverend Lovejoy of the Baptist Church would not have married them unless her previous marriage was null and void. The strict code of the local church in this time period did not allow for divorce. We found no evidence of a divorce from either Bellows or Stevenson. We are unable to tie him in with the local Stevenson/Stephenson families in Burrillville. He did marry Martha twice and stayed with her for over a decade, which was quite a feat for any of her husbands. Even Miss Forrester did not speak ill of him. His manicured nails and dandy dress, in her version, will always be remembered by us.

Now may be a good time to speak of John's son, Harry Jerome Dresbach Stevenson. Mr. Wilkinson feels there is a good chance Harry is the son of JWB. We do not know his reasoning for this except that both his mother and grandmother believe this was the case. Mr. Wilkinson's mother was Eva Ogarita Stevenson, and his grandmother was Ella Oretta [Wyman] Stevenson, who married Harry. According to family history, after grandmother Ella divorced Harry J. D., she burned much of Martha's materials including Martha's and Booth's marriage certificate. Mr. Wilkinson does not know why Ella divorced Harry. He suggests that though his grandfather was a loving and caring person, he was too much of a free spirit for Ella Oretta Wyman. He further states that his grandfather was at times an actor, sang very well, and was a part time waiter. Mr. Wilkinson found Harry in the 1910 census living in

South Norwalk, Connecticut. He died in New York City. According to Richard Merrifield, Harry's ashes were placed beside his mother in the Canterbury Plains Cemetery.

It was Miss Forrester's Uncle Harry who related much of their family history to her. Ogarita also kept in close touch with him, and suggested that he join her and Al Henderson to form a company of their own. We know Harry lived with Caroline and Alonzo on the Brown Farm as well as in the rented house with Stevenson and Martha in the late 1870s and early 1880s. Miss Forrester wrote that Harry was the best evidence that John Wilkes Booth survived the Garrett Barn. She shows Booth's pictures surrounding Harry's picture as proof of that statement. Through our eyes the resemblance does not appear to be that strong. How he got the name Harry Jerome Dresbach is another little story. As the author relates it, Rosalie Booth was in love with a lion trainer named of Frederick Jerome Dresbach, who met an unfortunate ending. Aunt Rosalie requested that Martha name Harry after him though it is an unusual middle name. There was also a Frederic Jerome in an American melodrama entitled the *American Fireman*. Edwin Booth appeared in this role at San Francisco Hall in 1853. Both *Ogarita/Sea of Ice* and the *American Fireman* were crowd pleasers for several decades. If the names were derived from the plays, then both Ogarita and Harry have stage names. Could John H. Stevenson or Arthur M. D'Arcy have been on stage in one of these pot boilers? Or was it John Wilkes Booth? There is the possibility of a stage connection, but we have failed to verify it.

Conclusion: Case of John H. Stevenson - unresolved

Case Seven Maggie Mitchell (1832-1918)

With all the conflicting material concerning Maggie Mitchell, we thought it necessary to call upon James O. Hall just one more time. (*We admit to being amateur detectives in the pursuit of the Burrillville and Maryland Booths . . . now we know we are late comers into both fields.) Mr. Hall wrote back that although Mrs. Rogers' letters were authentic, she often picked up some poor information. We learned there were two other actresses during the same period with the surname Mitchell, a Mary and an Eliza. It was Eliza who was first cousin to John Wilkes Booth. (*Mrs. Rogers quite probably confused Maggie with Eliza.) Eliza's stage career did not amount to much, and curiously, she died in India. John Wilkes Booth was said to have died in Bombay after his escape, but we will not chase that will-o'-the-wisp.) Maggie Mitchell was born in New

York City, June 14, 1832 as Margaret Julia Mitchell, daughter of immigrants from Scotland and England, Charles S. Mitchell and Ann Dodson. Maggie died in March of 1918.

Conclusion: Case of Maggie Mitchell - Resolved.

Case Eight Charlotte Saunders Cushman (1816-1876)

Another actress mentioned, Charlotte Cushman, was born July 23, 1816 and died February 18, 1876. Miss Cushman and the various names associated with her surname as written by Alonzo and others who record thespian activities have been mentioned previously.. An attempt was made to research Miss Cushman's background to verify whether any of Alonzo's "Cushmans" belonged on her particular family tree.

Sources: *(1) Henry Austin Clapp. Reminiscences of a Dramatic Critic. Boston and New York: Houghton, Mifflin and Company, 1902. (2) Edward and Jane James. Notable American Women - 1607-1950: A Biographical Dictionary. Cambridge: Harvard University Press, 1971. (3) W. T. Price. A Life of Charlotte Cushman. New York: Published by Brentano's, 1894. (4) Emma Stebbins. Charlotte Cushman: Her letters and Memories of Her Life. Cambridge: Houghton, Osgood and Company, 1878.*

Miss Cushman, who was born and died in Boston, was the daughter of Elkanah and his second wife, Mary Eliza Babbit. The Cushmans were descendants of Robert Cushman, business manager for the original Pilgrims who settled in Plymouth, Massachusetts, in 1620. Charlotte's own father was a merchant in the West Indies trade and suffered a "reversal" in business. He died at age 72 in 1841 and had six children from a previous marriage. Her mother was forced to support the family by running a boarding house, and the children were encouraged to support themselves, an accomplishment which the actress did rather well. In fact, after her career was successful, she supported much of her family for the remainder of her life.

Her maternal descendants, the Babbits, were also an old New England family who lived in Sturbridge, Massachusetts. A Dr. Erasmus Babbit was the second practicing physician in Sturbridge. There are a few familiar surnames among Miss Cushman's ancestry, but none we can definitely tie in with the Benchley/Brown/Mills families. Miss Cushman and Martha are alike in descending from early settlers in the colonies with their fathers associated with the sea and trade. Both of these ladies share the strong personalities and the strong almost masculine qualities needed to support their families under all kinds of circumstances.

Miss Forrester has Ogarita receiving a long sandalwood box inlaid with mother-of-pearl given to the budding actress after her first stage appearance with Charlotte Cushman in *Macbeth* in Boston in 1875. We discovered this in the lengthy article in two installments from the *Saturday Evening Post.* (*We were only given a portion of the article by the sisters and sent for the remainder from University Microfilms International, Michigan.) Miss Cushman was known for her remarkably generous and thoughtful nature. It is possible Ogarita received this box if she were indeed "Miss Wilkes" in that production. Again, it is Miss Forrester who casts doubts on her family history as she exaggerates beyond belief. In this particular article, she mentions an association with just about every major stage personality of the time period excluding Edwin Booth. This is a prime example of the dangers of exaggeration and fictionalizing of the more prosaic "truth." Some of the incidents she writes about may well have some basis in fact, but who will take them seriously as she has destroyed her credibility with excess. Still, it is a tribute to her artistry that we end up with the nagging thought that perhaps some of what she writes is true.

Conclusion: Case of Charlotte Cushman - Resolved

Case Nine Ogarita Elizabeth (Rosalie Booth?) [Bellows] Wallingford/Hills Wilson Henderson (1859-1892).

Our limited knowledge of Ogarita is from her daughter's portrait, a few letters written to family members, memories of her from Burrillville residents, her divorce papers, and a few newspaper articles concerning her death. There is an article dated May 30, 1890 from the *Columbus Dispatch* in Ohio with high praise of her acting ability. Despite vital statistics and the above pieces of information, we cannot capture the essence of young Zola's mother. There is much contradictory material concerning the young stage actress, Miss Wilkes, also known as Rita Booth and Rita Henderson. She signs her name as "Rita" a good part of the time. It is obvious from Miss Forrester's writings that she adored her mother and was happiest when she was with her on tour involved with the excitement and glamour the stage has to offer. The discomfort of the hotel rooms and the long train rides fade, compared to the adventure of being with her mother and other theatrical people.

On one side, Miss Forrester sees her mother as a lovely, softspoken and gentle woman who stood out "aloofly" amongst the other actresses. Then we read of her risqué behavior in town and on stage at the *Theatre Comique*. Martha wrote that Ogarita was ill a great deal of the time, growing up with colds. This, along with her strenuous life on the road, might have aided in her rather early death. She is a close friend to her mother and vice versa. After Martha dies, she seeks strength and comfort from her family members: Caroline, Charles, and Harry. Although, Ogarita can be a bit caustic when speaking of Alonzo and Caroline. There is a sadness about her as she writes to her younger brother, Harry. Her marriage to Al Henderson was not all that happy, and they were apart a good deal of the time. At one point, he makes a definite break, though he sends her money for the children. We have never been fully satisfied with the account of a Harvard student, George Wallingford Hills, being young Izola's father. But, then we have not asked the family for information on this. It was never our intent to document Ogarita's life except for her contact with the Burrillville lore and the possibility of her being John Wilkes Booth's child.

An accounting of Ogarita's active career trooping arrived. These dates and places were actually from her letters to her brother Harry Stevenson, twelve years younger than she.

1877 - Bath, ME with Grace Cartland. (*This suggests her career was off the ground before young Zola was born and before her marriage to Wilson. This does fit into Burrillville lore that she was a budding actress.)

1881 - Pascoag, RI - Where Zola and Elmer are upstairs playing. (*We suppose this is in the Wilson Place during her brief marriage to William Wilson. Who Elmer is, we do not know.)

1884 - Chicago, IL - Zola, six years old, is with her mother and manages the matter of meals, etc. for Ogarita.

1884 - Chicago, IL - Al and she saved money last year on the road but have not been able to do so this winter.

1886 - David City, Nebraska - She asks Harry to write her.

1887 - Chicago, IL - West Madison St. - She wants to start a company and asks young Harry to join them.

1887 - Duluth, MN - June - She receives a good notice with Mr. Miln in the closet scene from Hamlet.

1887 - Miles City, MT - June - One night stand.

1887 - Butte City, MT - She misses Zola and will take her next season with her.

1887 - No date or place - Al sent her some money for costumes. She expects to play "Desdemona and Francois in Richelieu." Many parts to learn.

It is quite clear that Ogarita is with touring companies a good deal of her life. She reputedly played in Boston, but there is no evidence verifying this except a Miss Wilkes who appeared in *Macbeth* in 1875. We read that a Rita Booth was a member of the Boston Comic Opera in 1890 with her husband as director. Her career could be summed up as a secondary actress of some renown. Our actual interest is in her real life role as Booth's daughter. She did not claim to be Rita Booth until the latter part of her career. Miss Merrifield wrote to Mr. Kimmel suggesting that Ogarita was in rough straits and needed the attention and/or the notoriety it would bring.

Miss Forrester writes that her mother would not talk about the Booth connection and asked young Zola not to mention it to anyone while they were on tour. We recall her whisking the twelve year old away from the Gilmans after Zola revealed the family association with John Wilkes Booth. The impression from Miss Forrester, herself, is that Ogarita is not that sure of the claim. Her mother shies away from any talk of the Booth family until quite late in her life. One senses that Zola's information came from her grandmother, Martha. This is not to say it was untrue, but it remains a question mark in just about everyone's mind who has read or knew of Martha Mills and the Booth affair. We read in Miss Forrester's *Saturday Evening Post* story that Charles Bellows, whom she ignores in her family history, is Ogarita's half-brother . . . they have different fathers. Did she really know whose child Ogarita was? There is no reference to the Booth episode in the above article. Despite all, Ogarita, like Martha, has eluded us. We do not really know who her father was except that it was not Charles Bellows.

Conclusion: Case of Ogarita Elizabeth (Booth) [Bellows] Wallingford/Hills Wilson Henderson - Unresolved.

Case Ten - Izola Louise [Wallingford or Hills] Forrester Merrifield Page (1878-1944).

This is a good time to bring back Miss Forrester to summarize our last findings on her life. Sometimes we regret having read *This One Mad Act* as early as we did. If we had not done so, on the other hand, a reference point for our investigations would be missing. It was never our purpose or intent to decimate Miss Forrester's accounting of her family history. The fact remains that her book could not be ignored while pursuing the Burrillville and/or Maryland Booths. Even the critics who damn her story are forced to admit to Miss Forrester's "all pervasiveness" and her "enticing writing style." After reading other literary efforts by Martha's granddaughter, we reiterate that she just goes too far in her anxiety to convince the reader of the validity of her subject matter, especially in regards to family history. Two of her articles follow:

Sources: *"Child Actress of the 80's" in the Saturday Evening Post, March 20, 1926 and "Green Pastures" in the Ladies Home Journal, May, 1927. Both by Izola Forrester. Acquired from the University Microfilms International, Ann Arbor, Michigan.*

We have referred to the "Child Actress" article many times. There are eleven pages of loving tribute to her mother, Ogarita, and the fond memories of her trouping days with her. (*Probably between 1884-1892.) It is apparent she adores her mother whom she sees as a long suffering, lovely and gentle lady. Her physical attributes are those beloved by the romantic age in which she lived. Long dark-brown hair (*black in the book) fine white skin, eyes dark brown, long in shape and heavy-lidded with an expression of sadness or dreamy aloofness reflected in them. She is slender and delicate with a soft and lovely voice. This is in sharp contrast to the items found in William Wilson's petition for divorce regarding her association with the "playing actors" of the Theatre Comique. Her grueling touring suggests there is a strength of purpose, if not toughness, within Ogarita to be able to endure the traveling show life she has chosen to lead.

We have read some rather harsh criticism of Miss Forrester and the way she saw her family. One critic wrote that the whole affair was humbug and that he was greatly surprised anyone took her seriously. He writes, *This One Mad Act* is a product of an eccentric grandmother and an equally eccentric mother written by a daughter who was obsessed with her family background (*Maryland Booth blood). Again, we agree to a certain point. But, the nagging doubt remains that there was some kind of an association with the Maryland and Burrillville Booths, if not the exact one Miss Forrester and her descendants would have us believe.

Her exaggerations are documented when she relates of tours with Ogarita and occasionally Al Henderson. Zola writes of an association with just about every major star of the day: Madam Janaushek, Miss Ellen Terry, Miss Marie Dressler, Miss Clara Morris, Mr. Joseph Jefferson, and Mr. Maurice Barrymore, along with lesser luminaries. We are told that young Zola even rides up Fifth Avenue in an open victoria with Miss Lillian Russell. Once upon a time, her stepfather, Al Henderson, was Miss Russell's leading man. One Christmas, young Zola was taken to the professional children's matinee at Tony Pastor's, "where he kissed us all and played Santa Claus with Aunt Louise Eldridge handing out gifts and Maggie Cline singing. . . ." (*Could the lady who was singing be the "Maggie" who corresponded with Ogarita,and not the more famous Maggie Mitchell? Maggie Cline has been mentioned in association with the theater in Providence and is probably Ogarita's friend of long standing. The name Louisa Eldridge is interesting. Eldridges lived in the Wallum Lake area and in Bridgeton not far from the Brown/Mills farm. On page 297 of Eleanor Ruggles, *Prince of Players*, another Louisa Eldridge is mentioned. She is traveling with Edwin Booth's touring company in 1882. To quote: "Louisa Eldridge, veteran trouper called 'Aunty' by everybody, would give us a song." Here is another possible association between Edwin and Ogarita. It would not be unusual for Ogarita and young Izola to bump into those who starred or were associated with Edwin Booth on stage. Ogarita has a relatively long acting career (*1875-1892).

Edwin Booth, born in 1833, and his possible association with Martha, still sits in the back of our minds. This is mainly due to the open hostility towards him displayed by Martha's descendants. Miss Forrester notes that she had never seen Edwin on stage as her mother forbade it. Her explanation is that Martha and Edwin had had a feud of some kind. There is also the possible association between Martha and Dr. Erasmus Miller, who took care of Mary Devlin Booth in Dorchester. We are not suggesting a liaison between Edwin and Martha, but some sort of confrontation or unpleasant affiliation.

In this particular article, Miss Forrester does not bring the name or figure of John Wilkes Booth into the picture. She does say that Charles Bellows was her mother's half-brother. This is quite probably true as we know that seaman Bellows is not Ogarita's father, but was possibly the father of Charles Alonzo Bellows. These are examples of the maddening bits of verifiable information that Miss Forrester occasionally gives. It keeps our hopes up when fact and fiction begin to blend occasionally. Charles is not her favorite uncle as he failed to meet young Zola in New York City when she arrives by train from the West and alone. Her uncle is somehow working in the theatrical world but not in the legitimate theater, the author adds scornfully. Apparently, he handles the curiosities paraded across halls and stages for the public's entertainment. In this episode, Charles is transporting Old Chief Thunder Cloud and his people to a stage engagement in Fall River, Massachusetts. Uncle Charles tells Zola that Thunder Cloud fought at Custer's Last Stand beside Sitting

Bull. Miss Forrester writes seriously that she did not realize the significance of his statement at that time.

Zola recalls her final parting with her mother and ends the article with, "I am glad that I was her child." The love she bears for her mother is almost painful to read both in *A Child Actress* and in *This One Mad Act*. In a sense, it is refreshing to read of such devotion.

"Green Pastures" is the story of a young sailor with a terminal illness coming home to die. Both Canterbury and Burrillville residents saw their town depicted as the locale, "Green Pastures." We see the component parts of Canterbury, Pascoag, and Crawford Notch, New Hampshire, as the setting for this story. Along with Mr. Clarence Barnett, we saw our Fountain Square, ice cream parlor, the Brown farm and the Pascoag Race Track . . . most of which do not exist today in the Town of Burrillville. Miss Forrester's characters and backgrounds lead us to believe she spent some time in Burrillville, both as a child and as an adult. (*She died in Keene, New Hampshire, according to her death notice in our local paper, *The Woonsocket Call*. To quote this newspaper, "Mrs. Izola Forrester Page, 64, author and scenario writer and great granddaughter of John Wilkes Booth . . . A native of Pascoag, RI, she played child's parts on the stage with her mother, the late Ogarita Booth Hills and later wrote feature articles for newspapers and magazines . . . She is survived by her husband, Mann Page, a well known stage director, four daughters and two sons.")

This story contains a few familiar family names spliced with others we do not recognize, which is not a crime in fictionalized writing. In fact, it is a trick of the trade to make composites of places and characters which exist or did exist. Miss Forrester tells a good story. We cannot find fault with her work as fiction. There was little else in the scenario that would add to our investigation. Liz Fairbrother, curator of the Canterbury Historical Society, has continued to send us articles written by Miss Forrester and other items of interest she finds in the files of Charles Underhill, the late historian of Canterbury. She also arranged a meeting in her town for several who were interested in the subject of Martha "Izola" Mills and John Wilkes Booth.

In the restored home of Al and Amanda Amundsen, we sat at the long table in front of a sizable New England fireplace which kept us warm, along with the hot tea we sipped Unfortunately, the sisters from New Hampshire were unable to attend. It was a rare treat to chat all afternoon on a subject which infatuated all of us even if from different perspectives and concerns. Liz was there and brought more information for us to ponder at our leisure.

Here are a few of the things that we learned that day at the Wright's Mill Farm in Canterbury. Mr. Charles Underhill carried on correspondence with other historians, including James O. Hall, about the Martha and Booth lore as found in *This One Mad Act*. Most of them write rather disparagingly about Miss Forrester's book, with the exception of Mr. Hall. We smiled to read we were following Mr. Hall's footsteps in Canterbury, though a decade later. There were letters between Mr. Underhill and Richard Merrifield, who wrote that he spent his boyhood in Westminster (*a section of Canterbury) and graduated from Westminster High School in 1918. Richard recalled his teacher, the charming and gentle Miss Ruth Shorter, and his trips to Hoxie's to get ice cream. He also wrote of listening to Mrs. Barstow tell stories about his mother, young Zola. Mr. Merrifield recalled Deacon Barstow of the Westminster Congregational Church in Canterbury. (*We have heard of the surname Barstow before as Martha was housekeeper to George Barstow. The Bates and Dwight Barstow shared a Christmas dinner in 1886. There is a Barstow Road and there was a Barstow Foundry in Canterbury. It was also a Barstow who built the Music Hall in Providence. Perhaps we should also mention Barstow Wilson, friend of Edwin and Mary Booth.)

Liz had already put us in touch with Frances E. S. Bingham, church clerk of the Congregational church. From her we learned that Deacon Harold Barstow died in 1943. Richard Noel Merrifield, child of Richard Forrester Merrifield and his wife, Emma Brunnergraber, was baptized on April 20, 1928. So was Clarence Robert Joslyn, born in 1921, of Clarence Lee Joslyn and his wife Nita (*Ogarita or Rita) Merrifield. We knew this Ogarita died young and was buried along with her Uncle Harry and Martha Izola Bates on the plains in Canterbury. Looks as though Richard assumed responsibility of Mrs. Joslyn's child. It is a closeknit family. We thought Martha might have been affiliated with this church as the one on the plains had burned, but Mrs. Bingham could find no listing for a Bates in the early records. There was a Mr. and Mrs. Robert Bates of Binghamton, NY. (*Can this be just a coincidence as this is the New York area where the first Ogarita died and is buried.) They came to Canterbury in 1954, both Theological Seminary graduates, much interested in the evangelization of New England. A committee was formed in 1955 to see about bringing needy children to church and Sunday school. (*Sounds like history repeating itself. Interestingly, Robert Bates is on the committee along with John Cutts. This spelling may be the true one of Beatrice Hendersons' first marriage. Alonzo has it as Clutts in his writings.) We have also seen a picture of the midwife, Miss Frederica Olney, in a group picture. An attractive woman in the photograph and obviously in the advanced stages of pregnancy. Miss Olney was not listed in the Westminster Congregational Church records. She could have attended this church, but had not been accepted yet as a full member.

The busy church clerk also found the Olney family in the Carey Cemetery in Canterbury. Listed were:

Olney, C. F. died March 22, 1867 age 2 years.

Olney, Frederick died March 14, 1869 age 59 years.

Olney, Giles Herbert, infant son of Frederick & Olive, died May, 1856, age 10 months.

Olney, Jessie M. died January 1, 1867 age 14 years 11 months.

Olney, Olive S. died March 25, 1902 age 79 years.

Olney, Oliver D. (US Navy Civil War) (G.A.R.) died December 30, 1864 age 16.

Miss Frederica Olney is not listed here. But Liz Fairbrother found a School District report of 1856 listing all persons between ages four and sixteen. In this were listed Oliver and Frederica Olney, as well as their father, Frederick. This would put our midwife in the proper time zone. The Olney family is an old New England name in Connecticut and Rhode Island and is related to the Benchley/Brown/Mills family in Burrillville and other places in our state. We are not one hundred percent sure the Olneys listed here are relatives of the Afro-American servant who worked for Miss Crandall. Black families often adopted the surname of their former owners. The right time frame would put Olive Olney as the midwife except that Martha's assistant was buried with her on the plains. This matter is left unresolved for others to investigate.

At Wright's Mill Farm, there was much discussion of Martha's maternity home and where it was actually located. Originally, Mr. Tracy said it was a maternity home for wayward girls and then called it the "maternity hospital." The building may have been moved several times and was said to have been burned by vandals a few years back.

Before we leave Miss Forrester and her history of the family, a few finer points must be considered in reference to the validity of her account. The blending of fact and fiction occurs throughout her book and other writings. Critics tend to disregard the possibility of a fleeting romance between Martha and John and of his fathering Ogarita. They do admit to the plausibility that he fathered children in this manner. It should be remembered that the author is writing from memories of what she was told in childhood as well as the material gathered from her family and other resources. We see *This One Mad Act* as a composite of all these things. She spent thirteen summers in Canterbury from 1908 to 1921 writing this book and the remainder somewhere else until its publication in 1937. From her family we learned that the book was not the best seller she hoped it would have been. In fact, it is probably read more often today than when it was published. Still, it cannot be ignored. Anyone researching Booth's personal life has to contend with *This One Mad Act.*

As far as can be determined, young Zola lived at the Wilson place until the age of about three or four and then went to the Brown farm with Caroline. She probably went to Canterbury in 1885 or 1886 when not on tour with her mother. The strong and dramatic personality of her grandmother, and the stories she related to the highly imaginative child, left a vivid impact on the granddaughter. We read of the family's constant struggle to make ends meet and Martha's exaggerations to Alonzo and Caroline of their well being in Canterbury. We have no way of knowing whether Miss Forrester truly believed her grandfather was John Wilkes Booth, as glimpses of doubt surface now and then in *This One Mad Act*. Ogarita's stance, as revealed by her daughter, appears curiously ambiguous. She does not admit to it until the last few years of her life after Martha had died. Still, the author must have taken this somewhat seriously to spend her time researching the material available on Booth and tracking down people for interviews. When we asked Mr. Tracy at Izola Bates' gravesite if he believed this story to be true, his reply was similar to many, "Why would anyone want to be related to the assassin of President Lincoln?" Good question. In other words, why work so hard to have this dubious acclaim, if it were not true.

It is obvious Miss Forrester felt it necessary to romanticize her grandmother and mother, to distort facts, and deliberately mislead her readers by eliminating family members. She must have known of Arthur D'Arcy, as she included him in her story. She brings her own retribution down on D'Arcy's head by having him shot as a spy . . .this for "deserting my grandmother." Her own family admits that Miss Forrester was painting a portrait of her family through rose-colored glasses. None of which discounts the possibility of a fleeting acquaintance between Martha and Booth. Her family has sought to verify this relationship for many years to no avail. How does one document a brief romance except to suggest the possibility of its happening in a certain time and place? Exactly what we have attempted to do.

There are some choices to be made in regards to Miss

Forrester's book and the actuality of Booth being Ogarita's father.

1. Miss Forester believed this was the truth as told by her grandmother and others.

2. Miss Forrester could not find any real proof of Booth and Martha's affiliation and decided to write a "story" that would convince others of this relationship, while still believing it to be the truth.

3. She could not find any proof and began a complex fabrication to support her grandmother's contention, which has been perpetuated by family members even to the present day.

No matter which one is favored, it does not eliminate the possibility of a meeting between Booth and Martha. It is a Catch-22 situation.

It was interesting to read of the reaction of those in Canterbury when *This One Mad Act* was in circulation, according to Mr. Underhill's materials. It is a classic example of a community's response when one who has lived among them writes of their particular spot on this earth. Few believed any of the parts concerning Canterbury, though a few thought the Booth thing might have some truth to it. Mr. Underhill, who did a complete analysis of *This One Mad Act* with scrutiny and insight, said Miss Forrester was writing of a Canterbury in the 1900s and not one in the late 1880s. We learned she went back to Canterbury around 1908 and stayed in a house she shared with a family by the name of Moody for thirteen summers writing her book. No one believed she stayed there in the winter as the house was badly run down. No mention is made of her children being with her during this time period, though letters to Alonzo at that time would indicate otherwise. We did ask Miss Forrester's children whether they were there or not, and they answered they were farmed out in the Canterbury area. Town Hall deeds and property records have been thoroughly examined many times by those looking for Martha's or Mrs. Merrifield's ownership. They all end up with the same negative result. Just these incidents depict the difficulty in ascertaining the "truth" in any given situation. We did not intend to explore young Zola's personal life. We wished only to analyze her writings regarding her grandmother and the rest of the extended family. Miss Forrester's memory is as much loved and honored by her daughters today as she in turn remembered her own mother, Ogarita.

Conclusion: Case of Izola Louise [Wallingford/Hills] Merrifield Page - Unresolved.

Case Eleven Henry Johnson (1834-1944)

We have deliberately saved all the confusing and conflicting data on Henry Johnson til near the end of our summations of the personalities encountered in the Burrillville Booths. The only exception is Martha Louise Mills, who deserves a place all her own in our closing chapter/file. The information on Henry is typical of almost every one of our cases under study. He is both a real life individual and a character in Miss Forrester's *This One Mad Act*. Where does the truth lie? How is fiction separated from fact? As we present the material unearthed on Henry, the shadow play that has confronted us throughout our search to discover whether there is any basis in fact for the Burrillville Booth lore will hopefully be understood.

Henry is one of our most intriguing personalities as he is the only individual involved with Martha's extended family whom we actually knew. It was beyond our imagination that Burrillville's Henry Johnson would be a participant in the mystery we belatedly fell upon and decided to pursue. When reading *This One Mad Act* for the first time, we thought that Miss Forrester's Henry must be our own Henry Johnson. (*Henry's last name was never mentioned in her book.) Later, we asked several Burrillville natives to read the book to see whether they could identify any familiar persons, places or things. These people knew nothing of the Martha/Booth legend, but all were absolutely sure that our Henry was in fact Miss Forrester's Henry. His birth year would coincide with Miss Forrester's time frame of her grandmother's history.

In *This One Mad Act,* Henry is mentioned briefly in the beginning and occasionally surfaces throughout the story when the need arises. According to Miss Forrester, he was Aunt Sarah's son as well as servant and dresser to John Wilkes Booth. (*Aunt Sarah fled with Martha and young Ogarita to Baltimore and the Stevenson family after President Lincoln's assassination.) The implication is that Aunt Sarah and Henry are slaves of the Booth family. We are told that Henry rode with Arthur D'Arcy and Booth on secret missions for the Confederacy. Henry followed Booth into exile after his escape from the Garret Farm. (*Miss Forrester relates that a Confederate soldier, Gerald Boyd, stood in for Booth and was killed in the tobacco shed. Others maintain it was actually James William Boyd, who not only shared initials with the assassin but was mistaken for Booth and then shot in place of Booth.) John Wilkes and the faithful Henry eventually ended up in London. Booth then continued alone to Bombay, India. Henry, for some unknown reason, left his master in London and returned to America where he was employed by Edwin Booth, who was then living and acting in New York City.

A fellow Knight of the Golden Circle, a friend and fellow actor of Booth, ran into Henry in New York. Henry gave Booth's address to James or Jimmy Wells, a comedian, who had been a stock member of the Richmond Theatre where he first met John Wilkes Booth. Letters were exchanged between the two friends. Miss Forrester managed to locate Mr. Wells' son, Louis S. Wells, who was living in Seattle, Washington. In a letter to the author, reprinted in her book, he wrote that his father always said John Wilkes Booth was never captured. Booth's death supposedly occurred in 1879, probably in Bombay. Towards the end of her history, Miss Forrester suggested that Henry eventually went to Boston searching for his mother, Aunt Sarah. This does not fit in with the earlier suggestion that Aunt Sarah died long before young Izola was born. Naturally, we read this with great interest, especially since our Henry Johnson was affiliated with a Wells family in our community. Alonzo mentioned a Nancy Wells, who died in 1871 age 86 in Broomfield (*Colorado?).

Henry Johnson was a well-known figure in Pascoag. We both, as youngsters, recall Mr. Johnson walking up Church Street in summer and winter wearing a fur coat. He would say it was "for insulation against the heat and the cold." At recess, the children would run to hear what the tall black man had to say or to receive a shiny penny from his endless supply. He was known locally as "Mr. Johnson" and would tip his hat even to the smallest child when greeting them. He lived in the Buck Hill area at Wallum Lake in the old Wells house, where he chopped wood and did odd jobs for a living. He always said that as a child he had personally shaken hands with President Lincoln when the slaves were freed. Mr. Johnson lived to the ripe old age of 109 years. He was so well liked that the townspeople "saw to it" that a burial lot and gravestone were provided for this former slave in the Pascoag Cemetery.

From Dr. Harry Lee Barnes' *Wallum Pond Estates*, we discovered that Alfred L. Wells purchased a farm in September of 1869 from Esten Angell. Henry lived in a shack beside the "big house" until Mr. Wells died in 1910. In his will it was stated that "Henry could remain on the farm always." Our Henry Johnson finally moved into the "big house" and remained there until his death, even though the farm changed hands three times.

From Henry's own account in Burrillville records and in several newspapers, including the *Woonsocket Call*, we learned of his living as a slave in the South. He was born on a Richmond, Virginia,

Henry Johnson
Born in Richmond, Virginia, in 1834
Died in Burrillville, Rhode Island, in 1944
Photo Courtesy of the Burrillville Historical & Preservation Society

plantation whose owner had 560 acres and 150 slaves, including Henry's father, Frank. (*His mother's name is not mentioned in any of these records.) The owner's son went to war and was wounded. Henry watched the fighting from a hill in the Shenandoah Valley. After the war, the slaves were dazed by their freedom. Their former master, William Johnson, told them they were free to go or could stay and work as farmhands. Henry took off and went to sea, served as a cook, worked on the railroad, and finally ended up in Burrillville on the Wells farm. We are not sure when he arrived here, probably in the late 1880s. It is curious that Alonzo does not mention Henry Johnson in his journals, but they were in competition, both cutting wood and doing odd jobs for other people. Of course, Alonzo did not mention everyone he knew, but kept to those who were part of his family's activities. There were other colored families in the Buck Hill area, namely, Jacob Lewis and Prince Lewis as early as 1852, according to the highway bounds list of that time. In later years, Caroline hired one of the Lewis' to help work her farm.

When we read of Henry in Miss Forrester's book, it did leave us a bit unsettled. Again, the same old problem. Are there some threads of truth in her story? Or, is "our" Henry Johnson of Burrillville just a model for her Henry, servant of the Booths? If she visited her Uncle Alonzo on the Brown farm between 1911 and 1914, or spent any time here, she would have known about our Mr. Johnson.

There were people who lived in the outermost section of our area whose surnames Miss Forrester could have used which are connected with John Wilkes Booth. Ella Turner, whose real name was Ella Starr, was Booth's mistress in Washington. She was supposedly from Baltimore. After Booth's death, she attempted suicide. Ella later identified Booth's body on the "Montauk." She was held as a witness for the trial of the conspirators but was never called to testify. We can't place Ella Starr here, but we know that Ebenezer Starr (1817-1874) purchased the Mason/Buxton farm in 1837. His son, Lemuel Starr, a clock repairer, operated the farm after his father's death. The Starrs were not held in high regard as they "kept a large drove of pigs which were allowed free range in the woods during the day and were called in at night." Only the foundations of this farm are found today by hunters and those who explore the abandoned roads and trails of Burrillville. In Miss Forrester's article, "Child Actress," she mentioned her mother, Ogarita, had an actress friend named Hattie Starr..

Three names found in Burrillville have been associated with the assassin: Starrs, Wells, and Henry Johnson. Our problem is the old one. Which came first? Did the Booth Burrillville lore originate here locally with Martha adopting and playing her own role as later written by her granddaughter? Or, did Martha and Miss Forrester, at a later date, bring the story here with the townspeople adopting it as their own? Difficult to say. This case would end here except for the discovery of a paperback book in the Pascoag Public Library book sale box.

Source: *The Lincoln Conspiracy by David Balsiger and Charles Sellier, Jr. Schick Sunn Classic Books. (Los Angeles, California, 1977).*

The book is adapted from a screen play starring Bradford Dilman as John Wilkes Booth. It is a Hollywood script that purports to be based on fact from primary source documentation. We read the dialogue, in actual quotes, of Booth and all the other persons involved with the assassination and its aftermath. Nevertheless, it is of interest to us as Henry has a leading role in this version of the John Wilkes Booth story including his escape from the Garrett Farm in 1865. There is even a picture of Henry Johnson, valet to Booth, a cigar in his mouth and wearing a narrow brimmed hat cocked to one side of his head. The photograph startled us but not as much as the revelation of Henry's last name as being Johnson. (*Miss Forrester did not mention Henry's surname in *This One Mad Act.)* Our Henry Johnson in photographs at age one hundred is pictured with an unbroken nose while the young Henry in this book sports a broken one. Martha's, young Zola's and Ogarita's likenesses are also included, but Ogarita does not look like the Ogarita pictured in Miss Forrester's book.

After reading *The Lincoln Conspiracy*, we believe that Miss Forrester's handiwork, or a derivation thereof, is revealed in *The Lincoln Conspiracy*. Old familiar names which the reader found in our chapter/files find their way into this so-called history. On one of the sisters' visits to Burrillville, they mentioned the fact that their mother and father, Izola and Mann Page, had written a script for Cecil B. DeMille, but the depression cut their hopes of having it produced. And, we noted that Clarence Barnett, the former Burrillville fan of Miss Forrester, wrote that he had seen a movie with the script written by her. We asked family members about the resemblance between *This One Mad Act* and *The Lincoln Conspiracy.* The reply was that a member of their family had written a thesis on their mother's findings. Others took it, analyzed her original production, and then expanded on it for their own sensationalism. We were told to be careful about what we might read into it.

We could hardly believe our eyes while reading Sellier's and Balsiger's history. According to them, Martha is still the wife of John Wilkes Booth, a fact that everyone in that time period knew. But, it is she who is the southern spy and gets arrested in Tennessee. Booth has her released, but in the process becomes indebted to the Radical Republicans, who are the true originators of the conspiracy and the assassination. After the assassination, Booth along with his valet, Henry Johnson and a friend, David Henson—with whom the real life David Herold is confused—do not take the southern escape route where everyone would be looking for them. They head for his ex-wife Martha's home at Harper's Ferry. (*Did they think that no one would look for them there?) All four of them are spotted in Baltimore, Philadelphia, and New York. They always seem to fade away upon confrontation. Even though he is on the run, Booth continues pursuing the ladies along the way. In Philadelphia he marries a former girlfriend, Kate Scott. Henson and Henry accompany Booth to England where he marries another girlfriend, Marsha Burnley. (*Both Scott and Burnley were familiar names in our area.) Looking for greener pastures, Booth and Henson travel to India while Henry Johnson returns stateside. At some point, Booth's friend, Henson, returns to America and goes to Fort Wayne, Indiana, where he becomes a farmer. In the process, he changes his name to Edwin Henderson. (*Any relation to Alexander Henderson?)

While Booth was in London, he changed his name to John Byron Wilkes . . . not a very heavy disguise. The middle name, Byron, does interest us as this is the same one used when Booth reputedly married Martha in 1859. Difficult to believe that this is a coincidence. It should be recalled that the reincarnated Booth told Dell Leonardi that he married Martha in Baltimore and used the name something like James Brayton . . . which seems to be rather close to Byron.

To continue with *The Lincoln Conspiracy*, Henry Johnson eventually finds his way back to Boston and his mother, where they live out the remainder of their years. (*Did they come to Burrillville to live on the Wells farm? Our Henry Johnson never mentions his mother's name, though he said his father's name was Henry at one time and Frank another. The Burrillville Henry related that his family adopted their surname, Johnson, from the name of the family who originally owned them.) This "historical" novel contains so much outrageous misinformation that it is difficult to believe anyone ever took it seriously. Balsiger and Sellier have Junius Brutus Booth, Sr.

becoming intermittently insane after the assassination, though history has him dying in 1852. They also have Rosalie dying in New Jersey in 1880. She actually died in 1889 in New York City. We were warned not only by Miss Forrester's family but by leading authorities on Booth as well to "run not walk to the nearest exit" regarding the reliability of this book.

Still there is the question of whether it was Miss Forrester, along with some residents of Burrillville and many others throughout the USA, who fabricated these stories of the Burrillville Booths and the local lore. More importantly, why? Either our Burrillville Henry Johnson was Booth's valet or he was not. Our Henry's own story would contradict any ties with Booth. Someone who shook President Lincoln's hand after being freed, surely, would not want to be affiliated with his assassin. Are there any threads of truth woven amongst these distortions and contradictions? Common sense tells us no, but now and then we wonder.

Before we beginning our summation of the latest findings on Martha Louise Mills, we think it might be appropriate to repeat a few words from Charles Underhill's writings. After analyzing *This One Mad Act* and exchanging letters with historians of the day, he wrote that no one has the right to tell half-truths. It leads to much confusion which will be perpetuated to the end of time. How true this is, especially in this case, where no one can glean the full truth after so many decades of half-truths. The nagging doubts linger, and future generations may never really know the full answer. The truth about Martha and her relationships with the Booth family has not been discovered nor do we really know whether Henry Johnson of Burrillville played a role in her life.

Conclusion: Case of Henry Johnson - Unresolved.

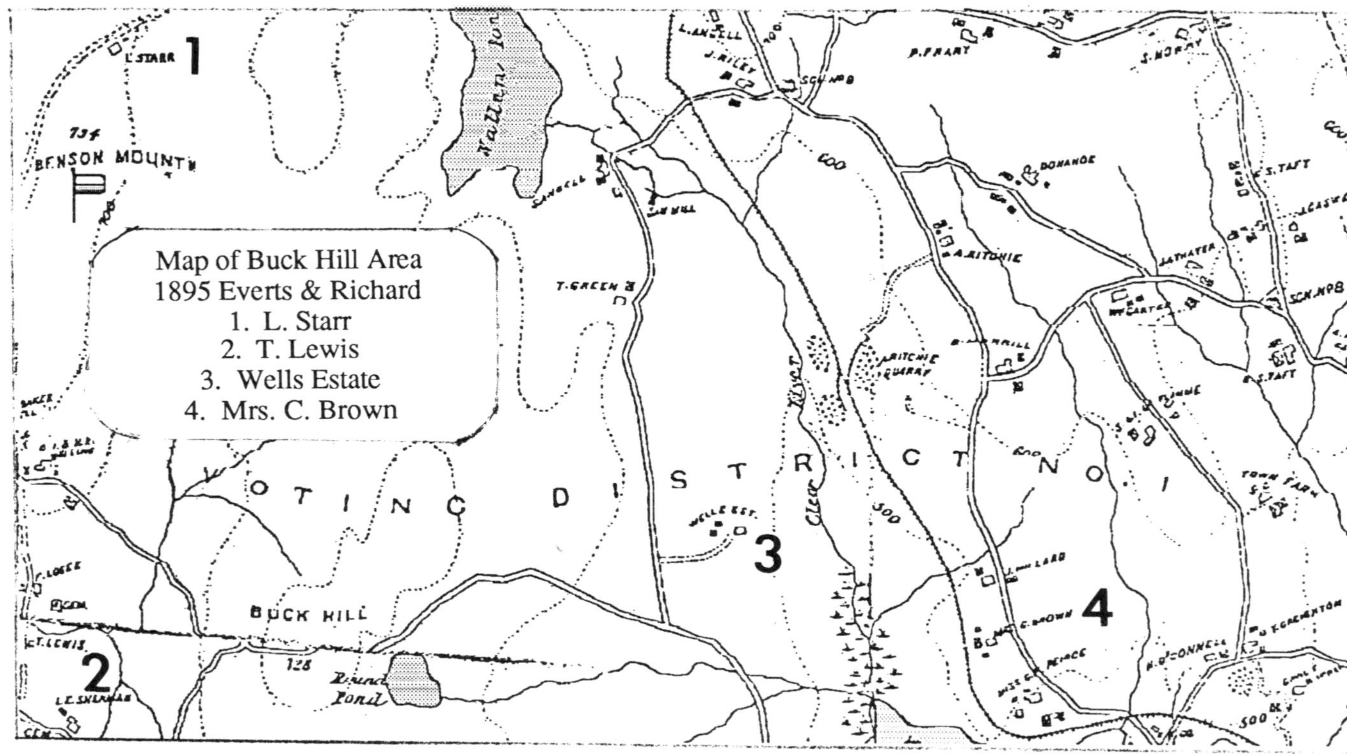
Map of Buck Hill Area
1895 Everts & Richard
1. L. Starr
2. T. Lewis
3. Wells Estate
4. Mrs. C. Brown
1
2
3
4
L. STARR
BENSON MOUNT
734
BUCK HILL
128
Round Pond
VOTING DISTRICT NO. I
T. GREEN
A. RITCHIE
A. RITCHIE QUARRY
DONAHOE
P. FRARY
J. RILEY
L. ANGELL
SCH. NO 8
S. TAFT
L.E. SHERMAN
WELLS EST.
TOWN FARM
600
500

Chapter/File 20

MARTHA LOUISE MILLS

Our elusive Martha's secrets are still escaping us even though our best has been done to unearth them. The unknowns she herself sought until her death have also eluded us. Much of her essence has been captured, but the real Martha is still a mystery. We have been unable to nail her down except with a few vital statistics and a great deal of hearsay and circumstantial evidence. Like the Benchley girls, Martha does pretty much as she pleases, although she appears to be more active in her pursuits. One of the unsolved mysteries is: Who actually brought her up from babyhood to young adulthood? It is still our contention that the Benchleys had a partial hand in this, but there may have been other families involved. The possibility of the D'Arcy family "adopting" Martha has already been explored. There are three other options for that honor, including two Smith families, one from Providence and another from Burrillville. The Smiths were more numerous than the Browns or the Mills in Rhode Island. Incidentally, the first settlers in Burrillville were the family of John Smith the miller.

The Smiths of Providence had to be considered after reading about Ogarita's birth at "Aunt Amy's" home at 13 Abbott's Lane in Providence in 1859. This information was given by Alonzo in a letter to Miss Forrester. It appears that Amy Benchley lived on and off with someone by the name of William Smith. An attempt will be made to follow the maze of census and directory findings on the Smith/Amy relationship. The first of these was a Revolutionary War soldier named William Smith who was tried for mutiny along with Beriah Bump and Arnold Benchley for protesting their pay. They were all subsequently pardoned in February, 1779. We assume the grandson of Sergeant Smith to be one William Arnold Smith who appears in Providence in the 1830 census. He is in the 1840 census, working as a carpenter, living with three sons and two females in Providence. William Arnold was between 40/50. Sons between 5/10, 10/15, and 20/30. Females, one between 40/50 (we assume to be his wife) and one 20/30. Three of these were employed in the manufacturing trade. The mention of William's three sons is interesting because Martha tells of a family with several sons who adopted her.

In 1847, Amey/Amy Benchley is living in her own home at 16 Nash Lane in Providence. In 1848, William A. Smith is listed as a widower living at 333 North Main Street, not far from Nash Lane. From the Providence 1854 Directory, both William A. and Amy are living at 16 Nash Lane. In 1859, William Arnold Smith is living with Amy Benchley at 13 Abbott's Lane at the same residence where Ogarita was born and at the same time.

In the 1860 census, William A. Smith and Amey Benchley are still at 13 Abbott's Lane, but William A. Smith is now a clockmaker and 55 years old. Amey is 76. Martha Bellows is listed here as the householder in the 1860 Providence Directory. How Amey fits into this arrangement and why Martha is living with them is another one of those mysteries. The assumption is that they have a close relationship.

Amey and William A., clockmaker, are there through 1862 and in North Providence in 1865. There is no indication that Martha stayed at Abbott's Lane as she is not listed after the 1860 directory listing. Amey and William moved back to Providence in 1870 at 13 Nash Lane near her first home. In the 1870 census, Amey is listed as a widow. When she dies of old age at the Dexter Asylum in 1878 in Providence, she is unmarried. We don't know what happened to William A. Smith, carpenter, widower, and clockmaker. There is the slim possibility that Martha was a part of this complexity for a brief time. Was William A. Smith the "father" who said, "don't darken my door" after Ogarita was born in 1859 . . . especially since Charles S. Bellows was not the father? A six month old Ogarita was living in Providence with the McNamara family sans Martha, according to the Rhode Island census records. And Martha, eight month old Ogarita, and five year old Harry Bellows are all in Boston in the 1860 Massachusetts census.

Alonzo mentions a William E. Smith, son of William Arnold Smith, born in North Providence in 1832. (*We need to be careful with the Pawtucket, North Providence, and Providence listings because the borders changed at various times. The early Pawtucket records are listed as being in North Providence. This does not lessen the confusion for those who do research, especially those foolish enough to deal with the Mills/Benchley/Brown/Smith families.) What William E. and William A. are to Caroline, we do not know. According to *Providence Births, Marriages and Deaths Volume III,* William E. was married twice, once in 1851 to Fanny J. Newson and in 1854 to Emily Reynolds.

We could not ignore the many entries for Smith in Alonzo's journals. These Burrillville Smiths are our second possibility for the family who raised Martha. They are somewhat less complicated than those affiliated with Amey and the Benchley family. Samuel Smith (1807-1886) and his wife, Merinda (1809-1888), had several sons and one daughter, Sarah Ann, born in 1833. (*Sarah J. [Smith] D'Arcy was listed as being 21 in 1850.) We have already noted one son, Cyrus E. Smith, born in 1843. We thought he might be the C. Smith who signed as a witness on one of D'Arcy's affidavits (*see Chapter/file 18). Elmer A. Smith born in 1841. (*Could he have possibly been the father of another Elmer whom Ogarita mentions playing with young Zola at the Wilson Place?) There was also a Fenner E. born in 1839, Edward L. born in 1846, Frederick A. born in 1850 and William N. in 1853. According to Alonzo, they were all born in Burrillville. The elder sons would have been in Martha's age bracket. Whether Martha lived with them at one time is unknown, though we do know she lived with William A. Smith and Amey Benchley in Providence.

The third possibility is a bit more tenuous in some aspects. Logic carried us to family number three, the Millers. Martha called her adopted family, Miller, though her references seemed to apply to the D'Arcy family. (*We suspect her little history was a way to get back at the D'Arcys or at least Arthur McNult D'Arcy and to soften the blow of his leaving her around 1869. This story was reputedly written in 1870?) She does say that, "I will say their name is Miller." The Miller name keeps cropping up in Burrillville. A Miller farm was for sale, and L. E. Miller, pharmacist, operated a drug store in Pascoag on Main Street for several years. This was mentioned in both the Canterbury notes and Alonzo's records.

While reading the *Prince of Players* by Eleanor Ruggles, we became aware of a Dr. Erasmus Miller caring for Mary Devlin Booth in Dorchester. Dr. Miller's wife said it was a pleasure to care for the dying Mary. Similar words were often heard from Martha in her letters to Alonzo telling of her nursing and of tending the dying. A tenuous connection, we know. (*We often thought that it was Edwin with whom Martha was involved rather than John Wilkes. Mainly because Edwin appeared in Providence and Boston much earlier than JWB. That idea was soon dropped.) Little more was thought of this until Alonzo's previous missing journal was examined one more time searching for names which were unfamiliar in our first one or two readings. It was rather a surprise to find the following listed: January 22, 1874. Erasmus D. Miller, Jr. married Emma L. Howe at St. Mary's Church in Dorchester by Reverend William H. Mills. (*Too much to be just another coincidence. Here is another Mills/Miller association which possibly brings us full circle back to Abraham Mills and his friend and fellow Samaritan, Barton Miller, who might have cared for his infant child after the death of Abraham's wife, Mary. We are not positive there was a Mary who died in childbirth. Martha and her grandchild mention her, but no mention from Caroline or Alonzo in the family history.)

Martha's medical associations have been pointed out in her letters to various people. The sign found in Canterbury attests to her medical knowledge. From where did her knowledge come? Miss Forrester has Martha establishing an emergency hospital in the Shenandoah home after it was confiscated by the Union Army. Out of mercy she aids the doctor during surgery and afterwards cares for the wounded. This story is questionable, but we suspect that Martha at one time worked in a hospital somewhere.

Contact is made with the New England Historic Genealogical Society in Boston with an inquiry about Erasmus Miller. Jacquie McClure in reference services was as happy as we with her findings. The marriage certificate of Erasmus D. Miller, Jr. to Emma L. Howe verifies Alonzo's writings. They were married in Boston January 22, 1874. The groom is 28, from Providence, RI, born in Dorchester, MA and is a clerk. The bride is also 28 and from Boston with no occupation. The groom's parents are Erasmus D. Miller and Louise. They were married by the Reverend Wm. H. Mills. Here we have a Reverend Mills marrying a Providence based Erasmus D. Miller whose father was none other than Dr. Erasmus Miller who cared for Edwin Booth's wife, Mary, in Dorchester.

From a *History of the Town of Franklin, Massachusetts* by Mortimer Blake published by the Committee of the Town in 1879 comes more on the Millers. Dr. Erasmus Darwin Miller, born April 7, 1813, in Franklin, youngest child of Dr. Nathaniel and Hannah [Boyd] Miller. Graduated from Brown University in Providence in 1832. Practiced in Franklin until 1838 when he moved to Dorchester. Has met with success especially in the the department of Surgery for which the Miller family have a peculiar proclivity and natural skill. (*Franklin is not far from Burrillville over the border in Massachusetts to the northeast of us.) Dr. Miller married Louise Clark, her first name also spelled Louiza. (*Could this be the source of Martha's middle name Louise or Lizola?) We did check the census records in both Franklin and Dorchester to see whether Martha might have been enumerated with the Millers. Our thinking was that she just might have boarded or worked for Dr. and Mrs. Erasmus D. Miller in her youth. The Millers did have several relatives and servants living with them, but none by the name of Martha Louise Mills.

Dorchester Births: Erasmus Darwin, son of Erasmus D. and Louiza on September 7, 1845. (*The researcher notes there were possibly more siblings born in Dorchester. This is the Erasmus mentioned by Alonzo in his journal. If there were no family connection, why would he place this amongst his listings? The names would not have been in the local papers in Burrillville as the wedding was in Boston. Evidently, Erasmus, a clerk, is working and residing in Providence, Rhode Island.) Dr. Miller's eldest brother, Dr. Lewis Leprelette Miller, was born in Franklin in 1798. He also graduated from Brown University in 1817, established a practice in Providence, RI, and was president of the Rhode Island Medical Society. His son Nathaniel also became a celebrated surgeon, studying in Europe during the Crimean war. It is very clear that the Miller family was well known in the medical community.

This is admittedly a shadow game, but there are a good many associations between the Millers and Martha. Alonzo reinforced our thin web of circumstance or coincidence. We have not been able to make any definite connections with Martha and these Millers, but it is a tantalizing thought. The following source provides us with some interesting geographical information which adds another connective tissue to our Miller theory.

Source: *Rhode Island Genealogy - Biography Volume II J. H. Beers & Co., Chicago 1908.*

The ancient town of Rehoboth in the Colony of Massachusetts included descendants of John Miller mentioned as early in records as 1643 and a Nathaniel Miller, born in 1672, either the progenitor or namesake to Dr. Nathaniel Miller, father of Erasmus Darwin Miller of Franklin and Dorchester. Rehoboth was divided into several towns, part in Massachusetts and part in Rhode Island. North Providence, Cumberland, and Pawtucket were the areas involved. In this part of Rhode Island "have dwelt for several generations the ancestors of Joseph Miller born 1865." Alonzo contends when Martha married Charles S. Bellows in 1855 she is "of Pawtucket." Despite lack of concrete evidence, we contend that

Martha was "brought up" in the "ancient town of Rehoboth" by persons unknown. The Millers, Smiths and/or Benchleys are a good bet. We note that the boundaries of Pawtucket, Providence and North Providence also moved at will as late as 1879. Martha's mystique and elusiveness have a good beginning in the maze of community changes along with the complexity of family relationships.

Descendants of Martha's family have not provided us with any place names except those of Burrillville, Canterbury, Boston, Baltimore and Providence. There doesn't seem to be any available reminders of her whereabouts prior to 1869 in family records. We have located her in the vital statistics on our own. This can be read two ways. Either Martha destroyed her records because of her relationship with Booth, or other family members have done so for various reasons. For instance, we are told that Ella Stevenson (*Harry's wife) threw away most of Martha's important documents including her marriage license and parts of Martha's biography after her divorce from Harry Jerome Dresbach Stevenson. We question why she was selective in destroying some of the material and not the rest. The biography was found by Miss Forrester in trunks in Ella's home in Norwalk, according to *This One Mad Act*. It does throw a shadow of doubt on the subsequent "history" written by Martha after 1869. Currently, the sisters (*Mrs. Colony and Mrs. Putnam) are transcribing their great-grandmother's diaries which appear to be more detailed and personal than Alonzo's journals. These diaries were written in later years by Martha. In conversation, we heard the remark made that Martha did not like New York City, though it was never mentioned again. We suspect she might have been there en route to Baltimore or when seeking the whereabouts of Harry D'Arcy.

Our inquiry about the birthplace of Martha's illegitimate son, born in 1852 and probably fathered by George Shepherd, was not answered. (*The Pawtucket Death Records list a George E. Shepherd, age 50, who died in 1896.) A locality would help us to pinpoint Martha's earlier life. This information on the illegitimate child came from Miss Merrifield as recorded in author Kimmel's second edition of *The Mad Booths of Maryland*. Searching through census and directories to find Martha L. Mills has been frustrating not because of the lack of names but for the abundance of them. In an 1850 census index of Smithfield, RI, we were pleased to see a Martha Mills. It was not our Martha but all the given names involved with her immediate family were here: Martha Mills, 53 born in 1797 with all except the younger children born in England. Sara Mills - 24. William Mills - 17. Abram Mills - 14. Samuel

Mills - 6. Elizabeth Mills - 29. James Mills - 29. Anna L. Mills - 2. Everyone is here except father Abram/Abraham. It is interesting that they are from England as in Martha's biography she writes that she was born in England . . . on a dark and cloudy night, of course. But, this again may be just romanticism so prevalent in the family genes. There were many Mills, Millers, Millards who either came to the colonies at an early date or in the mid-1800s. All of these names quite literally means "miller."

Martha is silent on her upbringing with the exception of her little story about her adopted family in Miss Forrester's book. Certainly, she must have had some contact with them unless she was disowned after her first marriage or after her affair with D'Arcy. Where do Caroline and Abraham fit into her young life? We have been disillusioned, not to mention confounded, by the contradictory information obtained from vital statistics in regard to Martha's birth, early childhood and young adulthood. We have been unable to find her birth recorded anywhere in the various communities associated with her life in Rhode Island, Massachusetts, Connecticut or New York . . . nor have we been able to locate a birth record for her father, Abram/Abraham Mills. Whenever another town, city or state was mentioned involving our Burrillville Booths, birth records for Martha and her father were checked . . . but to no avail. As mentioned previously, the first verifiable date on Martha began in 1855 with her marriage to Charles Still Bellows in Boston. The unreliability of vital statistics has proven to be less than helpful in our search.

The following material is being included as an example of how vital records can be misleading. We have included four marriage certificates, a death certificate and one notification of a correction. The first marriage certificate we received stated Bellows' age as 28 and Martha's as 23, making her birth year 1832 . . . as she was born in September and married in July. (*We had thought all along that she was older than she claimed to be in later official records.) Various vital statistics did not support this 1832 birth year. Repeated calls to city and state archives suggested there had been an "amended" birth year. The letter which came from Mary L. Sheehan stated the bride was 20 and the groom 24 on the original city marriage license. Shortly thereafter the "corrected" copy from the state archives arrived across our desk. This would make Martha's birth year in 1835 . . . still two years shy of her frequently claimed 1837 birth year.

Using the above information, it would appear we could proceed with our investigation using the 1835 date as the year for Martha's birth in a city, town or state recording. As more information flowed in regarding Martha's first husband, Charles Bellows, we noticed that all of his service records verified his birth year as 1827. (*See service death certificate. His father, Elijah Bellows, is from Vermont as was Fanny Bliss Wilson, wife of James Wilson. In fact, several other families living in the Bridgeton/Wallum Lake areas also claimed the granite state as their previous home.) If we accept the "amended" age of Martha when she married Bellows in 1855, then we have in incorrect age for him. There almost seems to be a conspiracy on the part of those who recorded the original information to cover, or at least to haze over, the exact dates associated with our elusive Martha.

Martha's marriage records to Stevenson in Boston do not contain the same material even from the same archives. Our copy obtained in 1989 has her father as Abram A. Bellows, whereas an earlier 1976 copy obtained by others has simply Abram A. There is always the possibility of a transcriber's error. If we had not received the 1976 copy, the assumption would have been that Abram A. Bellows was the name Martha recorded for her father. Census records can have as much variety as vital statistics. Two copies of the same 1850 Rhode Island Census are different. One has Betsey Benchley and Alonzo at one street address without Caroline, and the other has the three of them living together at another address. Which do we believe?

Since vital statistics perplexed us, we turned to street addresses, deeds and mortgages to see if they might reveal the secret whereabouts of Martha in her younger years. Martha was in Providence at 13 Abbott Street (*also known as Abbott's Lane) in 1859 and in 1860. Our next step was to spend some time in the tax assessor's office and at the archives located in Providence City Hall. We knew that Amey Benchley and William A. Smith also lived at this address on and off between 1850 and 1870. There was the possibility that Amey Benchley, William A. Smith, Martha Bellows, or Caroline Mills Brown might have owned this property. Unfortunately, identification of the exact location of the house on 13 Abbott Street or whether the building still existed was not possible. Old records pointed to the probability it had been located in Plat 5 in lots 71, 72, or 213 today. Assisted by pleasant and efficient office personnel and archivists, we scoured through old tax records, deeds and mortgages reaching back to the 1840s. There were no Benchleys, Smiths or Bellows listed anywhere, but we did come across surnames affiliated with the extended Benchley/Mills/Brown family.

A Phineas Mills owned many of the lots on Abbotts Lane

to the marriage of

John H. Stevenson and Martha L. Bellows

and that the following is a true copy of so much of said record as relates to said marriage, namely:—

Place of Marriage Boston, Mass.

Date of Marriage March 23, 1871

GROOM		BRIDE	
Name	John H. Stevenson	Name	Martha L. Bellows
Age	31yrs. Color - - - - - - - - - - - -	Age	33 yrs. Color - - - - - - - - - -
Residence	Boston	Residence	Boston
Number of Marriage	First Single, wid., or divorced	Number of Marriage	Second ~~Single, wid., or divorced~~
Occupation	Conductor	Occupation	- - - - - - - - - - - -
Birthplace	Cleveland O.	Birthplace	Stonefield, Conn.
Name of Father	Albert F.	Name of Father	Abram A.
Maiden Name of Mother	Adelaide M.	Maiden Name of Mother	Mary A. Mills

Name and official station of person by whom married: Rev. Wm. Bradley, Boston

Date of Record 1871

JOHN H. STEVENSON and MARTHA L. BELLOWS

and that the following is a true copy of so much of said record as relates to said marriage, namely:—

Place of Marriage BOSTON, MA

Date of Marriage MARCH 23, 1871

GROOM		BRIDE	
Name	JOHN H. STEVENSON	Name	MARTHA L. BELLOWS
Age	31 Color WHITE	Age	33 Color WHITE
Residence	BOSTON, MA	Residence	BOSTON, MA
Number of Marriage	FIRST Single, wid., or divorced —	Number of Marriage	SECOND Single, wid., or divorced —
Occupation	CONDUCTOR	Occupation	—
Birthplace	CLEVELAND, OH	Birthplace	STONEFIELD, CONNECTICUT
Name of Father	ALBERT L. STEVENSON	Name of Father	ABRAM A. BELLOWS
Maiden Name of Mother	ADELAIDE M.	Maiden Name of Mother	MARY A. MILLS

Name and official station of person by whom married: REVEREND WILLIAM BRADLEY

Date of Record 1871

Example of Inconsistent Vital Statistics
Last names of parents are included
on second inquiry but not on first.

CHARLES S. BELLOWS and MARTHA L. MILLS

and that the following is a true copy of so much of said record as relates to said marriage, namely:—

Place of Marriage BOSTON, MA

Date of Marriage JULY 30, 1855

GROOM	BRIDE
Name CHARLES S. BELLOWS	Name MARTHA L. MILLS
Age 28 Color —	Age 23 Color —
Residence BOSTON, MA	Residence BOSTON, MA
Number of Marriage FIRST Single, wid., or divorced —	Number of Marriage FIRST Single, wid., or divorced —
Occupation MARINER	Occupation —
Birthplace BOSTON, MA	Birthplace STANFORD, CT
Name of Father ELIJAH BELLOWS	Name of Father ABRAHAM MILLS
Maiden Name of Mother —	Maiden Name of Mother —

Name and official station of person by whom married: REV. S. STREETER, BOSTON

Date of Record 1855

CHARLES S. BELLOWS and MARTHA L. MILLS

and that the following is a true copy of so much of said record as relates to said marriage, namely:—

Place of Marriage BOSTON, MA

Date of Marriage JULY 30, 1855

GROOM	BRIDE
Name CHARLES S. BELLOWS	Name MARTHA L. MILLS
Age 24 Color —	Age 20 Color —
Residence BOSTON, MA	Residence BOSTON, MA
Number of Marriage FIRST Single, wid., or divorced —	Number of Marriage FIRST Single, wid., or divorced —
Occupation MARINER	Occupation —
Birthplace BOSTON, MA	Birthplace STANFORD, CT
Name of Father ELIJAH BELLOWS	Name of Father ABRAHAM MILLS
Maiden Name of Mother —	Maiden Name of Mother —

Name and official station of person by whom married: REV. S. STREETER, BOSTON

Date of Record 1855

Example of Inconsistent Vital Statistics
Ages of Bride and Groom change
on second inquiry.

CHARLES S. BELLOWS

and that the following is a true copy of so much of said record as relates to said death, namely:—

Name	CHARLES S. BELLOWS		
Date of Death	DECEMBER 16, 1869		
Place of Death	CHELSEA, MA		
Residence at time of Death	CHELSEA, MA		
Sex MALE	Color —	Single, Mar., Wid. or Div.	SINGLE
Husband or Wife of —		If veteran, specify war	—
Age 42	Occupation SEAMAN		
Birthplace	BOSTON, MA		
Immediate Cause of Death	DIS. OF HEART		
Due to	—		
Due to	—		

FATHER		MOTHER	
Full Name	ELIJAH BELLOWS	Maiden Name	SARAH
Birthplace	VT	Birthplace	ME
Date of Record	1869	Place of Burial	

Copy of Record of Death
of Charles S. Bellows

Dear Mrs. [redacted]

Re: Marriage Charles S Bellows and Martha L Mills

Please be advised that this office has checked the original marriage and intention of the above marriage and the ages are groom 24 and bride 20.

If you have any further questions, we suggest that you contact the Commonwealth of Massachusetts Archives at (617)727-2816.

Sincerely,

Mary L Sheehan

Mary L. Sheehan

Copy of letter verifying ages
on Charles' & Martha's Marriage Certificate

during the early 1840s. (*Could this have been a relative of Abram Mills?) Harriet and Elijah Baker owned property here in 1853 and 1871. (*The Baker/Cady family were mentioned by Alonzo in his journals.) A Perth Simmons in 1867 was located here. (*Thomas Simmons was Edward M. Brown's son-in-law and father to Alonzo's wife, Sarah.) We also have a John Miller located in Abbott Lane in 1855. (*Miller is another name which is mysteriously associated with Martha.) Levi Joslin and Ada H. Joslin appear here between 1891 and 1893. (*The Joslins figure prominently in both Alonzo's and Caroline's life stories.) In 1872, we even found an Elizabeth and Thomas Booth in the tax records. (*The Booths were intermarried with the Ross/Angell families in Bridgeton. Wouldn't it be something if Martha were raised by one of these Booths?) Fannie Carpenter, wife of Frank, and William Carpenter owned property here in 1889. (*Could this be our real Aunt Fanny? The Carpenters figure as prominently as do the Joslins in the history of our Burrillville Booths. It was Annie [Hopkins] Carpenter of Burrillville who named her daughter "Izola" in 1886.) There were not that many owners listed on Plat 5 in the earlier years, and they all seem to have some sort of connection with our mysterious figures. The fact remains, however, that apparently none of our ladies owned the house at 13 Abbotts Lane in which they lived.

Martha's use of the name "Izola" and the origin of it always seem to puzzle us. Two of Miss Forrester's daughters and their niece came to Burrillville looking for information on this name. We suspect Mrs. Shinsel was sent for the same reason in the 1970s. This indomitable researcher did find an Izola in Ross Village, Nora Izola [Angell] Hopkins. She was born in 1889 and the mother of Hazel Rosalie Hopkins. There is the possibility that Martha picked up the name in Burrillville and not vice versa. We can find no recording of that name earlier than the birth of Izola Louise Wallingford (Hills) in 1878. There are two other Izola's in Burrillville. Izola Elizabeth [Carpenter] Sherman born in 1886, and her niece, Vesta Izola [Carpenter] Dunn. Martha and Ogarita are somehow and in some way associated with the families in the Bridgeton/Wallum Lake/Buck Hill/Ross Village areas in the town of Burrillville. There are either strong friendships or a family relationship which we have not been able to verify, but it is certainly there. We wonder why Mrs. Shinsel found her way out to Burrillville, especially into Ross Village and the home of Florence Adeline [Angell] Taft. An attempt will be made to bare the family genealogy that hints of Martha's and Ogarita's involvement. We should mention that Brian Taft, grandson of Florence and nephew to

Hazel Hopkins, has tried to keep us straight regarding the intricacies of the intermarriages amongst these people. The following genealogy is courtesy of Mr. Taft, Miss Hopkins and various Rhode Island family histories.

The forerunner in the Angelle family was Randall Angelle born in 1767 in North Providence, son of Enoch and Amey [Randall] Angelle. Enoch was a sizable landholder in both Smithfield and North Providence. Amey died shortly after Randall's birth in 1767. Enoch married his wife's sister and fathered many children. (*Lydia Benchley, sister to Amey, Betsey, and aunt to Caroline, married into this second Angell family.) Randall married Marcy Angell of Smithfield in 1790 and at an early date was grazing cattle in Burrillville. He made his permanent home here on the Wallum Lake Road and fathered several children. All the familiar names associated with Caroline, Alonzo, Martha and Ogarita have intertwined with the Burrillville Angells. These include the families of the Estens, Wallings, Rosses, Salisburys, Wilsons, Millards, Hopkins, Smiths, Tafts and Browns. For example, Seth A. Ross, husband of Amey Ann Angell, was grandfather to Miss Hazel Hopkins.

We are interested in Seth A. Ross, whose children were named Adeline, Fernando, Maria, Edward, Earl and Frank. Edward Ross, who died in 1925, related all the complex family history and goings on in Bridgeton to Mrs. Nora Hopkins, his niece. A young Miss Hazel Hopkins overheard these discussions while recovering from chicken pox . . . which at that time meant spending weeks in a darkened room. She has retained and added to the family history throughout the years. Seth Ross traveled to Iowa and came back with the names of Fernando and Maria, not standard English names. There were a rash of Mediterranean names sprinkled amongst more austere Anglo-Saxon and Biblical names after this time. It was suggested this is when the name Izola came into being, though we have seen no written verification.

Smith Esten Angell's son, William Randall Angell, descendant of the original Randall Angelle, married Adeline Frances Ross. Their children were Florence Adeline [Angell] Taft born in 1879 and Nora Izola [Angell] Hopkins, born in 1889, mother to Hazel Rosalie Hopkins born in 1912. There were also two older sisters named Irene Myrtis and Viola Emily. We have heard echoes of these names in Martha's life story.

Nora's middle name came from the then three year old Izola Elizabeth Carpenter, born in 1886. This Izola's parents lived in Ross Village, Andrew and Annie L. [Hopkins] Carpenter. Annie Hopkins, born in 1855, was the daughter of none other than Hosea

Hopkins who lived on Buck Hill. Hosea Hopkins, as well as Everett Carpenter, worked for Caroline on her farm. Miss Forrester relates a story of Caroline hitching up the wagon and going up to buy baskets from Hosea who has a peg leg. Again, we have come full circle with dates and Miss Forrester writings. This does not tell us which came first, "Izola" from the complex Angell family or "Izola" of Pawtucket. It would be helpful to discover when Martha first used this name. The first time we saw it in writing was on Martha's death records in Canterbury along with young Zola's birth in 1878. The second time was in the *Danielson Transcript.* She is the first "Izola" but not the last. The name is still used in the present generation by Martha's great-granddaughter, Zola, from California. She is sister to Ros and Peggy. Apparently, they are still searching for the origins of this name.

There is another association with Martha and Ogarita in their relationship with Marthae Angell Hawkes of Burrillville who married George B. Ross in 1875. Her mother's name on the marriage record is listed as Celia Smith and father's first name is not legible. (*We can bet that the Smiths are related to the William A. and E. Smith associated with Amey Benchley in Providence and Pawtucket.) Marthae, also known as Mattie, had two daughters. Eva Ogarita was born in Pascoag in 1879 and died in Hopedale, Massachusetts, in 1937. (*Ella Wyman Stevenson also named her daughter, Eva Ogarita. This Eva was born in 1903 and is mother of our fellow researcher, Mr. Thomas Wilkinson.) Mary Darling Ross, her other daughter, was born in 1877 and died in 1976 in Burrillville. Mary gave birth to Martha Ogarita Sayles born in 1908 in Burrillville. In Alonzo's letters to Mrs. Izola Merrifield in Connecticut in 1911, we read that Mattie, who is still living in Ross Village, is asking about Ogarita's child and would like her to write. Did Miss Forrester ever get in touch with Marthae Angell [Hawkes] Ross to discuss the origins of the name, "Izola?"

There is little doubt in our minds that Martha and Ogarita are in some way strongly affiliated with our complex Angell family other than just the association by marriage of Lydia Benchley to Christopher B. Angell of Smithfield. Caroline was the niece of Betsey Benchley's sister, Lydia. It is a complex shadow play of names and somewhere in between lies the truth.

Two minor notations remain related to Martha "Izola" [Mills] Booth Bellows Stevenson Bates of Burrillville. In the 1930s and the early 1940s, there was a Bellows family from Boston who were living on the one remaining Wilson property near the dam and Ross Village. Myrtie Bellows was friendly to Florence Adeline

[Angell] Taft, though no one was privy to their conversations. It is unknown whether they were related to our Bellows. The elderly Mrs. Bellows moved to Foster, RI and never returned to Burrillville. In 1907 in the *Pascoag Herald,* we read of an Isola Remington marrying undertaker Varnum Steere at home, corner of Church Street and Irving Avenue in Pascoag. Varnum buried members of our Brown/Mills family in Bridgeton. As Miss Forrester relates in her book, Isola is the correct spelling if the name comes from the island in the lakes district of northern Italy. When all is said and done, the elusive Martha "Izola" has eluded us and her own descendants as well.

It is obvious we have been unable to tie up all the loose ends and resolve all of the contradictions found in the life of Martha Louise Mills. The material on Martha has been presented as found along with our ubiquitous commentaries and fluctuating opinions. The data unearthed and the information received pointed in one direction and then in another . . . just as any decent mystery should do. But, documentation of local lore is not an art form, and we cannot bring the mystery of Martha to an artistic conclusion. It has indeed been a shadow play of truth and untruth, of fact and fiction. It is apparent that Martha, her husbands, and some family members have purposefully been circumvent with us, misleading and withholding evidence which might have revealed a more complete picture of our elusive lady. (*The exceptions to that statement are Peggy Colony, Rosamond Putnam, Izola Allen, and Thomas Wilkenson, who have all been extremely helpful in our quest for the truth.) The vital questions in our minds are: Why was this done, and when did it all begin?

Did all of this subterfuge, distortion, and downright untruths begin in 1859 with Ogarita's birth? Was her father John Wilkes Booth, Arthur M. D'Arcy or someone as yet unknown? We are not satisfied with Miss Forrester's account of her grandmother's actions during this time period. The fact remains that we have been unable to identify Ogarita's father with any degree of certainty. Martha's first recorded use of the Booth name was with her marriage to John H. Stevenson in 1869 in Baltimore. (*Our thoughts on this have already been explored.) The true identity of Harry Jerome Dresbach's father also eludes us. Was Martha's son also the child of JWB, as Miss Forrester and other family members claim, or was he Arthur M. D'Arcy's son? There is always the possibility that he was indeed the son of John Horatio Stevenson. Martha herself has clouded the issue with conflicting entries in her personal records listing two dates for Harry's birth, 1870 and 1871. According to Harry, himself,

Stevenson told him he was not his father. We still cannot understand why Stevenson, the former cavalry man, detective, night watchman, clerk, bartender and soldier of fortune, allowed his wife to say she was Booth's widow. This same man gave his name to a child of either Booth's or D'Arcy's and lived with Martha for over a decade. Then, he silently slipped away so that she could marry Edwin S. Bates in 1881.

This whole scenario would make more sense if Stevenson and D'Arcy were indeed Civil War buddies and involved in some way with John Wilkes Booth and the Lincoln assassination. It would also appear that both Stevenson and D'Arcy were in on the story that Martha was the wife of John Wilkes Booth, and that Ogarita was "due" the gifts and money Aunt Rosalie Booth was reputed to have sent to the family. The intricate and confusing accounts which we accumulated not only from family records but from our own verifiable data make this tale an interesting one. It is because of our confirmed data that we have nagging questions regarding the shreds of truth scattered throughout the story of the Burrillville and Baltimore Booths and their association with each other.

There are two ways of attempting to "prove" local lore and local history. One way is to present materials that suggest the probability, plausibility, or possibility of what is accepted as being historically correct. The positive and accepted approach is to find and record verifiable data which points to the history and/or lore as having some basis in fact. The other is a negative approach, and not highly favored by historians, but one that still must be considered. It is the inability to discover verifiable data and records which would disprove the "history" as it is told or recorded. We have attempted both, but have still failed to resolve the mystery of Martha's life story.

Even though it was necessary to invalidate much of Miss Forrester's family history, we were unable to disprove that Martha Louis [Mills] Bellows had an affair with John Wilkes Booth. On the other hand, we were not able to prove that she did. The only conclusion that can be made is that there is only a slim possibility of our Burrillville Booth's family tree having some Maryland Booths upon it. There is still that nagging doubt in the back of our minds about the lack of positive information which would either confirm or reject the lore as it is known in our town. Is it all a complex fabrication on the part of many different people over a period of years? Or, is there some truth in this? Our chapter/file ends with the statement that the enigma known as Martha still keeps its mystery wrapped around her.

Chapter/File 21

FINAL WORDS

What have we really accomplished by this lengthy pursuit of the Burrillville Booths if most of our cases are still unresolved? It is our belief that a fairly complete picture of Martha and her extended family has been presented. To our knowledge no one has previously offered a written sketch of this woman's life with the exception of Miss Forrester's romanticized version. The slim possibility of Martha meeting John Wilkes Booth in Providence in 1859 has been suggested. We have stressed the activities of the Booth brothers, in particular John Wilkes, in the Providence and Boston areas. Miss Forrester's writings and methods have also been explored. These aided us in discovering the information and misinformation she brought to our investigation as well as the subtle hints provided. All of which helped us in our search for various family connections. Our intention was to present a broader view of Martha Louise Mills' life story. We believe this has been accomplished.

Critics may argue that our nets have been spread too far in the pursuit of the elusive Booths of Burrillville. We counter that ours is the first attempt to capture these particular "Booths." It was necessary to follow as many leads as possible. Authorities on JWB provided the information on his whereabouts while we concentrated on the dovetailing of time and place. Our search included fact and fiction concerning Martha and her extended family. Those who pursue Booth have been more than generous with answers to our frequent questions. They have not hesitated to provide us with material when requested. It was indeed fortunate to meet Martha's descendants who were willing to share their own many years of research. Of course, Alonzo was always looking over our shoulders and pointing out new clues in his journals when a calm fell upon our investigations.

A word to the wise might be in order to those who pursue historical facts. Our attempts to secure verification of information using the notes and/or references of others was frustrating. Records were not always where the researchers said they were. As one archivist wrote from Maryland, sometimes people are misled by the inaccuracies of an author who is not overly careful with his footnotes or references. This is one of the reasons we chose to place our sources before the material presented, which also kept our files in the promised progressive order.

One of the major culprits of misinformation involves the transcribing of written records to printed material found in city and state archives, especially in the matter of vital statistics. Not everyone's handwriting is perfect and mistakes are made in the copying of the information listed. At other times, resource materials located in a certain area a decade ago have simply disappeared. The new administration has no knowledge of the whereabouts of that material. Occasionally, it has simply been disposed of due to the ever increasing problem of space. Multilevel recordings by towns, cities, and states also led to confusion. Indexes did not jibe with their companion microfilms. The practice of microfilming actual records and documents on the national and state levels has greatly enlarged the researcher's field of study. This has also helped with the accuracy of the material by allowing examination of the original information. These systems are not perfect, although we do admit that there are more gains than losses for the pursuers of historical fact.

Our method of presenting the material by using source headings may come under fire by critic and reader alike. At times, the flow is uneven, and the reader is not always carried away by the logic of this presentation. Too often, it is the writer who puts the "facts" into his own fiction by the sheer force and weight of his own logic to provide a neat theme or theory without loose ends. We found this to be particularly apparent in the conflicting and often controversial writings of those who study JWB and the assassination of President Lincoln. Our own reactions to documented and undocumented materials have been stated, and our flights of fancy have been clearly labeled. It is apparent that we have changed our minds and/or stance at different times with the gathering and reviewing of our findings. We have not come to any definite conclusion in regards to John Wilkes being Ogarita's father. We want the readers to make up their own minds about the possibility or the plausibility. We hope our manner of presenting the discoveries as they came along was both enjoyable and intriguing. This method of unraveling the mystery a little at a time tends to offer a more honest and complete picture of the historical "truths" we were seeking.

There appears to be another "story" attempting to emerge from the framework of our investigations of Martha and the Burrillville lore. Strangely enough, we received the same sensation when reading Miss Forrester's *This One Mad Act*. There are too many family names, events, and places within the Burrillville story which crisscross with the historical accounts of the Maryland Booths. It is unlikely that Martha and Miss Forrester could have planted all the surprising information which has surfaced in our pursuit of the Martha Louise Mills' story. It has been suggested that Miss Forrester's accounts tend to negate a Martha/Booth affair. Much of her material has been proven erroneous not only by several critics but also by our own investigations. This alone does not prove that Martha's affair with Booth did not happen. There is also no definite proof that it did. Scholars and aficionados of JWB ought to consider an indepth study of Booth's associations, affiliations, and activities in Rhode Island as well as in our sister states of Connecticut and Massachusetts. We believe that any such study would uncover some familiar names, places and events mentioned in our research.

There is still much work to be done to correlate all the genealogy of Martha and Alonzo's families and friends. It might take another four or five years to finalize the intricate relationships. There are many more connections which need to be made in order to throw more light onto the suggested association between our Burrillville Booths and the Booths of Maryland. Our quest to discover who these Burrillville Booths actually were has not ended and our files have not been closed. The search continues with the hope that verification of the truth will be found.

Supplement

C/F 1 - p. 6

George W. Wilson, born at Pascoag on April 10, 1825, was a school teacher. Later he operated stores in Burrillville and Chepachet, Rhode Island. After reading the article found in *Representative Men and Old Families of Rhode Island* Vol. III, J. H. Beers & Co. (Chicago 1908), we thought this George W. might have been our George Wallingford, father of Izola Louise Wallingford. George W. Wilson died in Morenci, Michigan, on November 29, 1899. His death notice in the *Pascoag Herald* on December 15th that year mentioned George left for Morenci in 1853 where he operated a grist mill and store. (*His 1853 departure date would appear to eliminate George W. Wilson as a candidate for Izola's father. She was born in 1878 long after he had left this area.) This George was married to Harriet Potter of Chepachet, RI. Miss Forrester relates that George Forrester, her adopted father, was married to a Harriet Newell of Mayflower stock. Charles Still (Alonzo) Bellows was also residing in Michigan in 1887, the same year Izola Bates died in Canterbury, Connecticut. William Wilson went out to Morenci to visit his brother, George, in the late 1850s but returned to Burrillville shortly thereafter.

C/F 3 - p. 19

Ogarita's Birth Certificate. It is an unusual name which is often misspelled in newspapers and notices. This information was filed on "Jany 1860." Apparently, 13 Abbotts Lane is not her mother Martha's usual residence. Martha's birthplace is listed as Greenfield, CT, on this certificate. Wonder who filed this information?

COPY OF CERTIFICATE OF BIRTH

State of Rhode Island

Name of Child			
Oganita Elizabeth Bellows			
Sex: Female	Date of Birth: October 23, 1859	Local or State File Number: 312	
Place of Birth (Name of Hospital or Street Address): 13 Abbotts' Lane	City or Town: Providence	County: ----	RHODE ISLAND
Father's Name: Charles S.		Father's Birthplace: Boston, Mass.	
Father's Age: ----	Father's Occupation: Mariner		
Mother's Maiden Name: Martha L.		Mother's Birthplace: Greenfield, CT	Mother's Age: ----
Usual Residence of Mother: ----			

I HEREBY CERTIFY THAT THE FOREGOING IS A TRUE COPY OF THE INFORMATION ON FILE IN THIS OFFICE.

ISSUING OFFICE	Filing Date
State Office, Providence RHODE ISLAND	Jany 1860
This Copy Issued: March 23, 1989	Signature of Registrar: ACTING Roberta A. Chevoya

C/F 3 - p. 20

Pleasant Valley, Maryland, was a mustering out point for Union soldiers with severe injuries and contained a hospital unit. From *The Seventh Regiment Rhode Island Volunteers in the Civil War 1862-1865* by William P. Hopkins and published by the Providence Press in 1903, we read of many Rhode Island soldiers who were either "left behind" or discharged at Pleasant Valley. This area is approximately 35 miles from the Bel Air home of the Booth family. Martha is reputed to have lived here between 1865-1868. Could this be the spot where she nursed the Union soldiers and not at her Shenandoah Valley home? Apparently, Miss Forrester did not know that the Pleasant Valley area served as a military center. She had Martha "hiding" here from the problems of the world and writing poetry in a "secluded hamlet."

C/F 6 - p. 38

The attached article is mentioned both in *This One Mad Act* (page 81) and in George S. Bryan's *The Great American Myth* (page 365). According to Bryan, both the New York papers *Times* and *World* carried this notice on April 15, 1892. There is no evidence that Ogarita (*Rita Henderson) used Booth as her last name until the late 1880s. If she did use the stage name, Rita Wilkes, early in her career, it was a thin disguise. We question why she waited until after her mother's death in 1887 before using the Booth name.

APRIL 15, 1892.

WILKES BOOTH'S DAUGHTER.

Rita Booth, Character Actress and Wife of Albert Henderson, Is Dead.

Rita Booth, who is said to have been the daughter of Wilkes Booth, the slayer of President Lincoln, and who for some years has been the wife of Al Henderson, the well-known orchestra leader, died on Tuesday in Binghamton, N. Y., where she was playing in the company of Floy Crowell. The body was brought to this city, and the funeral will take place to-day.

Rita Booth was a clever character actress, and often declared that she did not wish to rise to any eminence in the dramatic profession, because she feared her relationship would bring unpleasant notoriety. She wore always a medallion locket containing the likeness of the ill-fated Wilkes Booth.

C/F 6 - p. 40

The Reincarnation of John Wilkes Booth. A Study in Hypnotic Regression by Dell Leonardi. We never did hear from the author, but the publisher gave us permission to use the material with "no direct quotes." Dell is another curious name associated with Martha's descendants.

C/F 6 - p. 45

Columbus Dispatch May 29, 1890. This article was received courtesy of Miss Forrester's daughters and was also noted in George Bryan's *The Great American Myth*. Ogarita and her husband, Mr. Alexander Henderson director of the Boston Comic Opera Company, are playing in Columbus, Ohio. The contents of this article are reviewed in the text. This is the first time we have seen the Booth-Henderson name used in print with the exception of family writings. The last few lines indicate that Ogarita is planning to make public the family papers and memoranda which link her with John Wilkes Booth. Izola Louise Wallingford Henderson would have been about twelve years old when this appeared in the *Dispatch*.

MRS. BOOTH-HENDERSON.

A LADY WHO CLAIMS J. WILKES BOOTH AS HER FATHER

Filling an Engagement at a Columbus Theater—What She Told a Reporter.

At the Globe Theater, with the Boston Comic Opera Company, is a lady whose name and family connection are inclined to impart a degree of interest to the general public rather more than ordinary. The lady's maiden name is Rita Booth, she now being the wife of Mr. Henderson, the director of the company. Mrs. Booth-Henderson, in a conversation with a reporter of THE DISPATCH, says she is a daughter of J. Wilkes Booth. She remembers her father distinctly, although but eight years old at the time of his death. She was asked concerning the truth or falsity of the recently-published statement of some lady living in the South, to the effect that her father, J. Wilkes Booth was not dead, but that the wrong man had been shot, on that eventful morning, more than twenty-five years ago, and she emphatically affirms that her father is dead, that he was shot at the time history records it, and that she saw his body a number of times before its burial.

Mrs. Henderson says her mother died about three years since, leaving her as the only child, yet she says she has two half brothers living. She was born in Richmond, Va., and has been on the stage more or less for the past fifteen years. She was leading lady with George C. Milne, the preacher-actor, a few years since, and late with Grace Hawthorn. She made her first appearance on the stage at the Boston Globe Theater, in a minor part. She first appeared in this city at the old Comstock, now Metropolitan Opera House, about seven years ago with Palmer in the "Danites." She appeared later with the Bennett & Moulton Opera Company, at the Grand, four years ago.

Mrs. Booth-Henderson has many of the characteristic features so marked in the Booth family and her facial resemblance, as well as her love for the stage, would seem to be strong evidence of the statement she makes. She states that she has a diary containing much important memoranda of her father's life and papers of his, and that at some time not far distant she will make them public.

C/F 12 - p. 105

Stevenson/Booth marriage in Baltimore, Maryland. Source: Baltimore City records. The record indicates this marriage was filed June 13, 1871 and that Martha (*not Izola?) has her initials as J. M. "J" for Mrs. John Booth?

MALE		FEMALE
STEVENSON, JOHN H.		BOOTH, MARTHA, J.M.
BALTIMORE	ADDRESS	BALTIMORE
AGE 28 COLOR WHITE	AGE	31 COLOR WHITE
SINGLE	CONDITION	WIDOW
BAR TENDER	OCCUPATION	NONE
	RELATION	
ISSUE MAR. 2, 1869	MARRIED MAR. 2. 1869	FILED JUNE 13. 1871
MINISTER DAN'L BOWERS		
REMARKS BK. 3-1-F-R-1869-72		FOLIO- 448

C/F 12 - p. 108

Source: Pension Office Records from the National Archives. Dr. Putnam's rather important letter suggesting he cared for the family of Charles Still Bellows for some time previous to Bellows' last enlistment. (Letter on the next page.) The Assistant Clerk of Superior Court, Edwin A. Wadleigh, swore to the good reputation of Dana B. Putnam.

State of Massachusetts, Suffolk ss.
Then Personally appeared the above nam
Martha L. Bellows, and made oath to
the foregoing statement by her su
scribed, on this 19th day of Novem
1870, before me, & I certify that
have no interest in this claim
Edwin A. Wadleigh
Asst Clerk
Supr Ct

I certify that I was the family Physician of the late Charles L. Bellows, whose widow Martha L. Bellows is an applicant for Pension, ~~and~~ for some three years ~~after~~ before his death until that I saw him just before his last enlistment into the Navy, that is to say in the Summer of 1868 and he was then in good and sound bodily health and always before that he had enjoyed perfect health in every respect, in my opinion, and had it been otherwise I would have certainly known it as I regularly attended his wife and children when they were sick and I believe his habits were correct. I am not related to claimant & have no interest in her claim.

D. B. Putnam M.D.

C/F 13 - p. 114

Baltimore City Directories - 1867-68 and 1870. This information was received from many sources: Mr. Wilkinson, the sisters, and by our own investigations. There are many Stevensons listed. John H. Stevenson, clerk, was also found in the 1867-1868 Baltimore City Directory living at 67 South Eden Street. Note the Robert A. Stevenson, chairmaker, living at 67 South Eden Street in both directories. Could this be John H's brother or father?

Stevenson Dr. James S. 134 n Exeter
Stevenson James, laborer, 125 Stirling
Stevenson James, salesman, 12 Fish Market
Stevenson John H. chairmaker, 303 e Eage
Stevenson John, police, 32 Anthony
Stevenson Dr. John M. 134 n Exeter
Stevenson John H. clerk, 67 s Eden
Stevenson J. M. sr. (J. M. Stevenson & Son
124 w Biddle
Stevenson J.M.jr. (S. & Sons,) 226 Madison
Stevenson Margaret, young ladies' school,
n Pine
Stevenson Nimrod, salesman, 127 Franklin
Stevenson Robert, police, 125 n Eden
Stevenson Robert, chairmaker, 2 e Lomba
dw 67 s Eden
Stevenson Stephen, sexton, 45 Stirling
Stevenson & Sons. (J. M. Stevenson, sr., J.
Stevenson, jr. Wm. H. Stevenson,) prod
com merchants, 165 n Howard

Stevenson Jno. K. engn'r U.S N. 340 e Fayette
Stevenson Dr. John M 134 n Exeter
Stevenson Jno. H condctr, 577 n Fremont
Stevenson John, police, 254 e Madison
Stevenson J. M. sr. 124 w Biddle
Stevenson J. M. jr. (S. & Son)226 Madison av
Stevenson Margaret, school, 28 n Pine
Stevenson Mrs. M. I. dressmkr, 577 n Fremont
Stevenson Mary, teacher, 28 n Pine
Stevenson Nimrod, salesman, 45 Mosher
Stevenson Owen, 214 w Fayette
Stevenson Robt. plasterer, 42 McElderry
Stevenson Robert, plasterer, 125 n Eden
Stevenson Robert, chairmaker, 242 s Caroline,
dw 67 s Eden
Stevenson Robt. A. chairmaker, 67 s Eden
Stevenson Robt. S laborer, 46 Bank

C/F 15 - p. 141

Edited portion of Martha's 1886 letter to Alonzo, where she mentions she was left a little money, which could have been received from just about anyone, either a relative or someone she befriended. For Alonzo to have seen it "in the papers" must mean it was either very noteworthy or in one of our local Burrillville newspapers. We searched these local newspapers from December through February, but found nothing mentioned. (*Martha often exaggerated her well being in her letters to Alonzo and Caroline from Canterbury. Our research found no evidence Martha owned property in Canterbury at any time. If she had been left some money, it might not have been a great sum.) These letters, for the most part, were received from Mrs. Colony and Mrs. Putnam, all but one had been transcribed by the same two ladies. We believe these are the original letters from Martha to Alonzo, and suspect Miss Forrester obtained them from her Uncle Alonzo when she contacted him in 1911. Martha's handwriting corresponds to the handwriting found on her government pension request. It would appear others had access to Alonzo's journals, including Martha and her granddaughter, Izola Forrester. A comparison of this letter and the last entry in Alonzo's Journal (see page 94) indicates they are both in Martha's handwriting.

Harry is well. and bids fare to be,
very good son. he is deeply interested
in religious matters. I suppose you
see by the papers a few months
ago. that I had been left a little
money, such was the case. I have to
let me a lonely place. Canterbury
a town like Burrillville. and my
new house is called the prettiest
place in the town. I have had
built. with a room in ...

C/F 16 - 154

This notice, possibly from the *New York Clipper*, date unknown, is courtesy of Mrs. Colony and Mrs. Putnam. It is a record of one of the last appearances of Charlotte Cushman on stage at the Globe Theatre in Boston on May 15, 1875. A Miss Wilkes stars as Donalbain in this production. Ogarita's descendants believe she began her stage career as Miss Wilkes. Her mother, Martha (Mrs. John H. Stevenson), and her family are living in Boston at that time. Ogarita "Booth" Bellows would be about fifteen years old.

THE GLOBE THEATRE PROGRAMME.

Proprietor and Manager ....Arthur Cheney
Stage-manager and Director....................D. W. Waller

This evening

MISS CHARLOTTE CUSHMAN

will impersonate her celebrated role of

LADY MACBETH,

assisted by

MR. D. W. WALLER AS MACBETH.

Immediately after the performance, MISS CUSHMAN will be presented with a testimonial given her by a number of her friends, on which occasion the presentation address will be delivered by MR. CURTIS GUILD.

SATURDAY EVENING, MAY 15, 1875,

last appearance on any stage of

MISS CHARLOTTE CUSHMAN,

supported by

MR. D. W. WALLER,

when will be performed Shakespeare's sublime tragedy of

MACBETH.

Duncan		Mr. J. C. Dunn
Malcolm	His Sons	Mr. Lin Harris
Donaldbain		Miss Wilkes
Macbeth	Generals in the King's Army.	Mr. D. W. Waller
Banquo		Mr. C. F. Fyffe
Macduff	Noblemen of Scotland	Mr. G. B. Waldron
Lenox		R. B. Darcie
Rosse		Mr. Stuart Clarke
Fleance, Son to Banquo		Miss Portia Albey

C/F 16 - p. 157

1860 Providence Directory, page 22, obtained at the Providence Public Library on Empire Street. (Directory is listed on following page.) This decidedly places Martha in Providence some time during the 1859-1860 period. Martha is also listed as head of the household.

PROVIDENCE [B] DIRECTORY

Belknap Oliver, moulder, h. 141 Richmond
Bell Frank W. cigarmaker, h. 149 Cranston
Bell John, shoemaker, 12 Hospital, h. 55 Elm
Bell William, fiddler, h. Barre, near Dale
Bellows George, carpenter, bds. 137 Carpenter
→ Bellows Martha L. Mrs. h. 13 Abbotts lane
Bellows Willard H. clerk, 69 Westminster, bds. 11 Thomas
Belvin John, blacksmith, bds 69 Eddy.
Benchley James, jeweler, bds. 61 Westminster
Benchley Samuel, carpenter, h. 61 Westminster
Benchley William, carpenter, bds. 61 Westminste
Bender Gustavus, silversmith, h. 25 Dean

C/F 16 - p. 156

An early appearance of J. W. Booth at the Pine Street Theatre in Providence is recorded on page 279 in Charles Blake's *An Historical Account of the Providence Stage*, published by George H. Whitney in Providence, RI, in 1868. The Pine Street Theatre opened on September 5, 1859 under the management of E. Varrey and W. A. Arnold. Mr. Varrey is also listed as a member of the stock company which kept the theater open between visiting companies and stars. Could this be the same Edwin Varrey mentioned in Francis Wilson's *John Wilkes Booth* published by Houghton Mifflin Company in 1929? On page 12 of this book, Wilson writes of that Edwin Varrey, is a fine actor and one of the best men, who liked John Wilkes Booth. Varrey was among the many stage associates of Booth who at first could not believe John Wilkes shot the President and thought it incredible that such a man could have done such a deed. If E. Varrey of Providence and Edwin Varrey from Wilson's book are one and the same man, then here is another Providence/Booth association.

C/F 17 - p. 167

Both Edwin and John appear to have had a close association with Orlando Tompkins, pharmacist and theater owner from Adamsville, Rhode Island. Eleanor Ruggles in *Prince of Players* has Edwin staying with Orlando Tompkins in Franklin Square during the last week of his appearance at the Boston Theatre (page 174). According to Miss Ruggles, Edwin was informed of his brother's deed by his "Negro dresser" in Orlando's home, Saturday morning after the assassination.

C/F 17 - p. 167

Joseph H. Simonds, Booth's business manager and friend, was said to have been from Fitchburg, Massachusetts. The City Clerk's office at 718 Main Street in Fitchburg sent us the above record for Simonds of that city during that time period. There is a John Simonds listed and his birth is in the right year, 1838. Could this be our Joseph Simonds? Ernest C. Miller in *John Wilkes Booth in the Pennsylvania Oil Region* writes that Joseph H. Simonds was a clerk in the Mechanic's Bank in Boston and an aficionado of the theater. Joseph was a friend of John Wilkes Booth in Boston before becoming JWB's business partner and manager in the oil fields of Pennsylvania. (*Miller's description of Joseph H. Simonds is similar to that of John H. Stevenson's description in Miss Forrester's Book.) Stevenson was listed as a clerk in Boston, Baltimore and Washington, DC, though we have not been able to place him at the Mechanic's Bank. In *Kings Handbook of Boston* by Moses King published in 1885, there is an Alvan Simonds listed as cashier of the Mechanic's Bank. This might be the same Alvan Augustus Simonds in the recorded family history of Mr. Abel Simonds of Fitchburg.

Mr Abel Simonds

Mary Caroline Simonds Daughter of Abel & Jane T. Simonds
born October 27. 1832.
[illegible] Todd Simonds Son of Abel & Jane T. Simonds
Born May 17. 1834
William Henry Simonds Son of Abel & Jane T. Simonds
Born June 17. 1836.
John Simonds son of Abel & Jane T. Simonds Born
November 27. 1838.
Alvan Augustus Simonds son of Abel & Jane T. Simonds

C/F 17 - p. 172

Divorce petition of William Wilson dated October 1, 1882 obtained from the records in the State of Rhode Island. (*The old court records are no longer stored at Providence College but are now located at the Judicial Record Center, One Hill Street in Pawtucket, RI.) This record indicates Ogarita was a member of the *Theatre Comique* in Providence in 1882. According to her husband, it was a "disreputable place." It was Ogarita who deserted William on February 2, 1882, and "still does refuse to live with him." The divorce was granted. William's divorce petition lists Ogarita's middle initial as "E" for Elizabeth and not "R" for Rosalie. It sounds as though William hired a detective to record Ogarita's activities. She does not appear to be the demure and aloof person her daughter, Miss Forrester, portrayed.

To the Honorable Supreme Court, next to be holden at Providence within and for the County of Providence, on the first Monday of October A. D. 1882.

Respectfully Represents William R. Wilson of Burrillville in said County, that he is a domiciled inhabitant of this State, and has resided therein for the period of fifty years next before the preferring of this petition; that he was married to Ogarita E. Wilson his present wife on the twelfth day of October A. D. 1879, and hath ever since on his part demeaned himself as a faithful husband and performed all the obligations of the marriage covenant: but that the said Ogarita E. Wilson hath violated the same in this: that She hath without just cause wilfully deserted your petitioner on the second day of February A.D. 1882. Since which time she ever has refused and still does refuse to live with him, and hath been guilty of other acts of misbehavior and wickedness repugnant to and in violation of the marriage covenant. To wit That she hath as a member of the Theatre Comique Company of play actors of this city, a miscellaneous company, appeared upon the stage of that Theatre a disreputable place as an actress at public exhibitions, dressed in immodest and unbecoming attire; And also on the Sabbath day in the month of July last past upon one of the Steamboats running from this city, at the public bar, thereon, drank Lager, and other beer, in the presence of a public assemblage, to the disgrace and scandal of your petitioner.

Wherefore your petitioner prays that a decree of this Court may be made divorcing him from the bond of marriage, and from the said Ogarita E. Wilson

William R. Wilson

C/F 18 - p. 182

Case of Sarah J. D'Arcy #47157 Pension Claim and depositions from the National Archives Military Records. This places Arthur D'Arcy in Boston in July of 1865 where he was being held in prison for desertion. Later he escaped.

Headquarters Department of the East,

New York City, 29 July 1865.

Bt Col J. A. Clarke, U.S.A.,
Military Com'r Boston, Mass.

Colonel:

The charge & specification against Private Arthur D'Arcy, 2d Mass Cav'y (Co I) forwarded by you on the 27th inst., have been sent for trial to Capt D. T. Corbin, Judge Advocate of Genl Ct Martl now convened at Gallops Island, B. H. You will please hold the prisoner & the witnesses subject to Capt Corbin's requisition.

By com'd of Maj Genl Hooker
Chs O. Joline
Bt Lt Col & A.D.C.

C/F 19 - p. 193

From *Commemorative Biographical Record of Fairfield County*, published in Chicago in 1899 by J. H. Beers & Co. page 78. (List is on next page.) The subject of this biography was the Honorable Charles Mills born February 25,1833. Listed as his father is John Mills. We believe Miss Forrester also found this particular record just as we did. John's wife Sarah's maiden name is listed as Batterson. Miss Forrester has John Mills' wife, Sarah, marrying a Batterson after this John's death. She lists them as the parents of Abraham A. Mills. According to the Pawtucket Death Records and the Rhode Island Seaman's records, Abraham A. Mills was born in 1820 in Southport, son of Joseph and Sarah Mills. There is no mention of an Abraham in this record of the Fairfield County Mills family.

John Mills (2), the father of our subject, was born at Greens Farms, in the town of Westport, where he followed farming for many years, his death occurring in 1855. For about thirty years he followed the trade of stone mason in addition to the management of his homestead. Like his father he was a Democrat in politics, and a devout member of the Congregational Church, the family having always taken an active part in religious work in their locality. His wife, Sarah (Batterson), who died in 1883, was a daughter of Burr Batterson, a well-known citizen of Westport. Our subject is the eldest in a family of three children, the others being John, a farmer and stone mason now residing in the town of Westport; and David, a carpenter in Bridgeport.

C/F 19 - p. 196

Source: *Old Families of Rhode Island* and *The Pascoag Herald*. Herbert M. Wilson was a bookkeeper in his Uncle Marvin's box factory in Webster, Massachusetts. He was born in Burrillville, educated at Mowry & Goff's English and Classical School in Providence. In 1878 (*the year of Izola Louise Wallingford's birth at the Wilson Brothers farm), Herbert returned to Burrillville and began to manufacture yarn and shoddy, operating the Wilson Mill until 1899. Problems ensued and Herbert skipped out to California in 1913. (*This information found in the local newspaper.) Since his mother's maiden name was True, we wonder whether the Dr. True Wilson, who collaborated with Miss Forrester to continue the story of Booth's escape from the Garrett tobacco barn, is a descendant of Herbert Wilson of Burrillville or Herbert, himself.

C/F 19 - p. 204

Certificate of John H. Stevenson's death in 1906 courtesy of Thomas Wilkinson. (Certificate is on next page.) Stevenson still claims to have come from Ohio, but lists his parents' birthplace as England. Other service data lists them as being from Cleveland. The street address is interesting as Mr. Wilkinson forwarded us information where Stevenson has two addresses on his pension file in 1875. The address listed for his death at 507 13th Street NW, Washington, DC, is one of the addresses and the other is at 26 Mott Street, Boston, MA. Apparently, he used the Washington address for quite some time.

CERTIFICATE OF DEATH. 1136
RECORD

No. of BURIAL PERMIT: 169,068

DISTRICT OF COLUMBIA. 16884

FULL INSTRUCTIONS FOR THE GUIDANCE OF THOSE USING THIS BLANK, AND SPACE FOR REMARKS MAY BE FOUND ON THE OTHER SIDE.

1. Date of this Death .... August 7, 1906
2. Full Name of Deceased .... John H. Stevenson
If an unnamed infant, insert full names of both parents.
3. Sex: MALE ~~FEMALE~~
4. Age: YEARS 66 MONTHS 0 DAYS 1
5. Color: WHITE. ~~COLORED.~~ ~~INDIAN.~~ ~~CHINESE.~~ ~~JAPANESE.~~
6. Conjugal Condition: ~~SINGLE.~~ ~~MARRIED~~ [illegible] ~~WIDOWED.~~ ~~DIVORCED.~~

AUG 8 [illegible]

Under sex, color and conjugal condition, strike out the words not applicable.
Under color, the term "colored" includes all of African descent, whether of pure or mixed blood.

7. Occupation .... Government Clerk
8. Birthplace of Deceased .... Ohio
9. Birthplace of Father .... England
10. Birthplace of Mother .... England

If born in the United States, give State, Territory or District; otherwise, give country.

11. Duration of Residence in this District .... 15 years
12. Place of Death .... 507 13th St NW. Washington, DC
DURATION
13. Cause of Death
PRIMARY Cerebral Syphilis & General Arterio-Sclerosis

C/F 19 - p. 208

From the *Columbus* (Ohio) *Dispatch* dated May 30, 1890. Courtesy of Ogarita's granddaughters. Rita Booth is listed as a member of the Boston Comic Opera Company and has received rave reviews for her role in *The Mikado* at the Globe Theatre.

AMUSEMENTS

To-night: The "Mikado" at the Globe.
Globe Theater.
"THE MIKADO."

"The Mikado," at the Globe, is in most excellent hands and the Boston Comic Opera Company has made a reputation here that will insure them a splendid reception when they return. To be able to draw two good houses daily for four weeks in mid-summer heat is sufficient evidence of the hold the Bostons have upon the music loving public of Columbus.

Notes.

Next week the thrilling four-act drama, "Just in Time," will be placed on the stage at the Globe.

Herr Eduard Strauss receives $2,000 per day for each day his orchestra performs in this country.

Messrs. Cornell and Graham will strive hard to make the lecture course next season equal, if not excel, the course just passed.

Mr. William Dixon has been tendered a very prominent position in the company Elmer Vance is organizing to play "The Limited Mail" next season.

→ Miss Rita Booth is said by those who have witnessed her acting at the Globe this week, to be the best "Katisha" seen in this city for several seasons.

C/F 19 - p. 210

Letter from Ogarita to her brother, Harry S., dated July 16, 1888. Courtesy of the sisters. Edited by the authors. This letter would indicate that Ogarita is in touch with Miss (Mrs.) Rogers once again. Note the use of the "Aunt Rosalie" and "Uncle Joseph" referring to John Wilkes Booth's brother and sister. She is writing to her younger brother, Harry Jerome Dresbach, and not to her older brother, Charles Alonzo Bellows. We assume Ogarita did get her address and visited Rosalie and Joseph Booth, as Miss Forrester recorded in *This One Mad Act*. The time element is crucial. We know Rosalie died at her brother Joseph's home on January 15, 1889. Apparently, Ogarita was in contact with "Miss" Rogers and now considers herself to be a relative of the Booths. We assume Martha did have correspondence and an association with Booth's old neighbor. It is disappointing to learn that the family does not possess any correspondence from "Miss" Rogers. Why would they destroy this evidence unless it were Martha who was "that widow who robbed poor Rosalie of all she had," according to Edwin Booth? Neither Martha nor John Stevenson would want that evidence around. If she did get money from Rosalie for whatever reasons, it could not have been a great deal as Martha struggles a good part of her life just to survive.

Minneapolis
July 16, 1888

My dear brother Harry,

I received your dear letter, ...

... I hear from Maggie every week. Such dear loving letters as she writes me.

Write me soon, all about yourself, you know how interested I am in all that concerns you.

I received a beautiful letter from Miss Rogers in Baltimore. You remember us speaking of her. She sent her love to you, calling you my little brother, she is going to find out Aunt Rosalies address for me. She is living somewhere in New York with Uncle Joseph.

Well dear, I'll bring this dull letter to a close.

God bless you dear. The children send love and kisses to dear Uncle Harry.

With fondest love from your loving sister,

Rita

C/F 19 - p. 212

Notice of Izola Page's death was discovered in a collection of newspapers donated to the Burrillville Historical and Preservation Society. It mistakenly states that Izola was the great-granddaughter of John Wilkes Booth when she actually would have been his granddaughter. Wonder who sent the notice to the *Woonsocket Call*? There must have been someone in the Burrillville area who knew Mrs. Izola Page and her reputed association with John Wilkes Booth.

Mrs. Izola Page, Famed Writer, Native Of Pascoag, Passes At 64

(Special To The Woonsocket Call)

KEENE, N. H., March 7 (AP)—Mrs. Izola Forrester Page, 64, author and scenario writer and great granddaughter of John Wilkes Booth, who died yesterday at her Keene home, will be buried tomorrow morning.

A native of Pascoag, R. I., she played child's parts on the stage with her mother, the late Ogerita Booth Hills, and later wrote feature articles for newspapers and magazines.

She came here to live from California and New York about five years ago.

She is survived by her husband, Mann Page, a well known stage director, four daughters and two sons.

C/F 20 - p. 226

Source: Massachusetts vital records and city directories researched by Shirley Redden in conjunction with the New England Historic Genealogical Society's research service. In our attempts to tie in Burrillville's Sarah Ann Smith/Sarah J. Darcy of Boston, we requested the following information on the D'Arcy's of Boston. Arthur's wife, Sarah, does not appear in the Boston city directories until 1867. (*Wives did not appear on these records unless they were widowed or engaged in a profession.) Sarah worked as an assistant at Adams School and boarded at 219 Chelsea in the home of John S. D'Arcy from 1871 through 1873. Our Arthur is not recorded in these directories after the 1865 listing at 3 Harmony Place, East Boston. (*This might imply that Arthur took leave of his wife during that time period.) The marriage between Charles W. D'Arcy and Sadie Perry explains the D'Arcy name on the Perry stone in Woodlawn Cemetery, Everett MA. Sarah J. (Smith) D'Arcy's death is recorded in 1892.

C/F 19 - p. 219

An article on Henry Johnson from the *Woonsocket Call* dated April, 1941, found in the Burrillville Historical and Preservation Society's collection of Burrillville news clippings. Miss Forrester has Henry as a dresser to John Wilkes Booth and Aunt Sarah, Henry's mother, as Ogarita's nurse. According to Miss Forrester, Henry returns to New York after leaving John Wilkes Booth in London, and serves as a dresser to Edwin Booth in New York. Eleanor Ruggles in her *Prince of Players* (page 174) has Edwin receiving the news of his brother's deed from his own "Negro dresser." This would predate Henry serving as Edwin's servant. Mr. Johnson's history in this article would appear to refute any and all of the above statements. The problem is we really do not know whether Henry Johnson of Pascoag was son of Martha's "Aunt Sarah" or whether either one of them were ever servants of the Booth family.

Even though the Civil war resulted in the liberation of the negroes, Johnson has no memories of unfair treatment.

"Mistress Johnson (the negro assumed the surname of his owner) was the kindest woman," he said. "There were never any whippings. And she would buy slaves, but never sell them. We ate well, too."

Until the time he was 19, Johnson says he never did any hard work, his duties being to help bring in the tobacco crop. Even after the Civil war, he did not leave, although given the opportunity.

50 Cents A Day

"We were given 50 cents a day. That was pretty good money. It's even good today," he said.

One of his proudest recollections is the trip he made to Washington to see Lincoln, not long before the ill-fated president's death.

There was reverence in the old negro's eyes and worship in his tone as his memory took him back more than 75 years to a never-fading image of the Great Liberator.

Eventually, he left the only home and the only life he had ever known to seek adventure in the north. He went to Tarrytown, N. Y., where he was employed on a reservoir project.

Later he obtained work as a cook both on land and sea. He was chef on a four-master, touching many ports, but mostly England—and the West Indies.

It was more than a half-century ago that Mr. Johnson took a walk, a long walk, a walk destined to end in New England.

He was in New Brunswick at the time and decided he wanted to see his then, only living relative, an aunt in New York. So he started out. Mile after mile and day after day he continued.

Job In Douglas

He found himself in Douglas, Mass., utterly penniless, and applied for a job—with a farmer. His wish was granted. He liked his new home so well he stayed for seven years.

Johnson never did get to see the aunt.

In 1894 he journey to Burrillville. At first he worked there on odd jobs, but in recent years he has kept close to his little home.

He hears well, sees well; in fact, is well. The old fellow boasts he's never been to a doctor or dentist in all his life. He still has curly grey hair and more than half of his teeth.

When a boy of eight, he lost three fingers when he placed his left hand where it shouldn't have been while an older brother was chopping wood. But even then he didn't go to a physician. The mistress bandaged his hand and he never suffered ill effects.

Mr. Johnson smokes but doesn't inhale. He seldom touches intoxicating liquors.

C/F 20 - p. 234

All three of Miss Forrester's daughters visited Burrillville in January of 1990, including Izola, Mrs. Harrison Allan, who resides in California. We returned to the local sites visited previously with Mrs. Colony and Mrs. Putnam. This time we located the original homestead and the Wilson family graveyard beside Wilson's Reservoir. Among the many things discussed among us were the current theatrical people who claim to be descendants of John Wilkes Booth. The sisters did not claim any of the lesser knowns to be their relatives. The origin of the name, Izola, was again discussed. None of us have truly discovered where the name originated nor when it first appeared in this area The earliest recorded documentation is still the 1878 birth of Izola Louise Wallingford (Hills) in Burrillville.

C

X

Y

Z